THE ROAD TO POWER

THE ROAD TO POWER
First published 2011
by New Island
2 Brookside
Dundrum Road
Dublin 14

www.newisland.ie

ISBN 978-1- 8484-0117-4

British Library Cataloguing Data. A CIP catalogue record for this book is
available from the British Library

Typeset by Liberties Press Ltd.,

Cover design by Mariel Deegan.
Printed by CPI Anthony Rowe

New Island received financial assistance from
The Arts Council (An Comhairle Ealaíon), Dublin, Ireland

10 9 8 7 6 5 4 3 2 1

THE ROAD TO POWER

How Fine Gael Made History

Kevin Rafter

NEW ISLAND

Contents

Introduction

Perhaps it is the ordinariness of the man that generated so much of the hostility. He is no intellectual like the late Garret FitzGerald. His ministerial record is far less substantial than that of John Bruton, Brian Cowen or Bertie Ahern. He doesn't have the business achievements of Albert Reynolds nor the national sporting record of Jack Lynch. In fact, there was little in his political curriculum vitae that merited his election as Fine Gael leader in 2002, not to mind that which justified thoughts of entering Government Buildings as Taoiseach.

Kenny's road to power has been very different to that taken by any of his predecessors as Taoiseach. He had to rebuild a party whose very existence was up for discussion. He had to convince its members that having spent as little as 18 out of the previous 80 years in office that they could be ballot box winners. And he had to battle with a hostile media class and a doubting public.

In a 1973 assessment of the first five individuals to lead governments in post-independence Ireland, academic and broadcaster Brian Farrell wrote, 'the man's own personality, experience and ambition to govern will affect his performance.' Of these three criteria, personality is the one that helped Kenny endure as a party leader. 'Always positive' is how Fionnuala Kenny describes her husband. It is a personality trait that was needed in abundance given the depressed condition of the Fine Gael organisation in 2002, and the long line of poor opinion poll results, which convinced most media commentators and political pundits that Kenny would never lead his party into government. But Kenny's positive outlook convinced him otherwise. 'I'm in this for the long haul; I've served the longest apprenticeship of them all. I intend when I get my trade qualifications to prove that we will provide the best government ever,' he pledged in a 2009 interview with this author.

This book takes up the story from the previous edition – *Fine Gael: Party at the Crossroads* – a period which includes George Lee's abrupt exit from national politics and Richard Bruton's unsuccessful attempt to oust Kenny. In responding to Lee and Bruton, Kenny displayed a toughness so frequently missed by political observers. Kenny has never been shy about taking tough decisions but his most significant contribution to the history of Fine Gael may well be the decision to so nakedly position his party as a populist and pragmatic alternative to Fianna Fáil. Rebuilt in the image of its longtime rival, Fine Gael was ready to take advantage of the dramatic economic decline after 2008 and the related collapse in support for Fianna Fáil.

As in the first edition, this book draws on background conversations with leading figures in Fine Gael. I am particularly grateful to those who found time in the aftermath of the general election in February 2011 to discuss not just the outcome but also to place context on the events since the first edition appeared at the end of 2009. Publication of Fine Gael's election blueprint strategy – discussed in chapter one – offers a revealing insight into how the party prepared for the 2011 contest: how it saw itself, its rivals and also the electorate.

Enda Kenny's period as leader of Fine Gael in opposition from 2002 to 2011 will ultimately become the first chapter in a later assessment that will now include his tenure as Taoiseach. From this vantage point it is possible to say that he was an unlikely party leader, but an effective and lucky one. Time will eventually judge the success of his singular political objective of making Fine Gael the dominant party in the Irish Republic.

Kevin Rafter
June 2011

1

The Election Blueprint

The internal Fine Gael plan that thrust Enda Kenny into Government Buildings is 47 pages in length. The confidential document, entitled '2010-2011 Election Plan', outlines the detailed strategy for positioning Fine Gael in the general election campaign particularly vis-à-vis Fianna Fáil and the Labour Party, and makes specific suggestions about the policy areas which Fine Gael needed to stress in order to win support from key sections of the electorate.

Work on the strategy document started after Richard Bruton's unsuccessful leadership heave in June 2010. The plan was framed not just against Fine Gael's internal divisions but more significantly – what its authors describe as – the 'worst economic crisis since the foundation of our State.' The final report marked 'confidential' landed on Kenny's desk in the aftermath of the 'Black Thursday' bank bailout announcement on 30 September 2010.

The authors believed that the economy would dominate the election campaign. Voters had but one question: 'How do we save our country from economic and financial disaster?' Brian Cowen's government had presided over the worst economic period in the history of the Irish State. Considerable thinking was given to how Fine Gael should approach the banking and fiscal agenda being pursued by the Fianna Fáil-Green Party coalition. The idea of another Tallaght Strategy was discounted. The Alan Dukes-led initiative, which offered support to the minority Fianna Fáil government from 1987 to 1989, was seen as having blurred the distinctions between the two main parties.

'A key goal of Fianna Fáil right now will be to wrap their arms around us and proclaim to the world that both parties are working together in the national interest. Our view is simple: If you are going to sup with the Devil, make sure you use a long spoon . . . Obviously we must do what is right by the country. But in doing so we must not in any way relent in our attacks on the Government. The country is in a terrible mess because of their gross incompetence.'

Fianna Fáil's already weakened credibility was further undermined by the State's withdrawal from the international money markets on 30 September 2010. The public faced higher taxes and deeper spending cuts to pay for the 'Black Thursday' recapitalisation plan, estimated at costing between €45bn and €50bn. The arrival of the International Monetary Fund a few weeks later only further loosened Fianna Fáil's long-time hold on the prize of being the State's largest – and most dominant – political party. Fianna Fáil was being punished in the opinion polls but the consensus in Fine Gael was that the economic collapse – and in particular the events of late 2010 – changed the political landscape not just for the government parties but also for the opposition. Fine Gael had to avoid 'broad generalisations or uncosted proposals' but also had to articulate a policy platform focused on a number of 'big ticket' proposals, the origins of which became the party's 'Five Point Plan'.

In the late autumn of 2010 Fine Gael's confidential Election Blueprint concluded that the party had to adopt a robust approach to Fianna Fáil, which – regardless of the record on the economy – would do everything possible 'to rubbish our party, our politics and our leader.' Any failure to take the attack to Fianna Fáil was also seen as leaving room for the Labour Party to exploit: 'Given the huge anti-government sentiment in the country we simply cannot allow Labour to assume the mantle of prosecutor-in-chief of the government.'

Fine Gael had to fight the election by attacking Fianna Fáil's record, while at the same time competing with Labour to be identified as the main party of change. The report makes clear that both Fianna Fáil and the Labour Party were Fine Gael's opponents irrespective of talk of a coalition deal with Eamon Gilmore's party. The objective was to put both rival parties on the defensive. The recommendations, as set out in the report, included:

- 'A need to be prepared for the viciousness of the Fianna Fáil attack. There is no low to which they will not stoop;
- A need to understand and counter Labour's more subtle approach;
- A need to be prepared to offer both positive and negative messages to the electorate;
- A need to attack the Government aggressively, otherwise Labour will outflank us;
- No attack will be left unanswered.'

Many senior figures in Fine Gael expected a general election within a matter of months, possibly even towards the end of 2010, if the government collapsed over its budgetary strategy. Although the strategists did not believe Brian Cowen's government would last to the summer of 2011, they noted that if the coalition was still in office at that stage, Fine Gael would have to revise its overall strategy. They considered a scenario of having to fight the outstanding Dáil by-elections and a Dublin mayoral election in the first half of 2011. But they also considered the possibility that the Fianna Fáil-Green Party coalition could remain in office until the early months of 2012. An appendix in the Election Blueprint document was devoted to this scenario, which would have meant contesting a presidential election in late 2011.

Against a background of continuing political uncertainty Fine Gael was preparing for all electoral eventualities. Posters and leaflets were already printed in the event of an early contest. All candidate selection conventions were to be completed within 72 hours of the dissolution of the Dáil. The first draft of the party's manifesto had been prepared in the autumn of 2009 – when there were initial doubts about the government's viability – and the document had been revised and updated in light of the changing economic environment.

The confidential report '2010-2011 Election Plan' contained specific recommendations for how Fine Gael should contest the general election and even included a proposal to establish a 'Transition Team' to frame an agenda for the first 100 days in government. There were only two members of the Fine Gael parliamentary party involved in writing the crucial document. Both were Kenny loyalists: Frances Fitzgerald, a former TD who was now party leader in Seanad Éireann; and Phil Hogan, the Carlow-Kilkenny deputy who had become Kenny's most influential advisor, and who several months earlier had masterminded the campaign against Bruton's attempted coup.

The 14-member Working Group was chaired by Frank Flannery, who had been central to the rebuilding work after the 2002 election defeat and who was now Fine Gael's director of organisation. Membership included other influential party figures: Mark Mortell, another long-time party advisor and businessman who would play a key role in readying Kenny for the electoral hustings in 2011; Ciaran Conlon, a former public relations executive who had worked as Kenny's communications advisor since 2003, but who was taking on a new role to implement the election strategy plan; Mark Kennelly, the leader's chef de cabinet and a party official for two decades; Tom Curran, the party's general secretary who joined from Macra na Feirme in 2002; the party's Dublin director organiser Terry Murphy, who had worked with the party since 1996 having arrived from the Eastern Health Board; and Mari Hurley, a financial accountant who had worked with Sherry Fitzgerald and a number of internet development companies. Key members of the party's research team were also involved in drafting the crucial document: Andrew McDowell, Fine Gael's director of policy who joined the party in 2006 having been an economist with Forfás; Joan Mulvihill, and a former Young Fine Gael president and party research officer; Cambridge University graduate and former investment banker, Sean Faughnan.

Kenny had given the Working Group a specific brief: prepare a blueprint 'to fight and win the next general election and arising out of that election for Fine Gael to be the largest party in the Oireachtas'. The terms of reference were clear; less obvious was how to unite Fine Gael for the electoral contest. The report was very much framed against the lingering bitterness from the recent heave. Kenny had sought to downplay the divisions at the parliamentary party 'think-in' at Faithlegg House in Waterford in early September 2010. 'Its fair to say Fine Gael came through a difficult time in the summer. The party is strong enough to have dealt with its decision within its own rules and we've moved on,' the Mayo man said.

At that stage there were still mixed messages for Kenny and for Fine Gael in the opinion polls. Support levels for the main parties were relatively stable in the Red C series in the *Sunday Business Post*. Fine Gael had actually rebounded in the June 2010 poll taken in the aftermath of leadership heave; party support was up three percentage points to 33 per cent. But any sense of comfort at the reversal of the recent decline was tempered by Labour's best-ever showing in a Red C survey at 27 per cent. Fianna Fáil was at 24 per cent in June 2010, and the party retained the same level in the next poll in the series in September 2010. Fine Gael was at 31 per cent (down two points) while Labour was at 23 per cent (down four points).

But another post-summer opinion poll brought bad news for Kenny. Labour had consolidated its position as the leading party in *The Irish Times* series – the party was up four percentage points to 33 per cent. Fine Gael's support level at 24 per cent placed the party on level terms with Fianna Fáil. It was the lowest Fine Gael rating in the MRBI series since June 2008. The previous *Irish Times* poll had been used by Kenny's internal critics to force the leadership heave.

For senior figures in Fine Gael, the latest poll results made no sense. They questioned the methodology used and argued that the regularity in the Red C series offered a more accurate benchmark of the party's standing. But these arguments mattered little once the top-line poll figures, which were broadcast on RTÉ's nine o'clock television news, started to circulate in political circles early in the evening of 29 September 2010. Kenny was at a meeting of his parliamentary party in Leinster House when he received a text message with the poll findings. He read out the message to the meeting and the bleak news was met by stony silence.

There was newspaper speculation about another challenge, but in Fine Gael there was little appetite to reopen the leadership issue. Senior party figures strongly dismissed talk of a new crisis. Michael Noonan claimed there was a temporary surge in support for Labour but that Fine Gael would still be the largest party in the next Dáil. Leo Varadkar said it would be foolish to overreact to individual poll results.

There was significant annoyance when former Fine Gael minister Gemma Hussey entered the fray. Hussey described Kenny as a 'good and decent man' but said that the time had come for senior party figures to tell the leader to 'go quietly'. Unnamed members of the parliamentary party briefed the Sunday newspapers on 3 October 2010 that a move was underway to dump Kenny. But there was little substance to the speculation. Kenny was critical of continued media attention on his leadership and the use of comments from a handful of unnamed malcontents to maintain speculation. He had no plans to quit: 'I do intend to be the next Taoiseach and I intend to provide the hardest-working government in the history of this State because that's what it's going to take to sort out this problem.'

Kenny was helped by the fact that the polling findings were overshadowed by the dramatic 'Black Thursday' bank bailout announcement and ongoing public debate about the scale of the required fiscal correction. The poll performance was discussed at a parliamentary meeting on 6 October 2010. The meeting was notable for the attendance of Mark Mortell, who had recently accepted an invitation from Kenny to take a full-time advisor role.

Mortell listened to over 20 members of the parliamentary party discuss the party's plight and he heard concern expressed about Labour's recent strength in the opinion polls. Like Frank Flannery, Mortell was one of the unpaid advisors cast aside by Noonan when he became leader in 2001. Both men returned, however, to support Kenny and were heavily involved with the party from 2002 onwards. In the aftermath of the leadership heave, Kenny accepted that he needed to refresh his team of advisors – he wanted Mortell to work full-time with the party until the general election was over. Many parliamentary party members were unhappy at the influence of the advisor tier, which had essentially run the party from Kenny's office from 2002 to 2007. But the increased size of the parliamentary party in 2007 brought a new dynamic to the internal power structures. It was one part of the resentment felt towards Kenny, and the heave had only made the situation more tense.

An opportunity to restructure the Leinster House operation arose over the summer months when political director Michael McLaughlin signalled that he intended to return to his consulting business. Mortell was not just another paid advisor; he had been a member of Fine Gael since 1980 and had also had been a local councillor in Wicklow. This long-time party involvement gave him currency with the TDs and Senators, even those who opposed Kenny. Mortell saw his primary role as steadying the ship. Staff were told their primary objective was to help the party's politicians to be successful. But he also had a message for the same public representatives. He spoke at the end of the meeting on 6 October 2010. He put the focus back on the party's TDs and Senators and urged them to use their passion to promote Fine Gael in the media and in the Oireachtas. 'There's an election coming and the only way into government is if you're up for this, but you have to be up for it together,' he warned.

A similar message was delivered in the confidential Election Blueprint report, which explicitly called for a united front and a consistent message: 'We are confident that our various recommendations can help the party maximise its vote at the next election. However, we also believe that none of our recommendations will make any difference unless FINE GAEL can present itself as a united party that is focused on the people of Ireland rather than on itself. . . No party that is focused on internal issues at a time of national crisis will succeed in persuading a skeptical [sic] electorate about its seriousness of purpose in resolving that crisis.'

The public sentiment from Fine Gael was that the party was united in the aftermath of the leadership heave, but the confidential assessment in the Election Blueprint report clearly highlighted ongoing internal divisions. In the case of promoting Fine Gael's policy agenda, the report noted: 'We do not believe that the Public Reps are currently doing enough. . .'. The challenge to the party's politicians was to put aside their differences: 'There are too many people in the party quietly whispering that many of our policies may never be implemented. This whispering has to stop.' The danger of not having everyone onside was spelt out very clearly: 'We cannot be half-hearted in selling our policies. Otherwise the voters/media will simply not take us seriously and we will throw away a major advantage over Labour.'

The report opened with two questions. Firstly, how should Fine Gael position itself before the election, particularly in light of the new political and economic realities? The answer to this first question came in a nine-point pre-election programme labelled 'Positioning To Win', which included the following recommendations:

1. FINE GAEL must present a UNITED FRONT and deliver a CONSISTENT MESSAGE.
2. FINE GAEL should publish its own PLAN TO REBUILD IRELAND.
3. FINE GAEL need to STRESS TEST our policies and SELL THEM internally.
4. FINE GAEL should talk about CHANGE in a way that is

true to our history and values.

5. FINE GAEL needs to use more EMOTIVE LANGUAGE.

6. FINE GAEL must articulate a clear distinctive VISION FOR IRELAND.

7. FINE GAEL needs to show that it is DIFFERENT FROM Fianna Fáil.

8. FINE GAEL must identify its TARGET VOTERS as quickly as possible.

9. FINE GAEL should define LABOUR.

Secondly, how should Fine Gael campaign in the forthcoming general election? This question was answered with another nine-point programme entitled 'Campaigning to Win', which contained the following recommendations:

1. FINE GAEL must focus on a very small number of BIG TICKET items.

2. FINE GAEL must ATTACK.

3. FINE GAEL should immediately establish a dedicated REBUTTAL UNIT.

4. FINE GAEL must stay ON MESSAGE before and during the campaign.

5. FINE GAEL needs a strong LAST WEEK strategy.

6. FINE GAEL needs to make key decisions on its NEW MEDIA strategy.

7. The Leader should establish a TRANSITION TEAM for Government.

8. FINE GAEL needs a STRUCTURE to push through our Recommendations.

9. FINE GAEL should be ready for a SNAP ELECTION.

The strategy report accepted that more work was needed to get all the parliamentary party onside with Fine Gael's policy agenda and to show that the policies were properly costed. The party was expecting a vigorous Fianna Fáil attack on its agenda. Therefore, all party policies had to be 'stress tested' to ensure spending commitments were credible in light of the deteriorating economic environment. It was now accepted that with the changing economic situation, there would be 'considerable work done on both FairCARE and NewERA to prepare both policies for the rigours of an election campaign.'

Fine Gael's market research showed that the public was favourably disposed to the party's policy agenda, but that many people did not know enough about what the party was offering. Many within the parliamentary party argued that the Fine Gael narrative could not just be about pain and sacrifice – the party also needed to offer the public some hope. With that in mind, the election strategy blueprint argued that the message for the imminent election was two fold: 'a vision that shows we are both a fiscally responsible and a caring party.'

'We need to persuade people that FINE GAEL has a plan to create a better, fairer and more prosperous Ireland. We should be talking about fairness in health and education. About empowering the citizen, holding the bankers to account and reforming our political system.'

Hogan, Flannery and others on the Working Group were confident that the existing range of policies would allow the party 'to talk with credibility on all of these issues,' and that the party's policy platform on the economy, political reform and health provided a real advantage over the Labour Party. These senior Fine Gael strategists argued that in the new economic environment the party was actually better positioned than the Labour Party to benefit from the collapse in support for Fianna Fáil. Their analysis of the tumultuous political change was contained in the Election Blueprint report – and they believed that their recommendations would put Kenny into the Taoiseach's office.

The Key Voters

The party commissioned detailed voter research in early October 2010 'to identify our target voters and feed this information into our election planning process as quickly as possible.' The objective was to build a core constituency of supporters to deliver an overall majority of Dáil seats. There was sympathy with the conclusion that David Cameron had failed to secure a majority of House of Commons seats in May 2010 because the Conservative Party did not have a clear message for its targeted voters.

Fine Gael was proposing to build on its strong rural base as well as its appeal to voters who were fiscally conservative and urban voters who were angry at the economic collapse. The party believed it had already won back voters who were conservative in fiscal/economic terms – they 'returned to us from the PDs and need to be firmly anchored to FINE GAEL.' The view among Fine Gael strategists was that Labour's surge had been underpinned by 'Angry Urban Voters' who had moved away from Fianna Fáil but who had to date shown a preference for Gilmore's party over Fine Gael.

The Fine Gael handlers identified two key groups in the 'Angry Urban' constituency whose support 'could swing the election':

1. **Negative Equity Man** – a group comprising mainly skilled working-class, commuter-belt voters in the 20 to 40 age range, known as 'Breakfast Roll man', who had, according to some pundits, helped Bertie Ahern win in 2007.

   'However, things have not gone well for NE man since 07. Unless he's lucky enough to be still working he now eats breakfast every day in his own over-priced house in the commuter belt. He can't afford the mortgage but neither can he afford to sell. Like Breakfast Roll man he's non-ideological. Unlike Breakfast Roll man he's angry – he cannot believe that the bankers have got away with it – and he wants change. He's just not sure what change he wants. He wants to believe things will get better but doesn't believe anything the politicians tell him.'

'NE man is hard to reach. Neither he nor his wife/partner, who is just as angry, are big consumers of news. While policies like NewERA, with it's potential to create tens of thousands of . . . [skilled and unskilled working class] . . . jobs, should appeal to him he knows very little about it. NE man has switched from Fianna Fáil to Labour for many reasons: To register his disgust at what has happened; because Labour is seen to be strong on the banks and he likes Gilmore; because NE man doesn't see any real difference between Fianna Fáil and FINE GAEL. Labour's lack of detailed policies is not a major worry for NE man because he's not interested in policies.'

2. **Middle Class Liberals** – a group comprising middle-aged and older [lower, middle and upper class], soft left, suburban voters. The view in Fine Gael was that the party should have been performing better with this section of the electorate than the Labour Party. But recent polling data showed Labour marginally ahead of Fine Gael although the sample size under consideration in the Election Blueprint report was relatively small.

'The MCL are soft left suburban voters. They remember the 1980s and can't believe they're back. They are utterly appalled that their children may be forced to emigrate and, like NE man, they want to see the insiders who destroyed the country pay the price. Some of the MCL are out of work; most have seen their incomes drop; and almost all have seen their wealth decline as house prices collapsed. Although liberal leaning and very keen on the word 'fair' they feel that the middle class is, as in the 1980s, being asked to carry too big a burden. They know that change is essential and are looking for politicians with a clear vision for Ireland's future.'

'The MCL are big consumers of news and agree with the Commentariat's view that there is a lack of political leadership in the country. Since the MCL are liberal it is relatively easy for them to support Labour, particularly those who work in the public sector. They like Gilmore but many worry about Labour's lack of policies and what it might do in Government. They have not by and large warmed to FINE GAEL. They don't really know what we stand for and are not sure if we understand their concerns.'

The message delivered back to Kenny and other senior party figures from the Blueprint document was clear: 'We need to better understand why these and other voters have moved to Labour – and how we can win some of that vote over to FINE GAEL.'

There was a third group of voters which the Fine Gael strategists also sought to attract in greater numbers: women. Polling data showed that women were a greater component of the undecided voters by a ratio of 2:1. 'We are concerned that the very male image of FINE GAEL and the inability/unwillingness of the party to use more emotive language could lose us some of the women's vote at election time,' the Election Blueprint report noted. Fine Gael was polling well in the 18-24 age category mainly because the left-leaning youth vote was divided between Labour and Sinn Féin. 'Our challenge is to hold on to our youth vote, which is fickle, and ensure that is actually gets out at election time.'

The recommendation from the Election Blueprint report was for Fine Gael to present a package of proposals to the electorate underpinned by a number of key messages:

1. FINE GAEL is the party of change that best understands the hopes and fears of the Irish people.

   The strategy was to develop a message of change which appealed to Negative Equity Man and also to the Middle Class Liberal. The view was that up to early autumn 2010 Fine Gael – 'helped by the government's incredible incompetence' – had succeed in telling a negative story about Fianna Fáil but 'unfortunately, FINE GAEL has not yet developed a compelling Narrative for itself.'

   The Fine Gael narrative for the general election had to achieve two things. Firstly, the party had to better connect emotionally with the electorate. 'We need to express the voters' outrage at what has happened. Unless we do so clearly and strongly why should the electorate believe us when we say we will change things?'

The message was to contain outrage at the collapse in the Irish economy – 'destroyed by a toxic mixture of incompetence, venality and self-interest' – and it had to state the unacceptability of unemployment, emigration and the decimation of 'the wealth of middle Ireland and our pensioners. . . .' The message had to express how unforgivable it was that those responsible for the crisis, the government and the bankers, had not been held to account.

The message had to be married to a plan to change the country. The policy areas identified were economic renewal, creating 100,000 jobs, dismantling the Health Services Executive, and reforming the political system.

'Our watchwords should be conviction, confidence, and competence. As importantly we should tell the Irish people what we will not do, e.g., we will not put a single extra penny into Anglo beyond X amount.' The document stressed that Fine Gael's manifesto had to include a commitment that the party would 'stop pouring money in the black hole that is Anglo Irish.'

2. FINE GAEL has a clear VISION of the kind of Ireland it wants to create.

Fine Gael's overall policy agenda was divided into three specific areas: an enterprise economy, a fair society and political reform. Firstly, the idea of an enterprise economy was stressed as a vital component of the Fine Gael policy agenda. 'It will differentiate us from Labour and should appeal to our fiscal/economic conservatives. We also need to find a way to sell NewERA and its job creation potential to Negative Equity man.' Secondly, the party's challenge was also to ensure that 'Labour does not monopolise the word 'fair'. There was a belief that the party's Fair Society proposals in health and education would win support from Middle Class Liberals. Thirdly, Fine Gael had to convince the electorate that the party was serious about political reform. 'The New Politics is absolutely crucial to FINE GAEL's overall message. If we can convince voters that we are serious about reforming politics they just might believe we are also serious about the rest of our change agenda.'

Fianna Fáil and the Labour Party

Right from the beginning of his leadership in 2002 Enda Kenny sought to position Fine Gael as a pragmatic and populist alternative to Fianna Fáil. His view of Irish politics was encapsulated in a short passage in a strategy report prepared by Frank Flannery as Fine Gael sought to carve out new electoral space in the aftermath of the 2002 meltdown election. 'Forget about history, traditions, places in history, famous old faces, and political records. Forget about traditional constituencies, old faithful lobbies, and old allegiances. In the world of 21st-century politics, the voters out there could not care less.' Indeed, the entire period of Kenny's leadership had been driven by a singular objective; replacing Fianna Fáil as the largest party in the State.

Throughout Kenny's tenure as Fine Gael leader, Fianna Fáil was the benchmark. The assessment was that Fianna Fáil had not been electorally successful because of a remarkable political ideology but because the party was 'a populist holdall party' capable of permanent reinvention to become 'everything and anything when required'. Fianna Fáil was envied for its success, which was seen as having been achieved by putting image over substance, and Kenny's Fine Gael from 2002 onwards set out to replicate this model. The party was not interested in debates about political ideologies; rather it researched what the voters wanted and then in a simpler way it delivered these policies. Whatever needed to be done, would be done.

There was no serious debate about ideology – the party was interested in capturing what it called 'the progressive centre' – the focus was placed on winning power. The reorganisation report from 2002 was blunt about the objective: 'the only coinage any political party has at the end of the day is how many votes it gets'. Fine Gael under Kenny was intent on following the market for votes. The means of achieving this reality was a confident, relevant and responsive modern political organisation – and one that had no fixed view on ideology. The strategy was to turn Fine Gael into a version of Fianna Fáil as the new dominant market leader – as understandable as Pepsi replacing Coke, Yahoo replacing Google.

Despite Kenny's lack of interest in ideology, he had actually sought to define Fine Gael in a speech to the party's youth organisation in July 2010. But interestingly he did so by considering the interests which the two main parties represented:

'Fine Gael is the party of the people. Fianna Fáil is the party of the insiders. Fianna Fáil, the so-called Republican Party, has become the party of the insiders – the bankers, developers and bureaucrats – who helped break our economy. Today it is Fine Gael that is the true party of the people. Unlike Fianna Fáil, we owe no favours to Big Business. Unlike Labour, we have no institutional links to the Big Unions. We are beholden to no one except the citizens of this country. . . we will do what we think is right for all of Ireland's people and not just the privileged few.'

Not unsurprisingly, discussion in the 2010 Blueprint document returned to this familiar Kenny theme about creating difference from Fianna Fáil: 'FINE GAEL has traditionally been reluctant to define itself. Unfortunately the lack of a distinctive FINE GAEL identity is now hurting us badly by allowing the media/Labour to tar us as Fianna Fáil-lite. Our failure to define ourselves has simply allowed others to do it for us. The normal way for a political party to define itself is by reference to ideology. But in Ireland the three main political parties are, like the electorate, broadly centrist in views. Moreover, it's not clear that defining ourselves as either left or right makes sense. The global crash and Ireland's economic collapse were both caused by massive weaknesses in the institutions and ideologies of both the Market and the State.'

Ahead of the 2011 electoral contest, Fine Gael sought to create difference from Fianna Fáil in three ways:

- By positioning itself as the party of economic competence against its larger rival – 'the party that destroyed our economy.' The confidential report noted that Fine Gael had 'to push this as the most important difference between us and Fianna Fáil.' In this speech to Young Fine Gael, Kenny argued, 'for the second time in a generation, Fianna Fáil has led the country to the edge of bankruptcy. . . while we cannot claim perfection on our record in opposition, we have called it right on a range of the big issues: on benchmarking, on the over-dependence of the public finances on the property bubble, on the failed banking policies of the government.'
- By positioning itself as the party of change against its larger rival as 'the party of the failed status quo.'
- By positioning itself as the party that would do right by the country and its people whereas Fianna Fáil 'will do what is right for the party and its friends.'

But it was not just Fianna Fáil that Kenny's party was concerned about in late 2010. There was still nervousness in Fine Gael at the strength of opinion-poll support for Labour. An election narrative for Fine Gael vis-à-vis both Fianna Fáil and the Labour Party was set out in table form in the Election Blueprint strategy.

The relationship with the Labour Party was uneasy: 'It is absolutely vital that we do not allow Labour to present itself as the sole party of change. . . the reality is that Labour is actually quite a conservative party that tends not to favour radical change.' Explanations for the increased support for Labour were offered: 'Up till now Labour has very successfully exploited the politics of

Figure 1: A Possible Narrative for FINE GAEL

1. What should FG tell voters about itself?	2. What should FG say about FF?
• The party that *will* rebuild Ireland • The party that *will* bring real change to Ireland in the national interest • The party that *will* make sure the bankers don't get away with it	• The party who destroyed Ireland and have no vision for the future • The party of the failed status quo • The party of Insiders who poured your money into Anglo **What should FG say about Labour, if necessary?** • Where's the beef/substance? • The high tax/hard left party • A possible FF coalition partner
3. What will FF say about FG?	4. What will FF say about FF?
• A broken party that won't take hard decisions • Their figures don't add up **What will Labour say about FG?** • FF lite • They don't understand you (the voters)	• We made mistakes (so did FG/Lab)… but we took the hard decisions • The party of "green shoots" **What will Labour say about Labour?** • We were right about the banks • We will create a fairer Ireland

outrage. It has been able to reflect and articulate the anger of people better than FINE GAEL. But we are now moving into a different stage of the political debate when the pressure will be on parties to be honest about what needs to be done and to spell out their solutions. FINE GAEL can in our view reap a big political reward if we are seen to project strength and competence by taking a leadership position.'

There was a real belief in the Fine Gael hierarchy that 'Black Thursday' changed the political landscape – and in their favour. (Indeed, it was a correct assessment, and there would be future political benefit for Fine Gael after the IMF intervention.) Gilmore's party was seen as having gained its initial boost in support from 'broad generalisations' and on the back of uncosted proposals. 'We can finally smoke the Labour party out and demand that they answer the hard questions. This is what we did in the early 1980s and it resulted in FINE GAEL's biggest-ever victory and a poor result for Labour.'

The strategy was to define Labour in a manner which assisted in cementing the view that Fine Gael was the only alternative to Fianna Fáil in terms of leadership and in terms of having the policies to deal with the recession. Several potential routes to foster negative public sentiment towards Gilmore and his party were suggested:

1. Labour was a soundbite party without policies.
2. Labour was a hard left party where the trade unions had a very powerful say.
3. Labour was a high tax party evident by the fact that 'Gilmore has talked a great deal more about tax increases than spending cuts.'
4. Labour is Bertie-lite. 'We can ask whether Gilmore is just another Bertie Ahern – another supposedly "nice guy" who won't take hard decisions.'
5. Labour is a potential coalition partner for Fianna Fáil.

The report recommended that Fine Gael's research team start work on 'a detailed analysis of Labour's policies and statements by its senior members' and compile 'an extensive dossier on Gilmore' in readiness for the televised leader debates.

But there were some aspects of the Labour Party proposition which the Fine Gael handlers sought to adopt for themselves: 'One of the reasons why Labour has significantly improved its position since the last election is that it uses emotive language to connect with the voters. We, by contrast, tend to use language that is policy and fact-driven.' The proposal was not to transform Fine Gael 'into the "touchy feely" party of Irish politics,' but in several places in the Blueprint document mention is made of the need to display a stronger understanding of the wider public's mood.

Learning from past mistakes

Party strategists were keen not to repeat lessons from recent election failures. The main reference election was seen as the 1992 contest, which like the imminent election was labelled a 'change election' whereby the electorate was tired with Fianna Fáil following a period of fiscal austerity and political-business controversies. 'In theory, '92 was a huge opportunity for Fine Gael. In reality, it was a triumph for Labour and a disaster for us.' The election outturn in 1992 saw Albert Reynolds leading his party to its worst ever seat total – 68 seats, a loss of 9 seats. But Fine Gael failed to prosper at the expense of its traditional rival. The party lost 10 seats. The big winners were Labour/Democratic Left who combined, took an additional 15 seats, while the Progressive Democrats won 6 extra seats.

Learning the lessons from 1992, and why Labour gained and Fine Gael did not, was seen as crucial for the contest 20 years on. Seven key lessons were identified to avoid a repeat, and were outlined in the report as:

Lesson 1: Attack. Attack. Attack.

1992: FINE GAEL in 1992 decided to run a positive campaign. Labour, by contrast, was unrelenting in its negative attacks on the government, while remaining vague on its policies for government (sound familiar?). Their approach worked – ours didn't.

Lesson 2: Let's be passionate about change.

The dominant FINE GAEL positive message in 1992 was change backed-up by a range of concrete policies. However, post-election research showed that the great majority of voters dismissed our talk of change as little more than empty rhetoric. The people simply didn't believe us.

Lesson 3: Don't underestimate the 'Gilmore for Taoiseach' message

Labour's '92 campaign hammered home one key message: Spring for Taoiseach. As a result of FINE GAEL's Tallaght Strategy, Spring was able to position himself as the real leader of the Opposition, a perception reinforced by his role in Robinson's election as President and his strong performances in the Dáil. FINE GAEL completely failed to develop a clear message on Labour.

Lesson 4: A clear communication strategy for the Leader is essential

FINE GAEL in '92 paid relatively little attention to developing a clear communications strategy for John Bruton. The dominating image of Bruton – a prosperous FINE GAEL farmer – went largely unchallenged and helped undermine the FINE GAEL change message, particularly among Dublin's middle class.

Lesson 5: Let's not become the meat in an ideological sandwich

While the Left were hitting us on one side, the Progressive Democrats also won seats in 1992, many of them at our expense.

Lesson 6: No mixed messages

FINE GAEL decided that '92 was going to be a 'policy' election and the party's communications strategy was developed on this basis. However, the whole policy message was fundamentally undermined by Bruton deciding that he would focus on the idea of a Rainbow coalition in the early days of the campaign. This was despite the party having failed to develop any clear communications strategy around the Rainbow coalition concept.

Lesson 7: The Last Week

As in 2007, FINE GAEL lost steam in the final stages of the '92 campaign. Nor were we able to respond effectively to Fianna Fáil's negative campaign in the last week.

Leadership

Enda Kenny was an unlikely leader of Fine Gael but throughout the period since 2002, he had proven to be a lucky party leader, and an effective and durable one, whose achievements were often underestimated. Following his surprising election as party leader; he focused on the areas where he could make a difference: reorganisation of Fine Gael, raising money and seeking out new candidates. He brought stamina and commitment to an unrelenting job of endless late nights and early mornings. And in this post-2002 period every meeting was the same – listening to the anger of party activists as he delivered encouragement to counter their defeatism and eliminate the loser mentality. During the 2007 general election Kenny proved that his likeability was not artificial and that he was a natural campaigner. He held his own against the most successful political leader in contemporary Irish politics, and delivered electoral success for Fine Gael but not government.

Kenny, as mentioned previously, had shown no interest in ideological debates. His ambitions were aspirational, which left room for pragmatic decision-making. 'To change Ireland for the better. And to be able to say when I've done my work with Fine Gael and as leader of the country I'm going to leave Ireland a better place. And from that perspective each citizen is central to the kind of politics that I practice,' he said in a 2009 interview with this author. Such vagueness dominated his comments during the 2001 and 2002 leadership contests. But the policies that Fine Gael subsequently adopted pointed to a deliberate strategy of positioning the party as a populist and pragmatic alternative to Fianna Fáil.

Under Kenny, the reinvention of Fine Gael was the theme but the intention was always clear: in a post-ideological political environment, Fine Gael would only succeed if the party was transformed into a version of Fianna Fáil; the future was – in the words of the 2002 strategy report – 'in combining the best facets of Fianna Fáil populism with a rejuvenated expression of the great ideals which Fine Gael stands for.' The party mirrored Fianna Fáil, and the reoganisational work after 2002 meant Kenny's party was poised to take advantage of a serious decline in support for the larger party.

Doubts about Kenny's ability persisted from the day he was elected leader of Fine Gael. Despite facing down his internal opponents in June 2010, the same questions were still being asked. In the September 2010 Red C poll 43 per cent of voters claimed they were more likely to vote for Fine Gael if the party changed leader. The continued focus on Kenny's leadership irritated those in his inner circle. 'That was the narrative for the whole duration of Kenny's leadership. Even *The Irish Times* included Richard in their poll. The narrative was essentially that Enda was leader at Richard's discretion. And some people in the parliamentary came to believe that narrative,' a party advisor says.

But ever the lucky leader, Kenny was about to benefit from tumultuous developments following the 30 September 2010 bailout announcement and Brian Lenihan's subsequent request for external support to the International Monetary Fund and the European agencies. The first indications of this fast-moving situation on public opinion came in late October 2010. The Red C pollsters described their survey as 'another watershed in the historical political landscape'. Fianna Fáil had gone through a tough two years since the autumn of 2008 but the party was about to fall further. The Fianna Fáil share of the first preference vote was at its lowest in the seven years that Red C had been surveying public opinion. The party's rating was down six points to 18 per cent. The result was a significant blow to Cowen and his colleagues. The Labour Party was up four points to 27 per cent while Fine Gael was up one point to 32 per cent. If this shift in the political environment was replicated on election day, it would deliver huge losses for Fianna Fáil and see Fine Gael arrive as the largest party in the State by some distance.

There was no coming back for Fianna Fáil – the international bailout in late November 2010 stripped the party of all pretences to the crucial mantle of economic competency. The unravelling of its historic political dominance became evident early in 2011 as Brian Cowen struggled to hold onto his leadership and while he survived a confidence motion, he was shortly to hand over responsibility to Micheál Martin as the grim reaper of an election loomed. Fine Gael's fortunes were on the rise as support for the Labour Party declined from its historic highs. In an end-of-year Red C poll, voters were asked which party they considered best equipped to handle the economy. Fine Gael was on top at 34 per cent with Labour at 23 per cent, while Fianna Fáil – like its own party support – was some way back in third place at 17 per cent.

During this time some political commentators remarked that Kenny had disappeared from public view. Michael Noonan and the party's other economic spokespeople were certainly dominating radio and television debates. 'It's bullshit that he was hidden,' a party insider says. But following his arrival as a full-time advisor, Mark Mortell had instigated a total overhaul of the party's communication strategy. Mortell judged that most people's perception of Kenny was influenced by what they saw and read in the media. But Kenny did not do himself justice in radio or television interviews. So a decision was taken to minimise Kenny's media appearances. Kenny was visible, but now on the terms largely set down by Mortell. Set-piece interviews were reduced. The strategy was to play to Kenny's strengths.

There is little doubt that Kenny had been a victim of 'pack journalism', where reporters feed off one another and reinforce their joint opinion. This pack-formed consensus that Kenny was not up for the job had persisted for several years. His mistakes were over-exaggerated and excessively dissected. His achievements too easily dismissed. Yet when people met Kenny, they saw a different individual from his media portrait. He had undoubted weaknesse: he was a poor media performer and he was a negative for certain sections of the electorate. 'He's very "west of Ireland". And that rural thing does grate with an urban audience and with women voters,' one Fine Gael official accepted.

Kenny is not an intellectual – nor does he claim to be one – but the June 2010 leadership heave had shown that neither was he the fool so often described by the media. Indeed, many of his long-time detractors finally accepted that he was an astute political leader with excellent instincts. Indeed, as a survivor, he shared many characteristics with Charlie Haughey. Both men were always at their best when under pressure and having to respond to tricky political situations. Kenny had displayed those survival qualities most recently when fighting for his job as Fine Gael leader and also in handling the fallout from the abrupt resignation of George Lee.

The Election Blueprint report addressed the leadership issue: 'any narrative for the party will not work unless the Leader can also answer one simple question in a convincing manner: Why do you want to be Taoiseach?'

'We suggest that the Leader should pitch himself as the People's Champion, the man who will make the right decisions to defend the people of Ireland from the Insiders and the Fianna Fáil cronies who have brought our country to its knees; from the threats to our national sovereignty in the wake of Black Thursday.'

Nevertheless, after almost nine years of media hostility, Fine Gael strategists were not expecting any favours from the media. The Election Strategy Working Group was concerned about media perception of Kenny, Fine Gael and the party's policies. Particular attention was devoted to opinion-formers, what they called the 'commentariat', and they went as far as explicitly defining this group as 'the most important opinion formers in the old and new media, including key editors, correspondents, columnists, academics and bloggers.'

The 'commentariat' was seen as having two important roles: firstly, 'they act as an important filter between FINE GAEL and the voters;' and secondly, 'perhaps even more importantly, many people in FINE GAEL look to the commentariat for validation of our policies/ideas.'

The task was to convince 'at least some of the commentariat' about the seriousness of Fine Gael's commitment to real change in

Irish society. The power of these opinion-formers was acknowledged: 'The fact that FINE GAEL did not receive any real support from major commentators for its banking policy undoubtedly diminished support for the policy internally, even though events have subsequently proven that the policy was broadly correct.'

The Election Blueprint made a number of proposals to overhaul the party's approach to communications, including preparing a specific new media strategy. The Fine Gael response was to have a comprehensive, rapid rebuttal strategy in place to avoid panic, and also to have their own attack agenda against Fianna Fáil and Labour policies. 'We cannot wait until the election is called for our Prebuttal, Attack and Rebuttal (PAR) approach to be adopted. Voters (and candidates) need to understand the nature of the campaign that will be waged by us. This will be a fundamental part of the FINE GAEL campaign.'

Staying 'on-message' had to become the core of the party's communication strategy before and during the election campaign to ensure that '. . . everyone, from the Leader down, stays strictly on message.' There were admiring references to the main themes from the 1992 Clinton Presidential campaign and the coherence of the message that the then Arkansas Governor presented to the American electorate:

- Change versus More of the Same – the main message.
- The Economy Stupid – the main concern of voters.
- Don't Forget Health Care – the key non-economic policy.

The challenge for Fine Gael was to develop an equivalent series of messages. An example was given:

- We Will Save the Country by Changing the Country – the main message.
- Jobs – the chief concern of voters.
- Don't Forget FairCare or New Politics – Fine Gael's key non-

economic policies.

The advisors wanted to build on Kenny's main strengths, which were identified as a genuine interest in and commitment to the people of Ireland; a steadfastness in the face of pressure; and a willingness to challenge established interests over issues like the Seanad, privatisation of state companies and reforming the health services. 'The plan wasn't to tell the voters that Enda was brilliant – they wouldn't believe that – but we had to make them see that he could do the job,' one Fine Gael strategist says.

An outline of a narrative for Kenny was presented with scenarios dealing with all the main party leaders. Labour would present Kenny as 'a nice guy who doesn't connect,' while Fianna Fáil would focus on the post-heave divisions in Fine Gael and Kenny being 'weak on policy'. The counter argument from Fine Gael was to present Kenny as 'a strong leader with a clear vision' and 'The People's Champion'. When attacking Cowen, Fine Gael identified three words – 'incompetent, arrogant and out of touch'. But the recommendation for Gilmore – undoubtedly conscious of a potential coalition partnership – was less strident: 'What should FG say about Gilmore, if necessary? All things to all men.'

The political situation was in so much flux that within weeks of the Blueprint document landing on Kenny's desk, a bailout from

Figure 2: A Possible Narrative for the Leader

1. What should FG tell voters about EK?	2. What should FG say about Cowen?
• A strong leader with a clear vision • The Peoples' Champion	• Incompetent, arrogant and out of touch **What should FG say about Gilmore, if necessary?** • All things to all men
3. What will FF say about EK?	4. What will FF say about Cowen
• Leads a broken party • Weak on policy **What will Labour say about EK?** • A nice guy who doesn't connect	• He's taken the hard decisions **What will Labour say about Gilmore?** • "Gilmore for Taoiseach"

the IMF was secured, the Green Party announced its intention to pull out of government and all the planning for an electoral contest with Brian Cowen as leader of Fianna Fáil was cast aside.

In the final Red C survey in 2010 the pollsters observed that 'the clear impact among voters in today's poll is that a previously perhaps uncommitted electorate is now beginning to crystallise their intentions.' With an election due early in 2011 the impact of the political upheaval in government and Brian Lenihan's austere IMF budget could be seen in the poll findings. The news for Fine Gael was good, as the Red C experts observed: 'Fine Gael fortunes are on the rise, as voters become more focused on an actual election. They remain the largest party in the state, and also have an upward trend in support over the past few months. Much is made of momentum in any election campaign and at present the party appears to have a steady upward growth in support. Their potential support is also the highest of any party, with over 60 per cent saying they may potentially vote Fine Gael; while their loyal support is also the highest with 21 per cent of all likely voters already saying they will definitely vote for the party.'

The February 2011 campaign was like no other in Irish electoral history. Fianna Fail was essentially a bit-player in the national narrative – a unique position for a party which had dominated Irish politics since 1932. Fine Gael ran a highly professional campaign in 2011. The party had access to considerable resources. Unlike four years previously, the Fine Gael frontbench were politicians with serious ministerial potential – Noonan, Hogan Varadkar, Coveney, Reilly and Shatter. Lessons had been learnt from the previous campaign and, in particular, the party's poor performance in the days before polling. The Blueprint plan had issued a clear warning: 'FINE GAEL has traditionally not been strong in the last week of a campaign. Yet this is exactly when many of the swing voters decide how to vote. FINE GAEL must ensure that this time, the last week is dominated by a strong FINE GAEL message and that we are not responding to the other parties.'

Previous elections had been dominated by the leaders' tour.

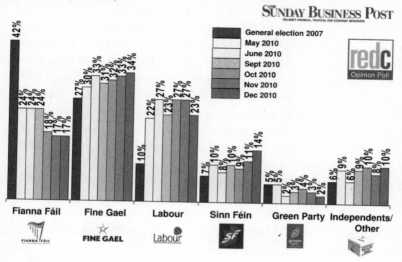

If there were a *general election* tomorrow, to which party or independent candidate would you give your first preference vote?
(Base: All adults WHO WILL VOTE 18+)

SUNDAY BUSINESS POST
IRELAND'S FINANCIAL, POLITICAL AND ECONOMIC NEWSPAPER

redc
Opinion Poll

Legend:
- General election 2007
- May 2010
- June 2010
- Sept 2010
- Oct 2010
- Nov 2010
- Dec 2010

Fianna Fáil: 42%, 24%, 24%, 24%, 18%, 17%, 17%
Fine Gael: 27%, 30%, 33%, 31%, 28%, 33%, 34%
Labour: 10%, 22%, 27%, 23%, 27%, 27%, 23%
Sinn Féin: 7%, 10%, 8%, 10%, 9%, 11%, 14%
Green Party: 5%, 5%, 2%, 3%, 4%, 3%, 2%
Independents/Other: 6%, 9%, 6%, 9%, 10%, 8%, 10%

Kenny had been a success on the road, meeting voters and rallying the party troops. A winter election meant the opportunities available for such a tour were more limited than in 2007. There was also recognition that Kenny's availability would be more limited than previously with several televised leader debates. Considerable work was done preparing for the televised debates – a showdown with Vincent Browne on TV3 was rejected from the outset regardless of what terms the station proposed to get Kenny to debate with Gilmore and Micheál Martin, the new Fianna Fáil leader.

Kenny went into the three other debates as the most experienced of the main party leaders, although the media narrative was still that he was the one to watch for mistakes. Fine Gael strategists believed their offering to the electorate was more realistic than that promoted by the Labour Party, while Fianna Fáil was simply discredited. The issues and themes in the Election Blueprint document had been distilled down into a five-point recovery plan covering jobs, the budget, the health services, the public sector and political reform.

The party's message was clear: 'Ireland is in the middle of the biggest crisis in the history of the State. There are no easy answers or quick fixes. But we are optimistic that the road to recovery is there with the right leadership and the will to reinvent, re-imagine and reform our Nation. It is going to take hard work to get the country back on an even footing and to get Ireland working again. Fine Gael believes we can get Ireland working together.' Research showed that the five-point plan worked with the voters. Kenny kept it to the fore in the debates and even at one stage, when under pressure from Martin, advising the Fianna Fáil leader to look online for the information he was seeking.

The media loved the debates and the voters watched in sizable numbers, but they were less influenced by what they saw and heard. Before the final three-way debate between the leaders of Fianna Fáil, Fine Gael and Labour, one survey showed that fewer than half of all voters (47 per cent) said that the first three debates had had an impact on how they would vote. They were taking a much broader view – allowing their vote to be determined by coverage in the news media (71 per cent), the content of the party manifestos (68 per cent) and discussions with friends and family (58 per cent).

The much-anticipated 'Kenny factor' did not play with voters. Kenny performed strongly on the hustings and did well in the televised debates. There were strong visual images during the campaign when he met with European leaders including a trip to Berlin to meet Angel Merkel. There was a dramatic turnaround in the public's attitude to the Fine Gael leader. At the start of the campaign Kenny trailed both Martin and Gilmore in the voters choice as the best Taoiseach. But in the final Red C survey before polling day Kenny was ahead of his two rivals. 'Kenny is the leader that most people would now like to see as Taoiseach; with 35 per cent now supporting him, up a staggering 12 per cent since the start of the campaign,' the Red C experts noted.

The voters wanted stability and that was something only a government involving Fine Gael could offer. And the voters had come to accept that Kenny would lead this new government. The trend for Fine Gael had been very positive in the Red C series since the start of January 2011. The party had moved from 32 per cent in the January poll to 40 per cent in the final survey before polling day on 25 February 2011. There was talk of a single party Fine Gael government but the final Red C survey still saw Fine Gael somewhat short of what was needed for an overall majority of Dáil seats. Moreover, the final Ipos MRBI survey had Fine Gael support at 37 per cent. Kenny's party was set for a very good result but not enough to govern as a single party majority government.

Some months previously, the Blueprint Plan document spelt out the Fine Gael strategy to win an election that the party's senior advisors believed would 'be fundamental to the future direction of the country for a generation.' Their message to Enda Kenny was clear: 'We face an opponent who wrought havoc and destruction on a productive and dynamic economy. Ireland needs new direction, new policies and a new team to begin the rebuilding of the economy and our society. It is an election that must, in the national interest, result in a Fine Gael-led government.'

When the final ballot papers were counted, political history was made. Kenny had succeeded in his ambition in making Fine Gael the largest party in the State. Fine Gael won 36 per cent of the vote and took 76 seats. Fianna Fáil was not just defeated but on 19 per cent and with a mere 20 Dáil seats, the party, which Eamon de Valera had taken into government for the first time in 1932, was broken. The Labour Party had an excellent result but the talk of 'Gilmore for Taoiseach' had been misplaced.

And yet in dumping Fianna Fáil out of office the electorate had done as they had done previously in turning to a Fine Gael-led administration. Although on a more dramatic scale, the change of government in 2011 was merely a repeat of the outcome experienced in 1948, 1954, 1973, 1981 and November 1982. In each of those electoral contests Fianna Fáil was sent to the opposition benches while Fine Gael entered office to lead an alternative government.

There was political history but no revolution on 25 February 2011 – revolution implies a fundamental change in power or organisational structures. The Irish electorate actually reaffirmed their conservative nature. In rejecting Fianna Fáil they turned to another centrist, pragmatic party. But Enda Kenny had achieved his personal objective: Pepsi had replaced Coke, Yahoo had replaced Google – Fine Gael had replaced Fianna Fáil.

2
After Garret

The resignation of Garret FitzGerald in the aftermath of the 1987 election defeat left Fine Gael not just with a leadership problem but also sharply divided views about the party's identity and future direction. The struggle for the heart of Fine Gael was not easily resolved. Alan Dukes was given a little over three years before being forced to stand down as leader ahead of a no-confidence motion in November 1990. His successor, John Bruton, having withstood a leadership coup early in 1994 did not seem likely to see a fifth year as party leader. But then the unexpected collapse of the Albert Reynolds-led Fianna Fáil-Labour coalition in the autumn of 1994 led to the creation of a new government without a general election. Outside Áras an Uachtaráin, Bruton was asked how he felt at being catapulted into the Taoiseach's office. 'It's a bit of a shock,' he replied. His party opponents were in even greater shock, and many languished on the backbenches as Bruton enjoyed two and a half years leading the Rainbow coalition comprising Fine Gael, the Labour Party and Democratic Left. But being in office only brought a public pause to the Fine Gael leadership debate, and after the party returned to opposition in 1997 the internal battle which had been ongoing since the day FitzGerald resigned recommenced.

Fine Gael was seen as having stagnated after the 1997 general election. There had been a by-election victory in Cork South Central in October 1998 and a credible second place in the Tipperary South by-election in June 2000. But the party's national standing remained lacklustre. Opinion poll ratings were poor. The local elections in 1999 had delivered an increase in the party's first preference vote to 28 per cent and seven additional local council seats, but there were signs of trouble ahead. The party's deputy leader, Nora Owen, failed to win a council seat.

It was a tough time to be in opposition. Bertie Ahern's Fianna Fáil-Progressive Democrat coalition benefited from a national 'feel-good' factor. The economy was booming. The peace process was consolidated in Northern Ireland. Ahern and his coalition achieved consistently high satisfaction ratings. In 1998 after the signing of the Belfast Agreement, the government's satisfaction levels hit 73 per cent. A Fine Gael publicity campaign in late 2000 to draw attention to the downside of the economic boom backfired badly for Bruton. The 'Celtic Snail' campaign was supposed to tap into public dissatisfaction with 'poor quality of life' issues arising from unprecedented economic growth – traffic congestion, high housing prices and costly childcare. 'We'll grab the snail by the horns,' the slogan promised alongside an image of a snail coloured in green. But rather than troubling Ahern's administration, the ill-conceived campaign heaped public and media derision upon an already-struggling Fine Gael.

It seemed that there was little the main opposition party could do to improve its standing with the voters. Even the tribunals of inquiry at Dublin Castle – which generated damning revelations against Fianna Fáil politicians – had little impact on support for Ahern or his party. Fine Gael also had its own tribunal troubles. In April 2000 Frank Dunlop – a former Fianna Fáil government advisor and party strategist – revealed that he had paid 15 Dublin county councillors over IR£112,000 in connection with land rezonings. Fianna Fáil and Fine Gael were forced to establish internal party investigations. Six Fine Gael Oireachtas members told their party inquiry that they received money from Dunlop. They all said the donations were for political purposes and had not influenced their voting decisions. Bruton decided that another three party public representatives would be prevented from being nominated for the following general election unless they provided more detailed information in relation to payments received from Dunlop. The move was met by threats of legal action. The debacle made it difficult for Fine Gael to play the 'honesty' card vis-à-vis Fianna Fáil.

Bruton also added to his own troubles. In June 2000 he left open the possibility of disgraced former Fine Gael minister Michael Lowry regaining party membership. Lowry had resigned in controversy four years previously when journalist Sam Smyth revealed in the *Irish Independent* that businessman Ben Dunne had paid for an extension to Lowry's County Tipperary house. Further disturbing evidence emerged at a subsequent tribunal of inquiry which showed that Lowry's business arrangements had been designed to evade substantial amounts of tax. An investigation was also ongoing into Lowry's role in the awarding of a lucrative mobile phone license when he was a government minister – which when concluded in 2011 was damning of the former minister's role in the awarding process. But despite what was already known about Lowry in 2000, Bruton did not rule out his return to Fine Gael. He said that to do otherwise would have been 'unchristian'. The comments only added to growing frustration in party ranks although Bruton still had a coherent group of supporters including Phil Hogan from Carlow-Kilkenny and Enda Kenny, a long-time TD from Mayo who, like fellow loyalist Nora Owen, had served as a cabinet minister in the Rainbow coalition.

But another senior party figure, Austin Deasy, who had been a minister in the Fine Gael-Labour coalition in the 1980s, had had enough. In November 2000 the Waterford TD tabled a no-confidence motion in Bruton. Deasy did not consult his colleagues. His action caught Bruton's other detractors by surprise. They were not prepared for a heave. The motion was beaten but the leadership issue had not been fully settled. Many members of the Fine Gael parliamentary party were unconvinced that Bruton could turn around the party's fortunes. A growing band of critics were merely biding their time. Rumours started to circulate in early January

2001 about a private opinion poll testing support for alternative leaders. The results were said to be poor for the former Taoiseach.

An opinion poll in *The Irish Times* in late January 2001 eventually forced Bruton's opponents into action. The party's national support was at 19 per cent; its rating in Dublin was 11 per cent. Bruton's satisfaction rating had fallen to 37 per cent. The party was facing electoral disaster. 'The nightmare is just beginning,' one newspaper recorded. The endorsement Bruton had received from his colleagues only three months previously no longer mattered. Responding to the opinion poll results, Alan Shatter, a member of the party's frontbench, suggested Bruton should resign. Two party heavyweights, Michael Noonan and Jim Mitchell, were ready to force the issue. They had both served as senior ministers under Garret FitzGerald, and each had an ambition to lead Fine Gael. The two men were in agreement that the timing was right for a heave, and they went public together. Noonan predicted that Bruton would 'close down' the party if he remained as leader. Mitchell referred to Bruton as a 'weak currency'. The remarks incensed supporters of the former Taoiseach who argued that another heave was ill-conceived and would be hugely damaging to Fine Gael regardless of the outcome.

Bruton was not going to go easily. He had successfully survived an attempt to remove him in 1994 when – as in 2002 – poor opinion poll results motivated senior party members to act. Four frontbench TDs – Charlie Flanagan, Alan Shatter, Jim O'Keeffe and Jim Higgins – went to Bruton to seek his resignation. But Bruton had got wind of their plans and ensured that several of his supporters were present at the showdown. When the four plotters recognised the failure of their endeavour, O'Keeffe belatedly offered their resignations from the frontbench to which Bruton curtly replied, 'There's no need, Jim, you're all fired anyway.'

Eight years later, having enjoyed a successful term as Taoiseach but having failed to dramatically lift the party's electoral fortunes, Bruton's hold on the Fine Gael leadership was once more under threat. He opted to fight the challenge from Noonan and Mitchell calling on his colleagues not to 'desert the colours.' The Bruton camp knew the numbers were very tight; a narrow victory was the best they hoped for heading into the crucial parliamentary party meeting. Phil Hogan, a Bruton loyalist, admitted that a tie of 36-36 was a possibility. Nora Owen hoped for the best but told Bruton that he would probably be 'pipped'. Several undecided parliamentary party members only made their minds up during the meeting which lasted for seven hours. Mitchell proposed the motion. Noonan seconded it. Enda Kenny was the first to speak in favour of Bruton – the two politicians were friends and had shared an office together at one stage. Kenny was also critical of those responsible for the no confidence motion. In all, 48 of the 72 members spoke. Bruton was defeated by 39 votes to 33. Just three people changing sides would have given the former Taoiseach victory. Alan Dukes had resigned in November 1990 before a no-confidence motion was voted upon, so now for the first time in its history Fine Gael had directly removed a leader from office. Bruton made a dignified speech and predicted Fine Gael success at the next general election. But the party was deeply divided. The atmosphere in the party offices in Leinster House was hostile. Colleagues in the parliamentary party were not talking to each other.

Noonan had backed veteran politician Peter Barry in the leadership election following FitzGerald's resignation in 1987. He had long held ambitions for the leader's job, and supporters of Dukes – and later of Bruton – privately believed that Noonan had, for his own ultimate gain, never been fully committed to ensuring the party's success. Having played the waiting game for over a decade, Noonan was now in a strong position to lead Fine Gael. He had the support of a considerable section of the parliamentary party, and was the front-runner to succeed Bruton. But he was not the only candidate. Mitchell declared his intention to seek the position although he had an agreed platform with Noonan. Many in the party doubted that Mitchell would be a candidate when the nominations closed at 6 p.m. on Monday 5 February 2001. Noonan's alliance with Mitchell offered the party a 'dream ticket' of sorts. But whatever hope the Noonan-Mitchell axis had of avoiding a contest was dashed within hours of Bruton's defeat when Enda Kenny entered the contest. There would be no coronation for Noonan, something his backers were furious about.

There was considerable surprise at Kenny's ambition. He had been in Leinster House since 1975, had served for a short period as junior minister in the 1980s and as Minister for Tourism and Trade in the 1994-97 Rainbow coalition. But he had never made a big national impression. He had been a Bruton loyalist but he was not a political heavyweight in Fine Gael circles. Kenny was very popular, seen as excellent company, was always available when work was required at party events and by-elections; but, in truth, many colleagues saw him as a political lightweight.

'To be honest, I'm not sure many of us took his decision to run as very serious,' one senior party figure now admits. 'On the face of it the entry of Enda Kenny would seem to protect the Bruton votes. The Mayo man is the most popular deputy in the House but has not been noted either for his ambition or hunger for the job,' the Drapier column in *The Irish Times* observed. The unsigned weekly column was written by different politicians, and most likely in this case by a senior Fine Gael figure.

Following the Bruton defeat, Ivan Yates, a former Agriculture Minister from Wexford, was the most likely successor from among the former leader's supporters. But Yates, who was first elected in 1981 and had a successful bookmakers business, had grown weary of political life and wanted a new challenge. He indicated that he was not interested in the leadership, and not long afterwards announced his decision to leave political life at the next general election. Yates would have been a formidable candidate against Noonan. But with the Wexford politician's decision not to contest, Kenny saw his opportunity. He believed the interests of the party were best served by a leadership contest in which the members of the parliamentary party were presented with a choice. 'I felt a sense of anger at what had happened but the decision to run was my own,' he says. 'I genuinely felt that the time had come where I had to get up and be counted by my peers.'

Kenny came to his decision several hours after Bruton's defeat. It was 1.30 a.m. when he dialled the number of his home phone in Castlebar in County Mayo. His wife, Fionnuala O'Kelly, was asleep when the phone rang. 'I won't stop you but do you really want to do this?' she immediately responded. O'Kelly had worked with Fianna Fáil during the Haughey years so she knew better than most the difficult job of being leader of an opposition party, and especially one as divided as Fine Gael in 2001. Her initial reaction was also influenced by the impact on the family's life in Castlebar. If Kenny was successful, their lives would be transformed overnight. 'Do we need this grief?' she asked. The period since the end of the Rainbow coalition in mid-1997 had brought a degree of normality to the household with Kenny's life as an opposition deputy involving a more civilised working week, and more time at home with the couple's three young children. But whatever about her initial reaction, O'Kelly totally supported the decision to contest. 'I'm fully behind you,' she said as the early morning phone call ended.

A short statement declaring his candidature was issued. Kenny said he was running 'to provide a real choice for members of the parliamentary party' which, he believed, was in the best interests of Fine Gael nationally. 'Fianna Fáil have been in government for too long. I believe that the only viable, credible alternative to a Fianna Fáil-led government is a Fine Gael-led government, and I believe that I am the best person to provide a strong and credible alternative to the electorate when they next come to the polls,' Kenny asserted.

The Bruton wing of the party would have been expected to back the Mayo man but Kenny was anxious not to be seen as a candidate of the disposed leader. Support from all sections of the parliamentary party was claimed: 'I have received approaches from many members who both supported and opposed [the] motion of no-confidence.' But if Kenny had significant support, he appeared unwilling to show the strength of his backing. One supporter, Mayo senator Paddy Burke, said Kenny did not want party members to declare their support in public. 'He wants to unite the party. He will be talking to people in a private capacity. He has spoken to quite a number of party colleagues but he won't divulge their names. He is not putting pressure on anyone to publicly support him.' The intervention, however, only strengthened the view that Kenny did not have sufficient confidence in his own support base.

Kenny was trading on personal qualities well known to his colleagues. But even his closest friends in political life acknowledged a long career marked by a lack of serious achievement. 'He's very intelligent, extremely efficient and competent. He's honest and a good performer when he wants to be,' one Fine Gael colleague noted. The 'when he wants to be' assessment was widely shared. 'He has a lack of motivation and no natural presence. No one ever considered him for the job and we were quite taken aback when he announced his intention to go for it,' another Fine Gael source told the *Irish Independent*.

Most commentators dismissed the seriousness of Kenny's candidacy in 2001. One writer described him as 'a photogenic lightweight'. Columnist Vincent Browne raised doubts about his experience: 'And now out of the blue, comes a very nice fella, offering himself as leader of Fine Gael, Enda Kenny. His name would not have been the first or the second or even 23rd that would have occurred to me as a future leader of Fine Gael . . . But now that Enda Kenny himself has thought of the idea, maybe it is not so bad. Enda is a nice fella, maybe even a bit nicer than Bertie. He may not know much about BSE or decommissioning [...] or Ned O'Keeffe's farming practices or who is the Prime Minister of India or what is the capital of Djibouti. But people who meet him like him almost immediately.' While acknowledging that the Mayo TD was 'universally viewed as terrific company, a noted wit and as laid-back as a collapsed soufflé', journalist Miriam Lord delivered an equally devastating critique of Kenny's candidacy:

Just imagine the scene in the No-No-Noonan camp on Wednesday night after their defeat: like the dressing-room of the beaten county finalists after they've been hacked off the park by the neighbouring parish [...] Strong men and women are crying, from doughty full-back Nora to nippy winger Gay, who has exuded more moisture during his campaign than a burst main. They are a demoralised bunch. But not for long. Because somebody gets an idea. Always a bad sign in Fine Gael. 'Let's blow Noonan out of the water with a fresh, young candidate. A blonde. A big picture of a blonde on the lamp-posts would beat any airbrushed waxwork of Bertie. Now. Who fits the bill?' And they all look around at Enda, who is weeping quietly in the corner into the results of the recent TG4 opinion poll, which had him in third place behind party and constituency colleagues, Michael Ring and Jim Higgins. A shaft of moonlight shines through the broken window, bouncing off the golden hair of the dejected Mayo man and blinding his distraught colleagues. 'Indakinny!' they shout. 'Young and blond and will keep his mouth shut. He's the boy for us.' And so it came to pass that a mere stripling of fifty years of age, with twenty-five years of Dáil experience, emerged as the fresh, youthful face of Fine Gael, the young fella who will scupper the leadership plans of Michael Noonan and Jim Mitchell.

Few contenders for a senior political role had previously experienced the level of hostility heaped upon the Mayo politician. He also faced criticism from Mitchell that he represented the 'inert and conservative' section of the party. Throughout the short leadership campaign, Kenny attempted to counter the perception that he was a political lightweight. 'I don't know where this notion of Enda Kenny not having dealt with substantial issues over the years has come from. Just because one has a sense of humour and is not weighed down by the troubles of the world does not mean that one doesn't have a conviction or a competence to do the job in a proper manner.'

In media commentary Kenny was described as 'polished, photogenic, friendly, efficient'. One newspaper noted: 'Popular, witty and an accomplished raconteur and mimic, his personality would not spark a bitter campaign.' But little was actually known about Kenny's politics. Noonan had staked out positions on national issues as a senior minister and, like Mitchell, he was also a long-standing politician with a high public profile. Kenny, although a TD since 1975, was an unknown to most members of the public.

When questioned, Kenny gave away little about his political beliefs, not to mention any sense that there was an ideology in his approach to politics. His responses were vague, non-specific and, in truth, littered with universal political aspirations. Kenny promised that under his leadership Fine Gael would 'set new priorities for a wealthy nation that has so far shown itself incapable of offering proper standards in basic public services.' He outlined a list of general priorities. These included a pledge to end the sub-standard public health system; to target education spending and end the situation where one in six children left school without basic literacy skills; to tackle homelessness; and to deal with problems for carers and confront the crisis in childcare provision.

In his most memorable contribution during the 2001 party leadership contest, Kenny pledged to 'electrify' Fine Gael from the grassroots upwards. He promised to turn Fine Gael into 'a campaigning party' to tap into public anger at neglect in priority policy areas. He was not offering political redefinition or ideological overhaul. 'This row, if you like, was about lack of image, lack of style, a different form of leader, a new face,' he said, 'I have an electoral contact with people in a way that I believe Jim Mitchell or Michael Noonan do not.' With an almost ugly post-heave mood engulfing the deeply divided Fine Gael parliamentary party, Kenny promised to be 'a consensus builder and a team builder.' He described himself as someone who would provide 'a fresh face with a long political experience, somebody who has the energy and the stamina to reenergise and revitalise the Fine Gael electorate.' The message was clear: 'I don't carry any baggage.' His supporters played up the idea that their man could outdo Bertie Ahern in the contest of personality politics.

Mitchell was the public's favourite to succeed Bruton according to an IMS opinion poll. The former minister and Dublin Central TD had 30 per cent support among voters with Noonan on 25 per cent and Kenny on 17 per cent. However, among Fine Gael supporters the preference ranking changed. Noonan had more support among the party faithful than either Mitchell or Kenny. Some 32 per cent backed Noonan against 27 per cent for Mitchell and 25 per cent for Kenny. Intriguingly, reports of a private opinion poll on the Fine Gael leadership started to circulate. An opinion poll had been commissioned by supporters of Mitchell before the results of the January 2001 *Irish Times* survey which precipitated the heave against Bruton. Information from the confidential poll became public prior to the leadership contest. Just as in the IMS opinion poll, Mitchell was first choice to succeed Bruton with the public but Noonan was the favourite of Fine Gael voters. The private poll had been commissioned to test the strengths of alternatives to Bruton. The name of Ivan Yates was included but Kenny's was not, clear evidence that in January 2001 the plotters against Bruton did not rate Kenny as a credible threat. Not to be outdone, the Kenny camp produced the results of a telephone poll which suggested their candidate had stronger public support than the other candidates. The results had Kenny on 29 per cent, Noonan on 28 per cent, Mitchell on 22 per cent and 1 per cent for another Bruton-loyalist, Bernard Allen from Cork who had also entered the contest. But the poll gained little attention as it was based on a sample of 100 respondents.

Four nominations were eventually received for the vacant leadership position – Noonan, Mitchell, Kenny and Allen. The candidates were interviewed for a pre-recorded report on RTÉ's *Prime Time* programme broadcast the evening prior to the parliamentary party meeting. The programme gathered together a panel of floating voters to assess the responses of the four contenders to questions set by reporter, David Nally. Kenny stressed his ministerial experience and an ability to lead a team in revitalising the Fine Gael organisation. But when pressed on policy specifics, Kenny displayed a lack of confidence, stumbling through his answers. The panel was not impressed. The feedback included views that he was weak, a disaster, not clear, a sincere man with nothing specific to say and, most damning of all, 'an also-ran'. Nally asked the panel to rank the four candidates out of a maximum of 80 points. Mitchell confirmed his opinion poll showing by coming first with 55 points out of 80, Noonan received 52 points, Allen 44 and Kenny was last with 31 points.

Ahead of the leadership vote, half of the parliamentary party had not declared their allegiance publicly. Of those who had indicated a preference, Noonan had the support of 23 parliamentary party members, Kenny had 12, Mitchell had five and Allen had three. Noonan had the backing of several senior party figures including Alan Dukes, Frances Fitzgerald, Alan Shatter and Charlie Flanagan. The Kenny camp was claiming over 30 votes for their candidate – seven short of the number needed for victory. 'It's all to play for,' Kenny said. 'The battle will be won and lost in the corridors of Dáil Éireann.'

The relative weakness in Kenny's bid, however, was evident in a comment from Jim Higgins, another Mayo TD. 'Enda is in with a right good shout. It's a fantastic achievement to come from nowhere and build up a bloc of over 30 votes.' But being the candidate from nowhere did give some parliamentary party members something to consider when making their choice. 'Do I go for the fresh face or for the tried and trusted? It's a difficult decision,' said Donal Carey from Clare. Prior to the crucial parliamentary party meeting, Kenny had the public support of Jim Higgins and Michael Ring who were his constituency colleagues in Mayo, and senators Paddy Burke and Ernie Caffrey. The best-known names to declare support for Kenny were former junior minister Avril Doyle from Wexford and Dun Laoghaire TD Sean Barrett, a minister under FitzGerald and Bruton. He was also backed by John Perry from Sligo-Leitrim and John Farrelly from Meath. 'If John Bruton wasn't clicking with the public I don't believe either of the other three will. Kenny is a fresher face,' said Farrelly, a long-time friend.

When the parliamentary party met at 11 a.m. on Friday 6 February 2001 the pre-printed ballot paper circulated to each of the voters contained four names. But ultimately they were faced with a straight choice between Noonan and Kenny. Allen withdrew on the eve of the meeting having gained insufficient backing to mount a serious challenge. Speculation surrounded Mitchell's intentions particularly as he remained in close contact with Noonan during the contest. With the withdrawal of first Allen and then Mitchell the voting system was straightforward – the candidate with the most votes from the 72-member parliamentary party would win. Kenny's nomination was proposed by Michael Ring and Jim Higgins seconded him. Noonan was proposed by Charlie Flanagan and seconded by Olivia Mitchell. Besides the two candidates, only proposers and seconders spoke at the meeting. Kenny had the floor for about 20 minutes. His speech was described as aspirational. Noonan was heavy on specifics, not just for rejuvenating the party but also what politics Fine Gael would pursue in government.

The meeting lasted just over two hours and at the end of the voting process party chairman Phil Hogan announced the result. Noonan became the ninth leader of Fine Gael. He won by 44 votes to 28. Kenny was the first to speak. He pledged the new leader his 'full and total support in the drive to take government from Fianna Fáil in the next election'. He raised a smile from his colleagues by quoting former party stalwart Patrick Lindsay who after an election defeat in 1938 remarked: 'They will never know what they missed.' Significantly, Kenny also admitted that the leadership election had been a 'soul-revealing exercise'. It was as if after a quarter of a century in national politics, the Mayo man had found a sense of ambition and purpose that he did not previously know existed within him. 'You only get the cards in life once, and you play them when they come. Because if you don't and if you live long enough you will always regret them,' he subsequently admitted. But it all seemed too late. He was now the beaten candidate. 'You should try it some time,' Kenny later joked with journalists as they asked for his assessment of the outcome.

Noonan promised to take the fight to Fianna Fáil and to offer the voters the option of an alternative government. 'Fine Gael is a great party and we're at our best when we're energised,' the Limerick man declared. There were high expectations for the new leader. 'I haven't seen this bounce in Fine Gael since Garret,' Jim O'Keeffe said. Noonan moved quickly. A new frontbench was announced. Mitchell was rewarded with the finance position and was also appointed deputy leader. Supporters of Bruton were overlooked including Nora Owen and the two other candidates who had expressed an interest in the leadership. There was surprise at the decision to demote Kenny. Some believe Noonan simply did not rate Kenny, others claim it was a vindictive reaction to the Mayo man's strong defence of Bruton and his action in causing a leadership contest. Noonan's decision went down poorly with those who had supported Bruton, and subsequently backed Kenny. 'There was a brutality in how the Noonan camp treated John and then there was a vindictiveness towards Enda,' one party veteran recalls.

Noonan and Kenny met for what was a short but direct meeting. 'He explained his position to me and I explained mine to him. I said I thought it was a mistake. I had contested an open leadership contest, not a heave,' Kenny recalled. Noonan insisted there was 'no personal animus' involved. Kenny knew the score. 'The winner takes all in this business,' he admitted. There were other reasons for disappointment. His constituency colleague Jim Higgins – who had run his leadership campaign – was given a frontbench position. Kenny was offered but refused to serve as a junior spokesman. 'I will speak on broader political issues. . . I can conduct my affairs from the backbenches with a lot of opinions.' Kenny told the media that the demotion sent out 'the message that you shouldn't contest democratic decisions to be made by the Fine Gael party'. As he spoke to reporters Kenny's mobile phone rang – the caller was Denis Naughton who had also been dropped from the new frontbench. 'You're a young man in politics, Denis. If you want to talk to someone about how to take a knock in politics, Kenny's your man.'

In the aftermath of his leadership defeat and demotion from the Fine Gael frontbench, Kenny returned to Mayo to regroup. Noonan started the task he had been elected to achieve – getting Fine Gael into government. The Limierck man was a seasoned politician with considerable ministerial experience. He promised to revitalise the party with the electorate. The route into government would involve a coalition arrangement with the Labour Party and possibly the Green Party. But Ruairi Quinn, the Labour Party leader, had other ideas. He committed his party to keeping its options open on possible government partners until after the electorate had had their say. While Quinn conceded that his preference was a return of an anti-Fianna Fáil coalition he rejected all overtures for a transfer pact with Fine Gael. From the outset, Noonan's task was made even more difficult in convincing the electorate that an alternative coalition led by Fine Gael was a possibility.

The new Fine Gael leader had just over a year to prepare his party for a general election due at the latest in the early summer of 2002. It very quickly became apparent that for the third time since Garret FitzGerald's resignation in 1987 the party had misjudged in changing its leader in search of electoral popularity. The public never warmed to Noonan, who showed no interest in healing the deep internal divisions in the party. A small coterie of advisors surrounded Noonan who cut himself off from most of his parliamentary colleagues. His tenure as leader was marked by poor organisation, ill-thought-out policy initiatives and the absent of a strategic sense of what would be politically beneficial for Fine Gael. In addition to these self-inflected problems, Noonan also turned out to be a very unlucky leader.

Plans for a first triumphant Fine Gael Ard Fheis for the new leader had to be postponed when Ireland was hit by an outbreak of foot and mouth disease. The planned national gathering was replaced by a smaller conference confined to Dublin members, and Fine Gael's sense of doom and gloom was symbolised by the foam

mats soaked with disinfectant at the entrance to the RDS for delegates to wipe their feet.

Noonan was also hit by revelations linked to the tribunals of
inquiry. He was made aware of a $50,000 cheque which lay
uncashed in a safe in party headquarters that had been received
from the group which won the second mobile phone license.
Bruton had received legal advice that the uncashed donation did
not have to be revealed to the Moriarty tribunal which was investi-
gating the license as part of its continuing inquiries into the financial affairs of Michael Lowry. Noonan had a different view but news
of the $50,000 was leaked to the media.

Other embarrassing stories emerged: Fine Gael admitted that it
made illegal under-the-counter cash payments to its staff over a
nine-year period. The party reached a IR£111,000 settlement with
the Revenue Commissioners. It was also revealed that the party
benefited by around IR£90,000 from a 'pick-me-up' practise under
which donors picked up the bills for services provided to the party.
Fianna Fáil had had similar issues but had already dealt with the
Revenue Commissioners about the practices. The Fine Gael revelations were deeply embarrassing for Noonan. The party's political
opponents took advantage. One Fianna Fáil minister referred to
'systematic tax fraud in Fine Gael headquarters'. Noonan believed
people within Fine Gael were leaking information to damage his
leadership; he certainly had made internal enemies but he was also
suffering from his own unwillingness to ease the wounds in Fine
Gael.

Noonan never seemed comfortable as party leader – a classic
case of a media darling built up with high expectations who had no
real sense of what to do once the leadership position had been
secured. The run of controversies damaged his confidence. The new
party leader also had to deal with difficulties which emerged from
his role as Minister for Health during the Hepatitis C scandal in the
mid-1990s. The treatment of the women infected by contaminated
blood products was a huge political scandal. Noonan was forced to
issue several apologies for the insensitive manner in which those

involved had been treated. But he simply could not escape the affair. Early in 2002 RTÉ broadcast *No Tears*, a drama series based on the case of one of the women, Brigid McCole, a mother of eleven children, who had been infected with Hepatitis C through the infected blood product in 1977 and who on her deathbed in 1996 had been sent threatening legal letters by the State pressuring her to settle her legal action. At the time Noonan as Health Minister had asked in the Dáil whether McCole's legal team could have chosen a better candidate as a test case. Other women infected by the contaminated blood product were watching in the public gallery and walked out in protest at the remarks.

Noonan was not identified by name in the four-part television drama series but the character referred to as 'the minister' was portrayed in a highly negative light. 'I think so close to an election to make up for dramatic purposes events which never happened which portray me in a bad light is not only unfair but legally very risky for RTÉ,' Noonan said. The timing of the RTÉ broadcast just prior to a general election was seriously questionable in terms of editorial fairness but a weakened and divided Fine Gael was in no position to strongly challenge the national broadcaster. The controversy damaged Noonan especially with women voters, and dogged him throughout his entire term as party leader. At the Fine Gael Ard Fheis only weeks prior to the general election campaign Noonan again apologised for his role in the affair.

The Fine Gael victory in the Tipperary South by-election in June 2001 was the high point of Noonan's tenure, although as the vacancy had been created by the death of a sitting Fine Gael TD there was, in fact, no overall parliamentary gain. Noonan had been chosen by his party colleagues to turn around Fine Gael but the party's opinion poll ratings remained disappointing. Fine Gael never received a bounce from its change of leader. The party continued to languish in the polls. In March 2002, only weeks prior to the general election, Fine Gael support was at 20 per cent – a level which signalled electoral disaster.

Throughout this period, Kenny maintained a low profile. He

showed loyalty and in one of his few national media appearances admitted that Noonan had had 'a ferocious run of bad luck'. He was also interviewed about the tax and pick-me-up revelations. 'It's not just an embarrassment but it's blatantly wrong. Fine Gael should never have been involved in this.' Kenny said the poor opinion poll rating should 'galvanise' the party. 'This isn't a one-man band. The reaction should not be one of panic. Every member of the party has to get up off their butts and ask themselves what can I do about it.' But Kenny had reason for concern. Several local opinion polls in the Mayo constituency showed him battling to hold his seat.

As the election date approached, Noonan made one final attempt to secure an arrangement with the Labour Party. Ruairi Quinn noted the 'intensity of desperation' that came with the request but he was not interested in either a common policy agreement or a transfer pact. Quinn wanted his party to fight the election on an independent platform. 'This means neither of us will lead our party by Christmas,' Noonan forecast as the two men parted.

The economic performance during Ahern's first coalition government was unprecedented. In the 1997-2002 period annual GDP increases were in the region of 10 per cent while the rate of unemployment declined from 10 per cent to 4 per cent. All the main economic indicators moved in a positive direction – interest rates declined and the government finances swelled. Income tax rates were cut. Ahern had promised that his government would serve a full five-year term. On 17 May 2002, just weeks short of five years from the 1997 contest, the Taoiseach arrived into a near empty Dáil chamber to confirm his intention to seek a dissolution of the 28th Dáil. Fianna Fáil's campaign was slick, highly organised and very focused – the party promised to continue the economic boom with the slogan 'A lot done – more to do'. In the early days of the election, Fianna Fáil targeted the economic policies of the two main opposition parties. Its private research suggested that voters were less concerned about spending on health and infrastructure than ensuring that the next government did not pursue policies that risked economic growth. And Fine Gael gave Ahern's party plenty of substance to undermine its claim to fiscal responsibility.

Ahern was incredibly popular – almost three quarters of voters gave him a positive rating. Replacing Bruton with Noonan had not worked for the main opposition party. Fine Gael limped into the 2002 general election. The organisation of its campaign was a disaster. In a variation of the 'Celtic Snail' theme, Fine Gael focused on quality-of-life issues such as childcare, housing and traffic congestion. But the campaign made little impact with the voters who were more concerned with the money in their own pockets. Fine Gael's credibility was further damaged by ill-considered policy announcements including paying compensation to taxi drivers arising from the deregulation of the industry and also offering to compensate people who had lost money by investing in Eircom shares. The party also pledged not to increase income tax or capital gains tax. There was a promise to cut the tax burden on lower and middle income earners by €2bn. Finance spokesman and deputy leader Jim Mitchell said continued economic growth would pay for the party's tax cuts and spending plans. But the strategy was unconvincing. There was a real sense of a party desperately trying to buy votes. Any attempt by Fine Gael to claim the mantle of fiscal responsibility was lost.

Having ceded the economic debate, neither was Fine Gael able to capitalise on Fianna Fáil's continuing troubles at the corruption tribunals – after all, Fine Gael had its own problems at Dublin Castle. More importantly, the voters were unconvinced about the Fine Gael leader. When asked in an ICM poll in May 2002 who would make the better Taoiseach, 53 per cent opted for Ahern; only 13 per cent backed Noonan. One post-election survey showed that only 32 per cent of Fine Gael voters rated Noonan as the best leader. When the Fine Gael leader took a custard pie in the face while on the canvass trail the image seemed an appropriate analogy for the party's election campaign. Noonan continued to preach the message that he was confident about the future, and that he was the best leader to secure Ireland's future. But the voters delivered a damning verdict.

The first sign of trouble came from the count centre in Dublin North, one of three constituencies that used the new electronic voting system and was declaring its results the night before everywhere else. At a chaotic count centre, without even a proper platform for the candidates, the returning officer read out the names of the four successful candidates. Former Fine Gael deputy leader Nora Owen, who had represented the constituency for two decades, had lost out. The television cameras captured the impact of the dramatic defeat on an emotional Owen who was hugged by Labour politician, Sean Ryan. The defeat of a former minister with a high public profile left many in Fine Gael very uneasy as they waited for the opening of the count centres where the traditional ballot papers had been used.

The 2002 general election delivered a miserable outcome for Fine Gael. Middle class voters deserted the party. Given the results of pre-election opinion polls the seat losses were not unsurprising, but few had predicted the scale of the Fine Gael defeat. Big names fell all over the country. Owen was the first to go but others included former leader Alan Dukes, current deputy leader Jim Mitchell and Charlie Flanagan, a Dáil deputy for 15 years and son of the late legendary Oliver J. Flanagan. Eleven members of Noonan's frontbench including Paul Bradford, Deirdre Clune and Michael Creed lost their seats. The party's vote fell to just over 22 per cent – leading to the loss of 23 seats. The performance in terms of seats won and share of the first preference vote was the party's lowest since 1948. The Fine Gael share of Dáil seats – 19 per cent – was its lowest ever. The party's performance in Dublin was an even bigger disaster – Fine Gael received only one vote in every seven cast and ended up with only three seats out of the 47 on offer in the capital. In its traditional strongholds such as Dublin South East – the constituency of former leader Garret FitzGerald – there was now no Fine Gael TD; while in Dun Laoghaire – home to another former leader, Liam Cosgrave – the party lost both its seats and saw its vote fall by 16 per cent. Writing a post-election analysis, political scientist Michael Gallagher observed, 'the only room for argument over Fine Gael's result was about which word from the lexicon of gloom best described it. The thesaurus was well thumbed as labels such as meltdown, debacle, disaster, collapse and many others were wheeled out to do service.' In the end, Gallagher opted for 'catastrophe'.

Enda Kenny monitored the results from his home in Castlebar, watching the television and listening to the radio. The national situation was depressing, and throughout the day the message from his own supporters at the Mayo count centre was that he was in trouble. The situation was bleak when the first count results in the Mayo constituency were announced. The Fine Gael vote was down 11 per cent on the 1997 general election when the party had won three of the five seats. Kenny's colleague Michael Ring topped the poll but independent candidate Jerry Cowley polled well and Fianna Fáil looked assured of two seats. Kenny was in a battle for the last seat with his party running mate Jim Higgins, and Fianna Fáil were putting in a strong push for a third seat. By the end of the seventh count Ring and Cowley had been elected, and six candidates were chasing the remaining three seats. With 6,707 votes Kenny was 400 votes adrift of Higgins. 'I thought it was gone,' he says. Throughout the long day and early evening friends and family had called to Kenny's house. There were plenty of tears over the local drama and also for Fine Gael's national plight.

With this type of verdict from the electorate, there was only one route for a leader chosen by his party little over a year previously to win votes and office. At 9 p.m. on 18 May 2002 as ballot papers around the country were still being counted Noonan tendered his resignation as Fine Gael leader. In a television interview with RTÉ's Charlie Bird, Noonan admitted that the result 'was beyond our expectations and beyond our worst fears. It's been a seriously bad election result for our party.'

Shortly before midnight in the Kenny household, Fionnuala O'Kelly had gone upstairs to change her clothes before travelling to the count centre with her husband. The feedback from party tally-men was that Higgins would pip Kenny. But by the time O'Kelly returned back downstairs word had arrived that the distribution of the transfers of eliminated Fianna Fáil candidate Frank Chambers were going in Kenny's direction. Geography was playing a part as Chambers' support base was closer to Kenny than to Higgins – but the transfer advantage to Kenny was probably not enough to make up the 393 vote gap with Higgins. The uncertainty increased with a phone call Kenny received as he drove to the count centre. 'You might make it,' he was told. When the returning officer announced the results of the eight count, Higgins received 120 additional votes bringing his total vote to 7,220. Kenny's total increased by 600 to 7,307 votes. Higgins trailed his party colleague by 87 votes and was duly eliminated. Kenny's seat was eventually saved with a sizable transfer from his running mate. 'There was an air of unreality about the result. It was a huge relief that Enda had held onto his seat but there was no joy with Jim Higgins losing out and then there was the national situation,' one Kenny supporter recalls. In the end, the 87 votes separating Higgins and Kenny proved hugely significant in the next phase of Fine Gael's history.

3
Party History

The history of Fine Gael can be traced back to the foundation of the Irish State. Fine Gael itself was founded in 1933 arising from a merger of three existing organisations although the origins of the party are very much rooted in the controversy over the Anglo-Irish treaty agreed between the British government and republican leaders in December 1921. Divisions over the treaty resulted in a split in the Sinn Féin party. The anti-treaty side – many of whom would eventually form Fianna Fáil in 1926 – alleged a betrayal and rejected the treaty terms. Although defeated in the Dáil vote on the treaty they launched a military campaign. While contesting the Civil War the majority pro-Treaty side also set about establishing the new Irish Free State. The need to set up a new political party was down their list of priorities. The treaty split in Sinn Féin was confirmed in January 1922; private discussions about a new national party were only held the following December and the pro-treaty side only publicly reformed as a new organisation in April 1923. They gathered around the name Cumann na nGaedheal – Family of the Gaels – with William T. Cosgrave unanimously selected as their leader. Cosgrave was thrust into the leadership role following the deaths of senior figures, Arthur Griffith and Michael Collins.

Cumann na nGaedheal contested its first election in August 1923 securing 39 per cent of the vote. The party had an artificial majority in the Dáil as the anti-treaty side abstained from participation in parliamentary business. While De Valera continued to reject the treaty terms the new government embarked upon the challenge of State-building in an atmosphere of lawlessness. The British had departed and a replacement administrative system had to be established. The Cumann na nGaedheal government proved equal to the task. The list of domestic achievements included establishing the unarmed Garda Síochána and the Electricity Supply Board as well as promoting industrial policy through sugar production and the Shannon electrification scheme. It is to the enormous credit of this first generation of ministers that they succeeded not only in laying the solid foundations of statehood but they also secured international recognition for the new entity. By 1930, Ireland had won a seat on the council of the League of Nations.

Cumann na Gaedheal's electoral position took a serious hit in the June 1927 general election. The party lost 16 seats and it only had a three-seat margin over the newly-formed Fianna Fáil. But with De Valera's continued absence from parliament, Cumann na nGaedheal remained in office as a minority government. The situation changed after the murder of Kevin O'Higgins, a senior cabinet member, in July 1927. O'Higgins, who was not just Deputy Prime Minister but also Minister for Justice and Minister for External (Foreign) Affairs, was gunned down by the anti-treaty side. The murder was seen as an attack on the new fledgling democracy. The Cumann na nGaedheal government responded by forcing their opponents to participate in parliament. Legislation was introduced requiring all successful election candidates to take their seats and the contentious parliamentary oath to uphold the treaty. It was an action that secured the new State. But it also paved the way for De Valera's entry into the Dáil and, a few years later, into government at the expense of Cosgrave's party.

Cumann na nGaedheal remained in office after the September 1927 general election but only with the support of smaller parties and independents. When the party formed its final government it had a five-seat advantage over Fianna Fáil. By 1932 this situation had been transformed into a 15-seat advantage to Fianna Fáil and, following a snap election called in early 1933, the gap between the two sides had widened to 29 seats. Fianna Fáil had emerged as the largest party in Irish politics, and it retained this position at each general election from 1932 to 2011. The pro-treaty side – briefly after 1932 as Cumann na nGaedheal, and from 1933 onwards as Fine Gael – remained the second place party. Indeed, at each of the 23 general elections from 1932 to 2007 inclusive, Fine Gael was in Fianna Fáil's shadow as the second largest party in the State. The party also spent most of the last three quarters of a century on the opposition benches – enjoying only 18 years in government. The significance of the Fine Gael result in February 2011 has to be seen against this relatively poor background. Indeed, the longest sustained period in office was as Cumann na nGaedheal from 1922 to 1932. Not that Cumann na nGaedheal received an electoral dividend for its ten years in office. While the party was governing during the 1920s the anti-treaty faction that emerged as Fianna Fáil was building a nationwide organisation. Sean Lemass, Sean McEntee and others travelled the country recruiting candidates and putting in place a national organisational structure for De Valera's new party. When a general election was called in 1932 Fianna Fáil was in position to win.

But Cumann na nGaedheal did not help its own cause. Pro-treaty leader Michael Collins had predicted that the agreement would provide the 'freedom to achieve freedom'. But the pro-treaty side as Cumann na nGaedheal transformed during the 1920s into the party of the status quo. They became the defenders of the treaty opposed to amending the deal done with the British and happy to be known as the Commonwealth party. Fianna Fáil had a more radical policy prescription as it promised to dismantle the treaty and remove all symbols of the British presence in Ireland including the parliamentary oath and the position of the Governor-General as the representative of the crown. This radicalism of Fianna Fáil in contrast to Cumann na nGaedheal's conservatism was also evident in economic policy. While in office the Cumann na nGaedheal government pursued balance budgets. Decisions were taken without consideration of their electoral impact – for example in 1924, in order to reduce government spending the old age pension was cut from ten shillings to nine shillings a week. And prior to the 1932 general election the government sanctioned increases in income taxes and reductions in pay for gardaí and teachers – hardly a platform to win over voters.

After the 1932 general election a generation of politicians who had only known governmental office found themselves on the opposition benches in Leinster House. After the demands of government – and a decade of continuous effort to secure the stability of the new State – these politicians must have been exhausted. Initial hopes that the De Valera government would collapse were proven wrong as Fianna Fáil rapidly started to implement an ambitious programme including withholding land payments to the British and starting the process of dismantling the treaty. The pro-treaty grouping had also been concerned about the democratic intentions of the new Fianna Fáil government, and there were fears about unchecked republican activity targeting pro-treaty political gatherings. Shortly after entering office De Valera approved the release of IRA prisoners and lifted the ban on the military organisation. With renewed confidence, republicans took retribution on their enemies by breaking up Cumann na nGaedheal meetings. Clashes between rival factions, street fighting and running riots were commonplace.

Cosgrave and his colleagues were confronted with the need to rebuild a national organisational infrastructure, recruit new members and attract suitable candidates for future elections. Optimism was hard to discern. 'There is a very general and growing belief that Cumann na nGaedheal is finished,' one party official told Cosgrave. Cumann na nGaedheal needed to regain some initiative. There was an obvious attraction to a proposal to merge with two other opposition organisations – the National Centre Party and the Army Comrades Association (ACA). The National Centre Party was essentially a farmers' organisation whose leading members had supported Cumann na nGaedheal during the 1920s, one of whom,

James Dillon, later became leader of Fine Gael. It had emerged as the third largest party in the Dáil. According to historian Brian Maye, 'its almost identical policies and the increasingly polarised nature of politics drove it closer to Cumann na nGaedheal.' The link-up made political sense. There was a less obvious rationale for an alliance with the ACA – more commonly known as the Blueshirts – which had emerged with the objective of adopting a fascist system of government. The organisation also had an ambiguous attitude to the use of violence.

Such issues were, however, sidestepped in the heightened transition period when Fianna Fáil came into government for the first time. The Blueshirts offered energy and organisation to a demoralised Cumann na nGaedheal which had lost further ground in the 1933 general election, but the costs of the short-lived alliance were considerable. Its leader Eoin O'Duffy was chief of the police during the 1920s but was sacked by De Valera in early 1933. O'Duffy saw the Blueshirts as offering a counter to the revived IRA which was increasingly disrupting gatherings of pro-treaty groups. The Blueshirts shared many of the authoritarian trappings of fascist movements across Europe which made even more remarkable the decision for Cumann na nGaedheal – which consolidated constitutionalism after the treaty split – to align itself with an organisation so loosely attached to democratic principles.

The decision to offer the leadership of Fine Gael to O'Duffy was equally ill-considered. There was probably need for a leadership change but by any standards it was a bizarre move to replace Cosgrave – a man who was essentially Prime Minister for a decade – with O'Duffy, a controversial figure with an erratic personality, who was not even a member of Dáil Éireann. O'Duffy accepted the offer of leadership although the Blueshirts were an autonomous section within Fine Gael, translated as 'Family of the Irish', which was unveiled as the United Ireland Party – Fine Gael on 8 September 1933.

O'Duffy immediately embarked upon a nationwide tour to boost grassroots activity. He wanted a superior organisation to

Fianna Fáil. The strategy initially seemed to pay dividend. There was increased branch activity in Fine Gael and a strong turnout at the party's February 1934 Ard Fheis. O'Duffy's presidential address was a model of restraint. His fascist ambitions were downplayed. Whatever reservations existed within the old Cumann na nGaedheal leadership were kept in check. But tensions remained. One senior party figure resigned over what was described as O'Duffy's 'generally destructive and hysterical leadership'. The violence associated with the Blueshirts and continuing clashes with the IRA increased internal differences. Moreover, O'Duffy's nationwide activity did not deliver the expected electoral return – the results of the local elections in July 1934 were disappointing for Fine Gael. The unimpressive outturn provided sufficient justification to move against O'Duffy whose speeches were increasingly extreme. Cosgrave returned as leader in what was now in effect the old Cumann na nGaedheal trading under a new party name.

O'Duffy's short tenure as the first leader of Fine Gael was a disaster for the new party. As historian Fearghal McGarry recorded, 'although O'Duffy's extremism was not fully embraced by Fine Gael, its brief flirtation with fascism blemished an otherwise impressive commitment to democratic values dating back to 1922.' The Blueshirts alliance, while supported by many senior political figures, caused Fine Gael some ongoing embarrassment. The party had to live with the reality that some of its TDs had arrived in the Dáil chamber in the Blueshirt uniform while future leader James Dillon, responding to comparisons with other fascist movements in Europe, reminded Fianna Fáil that, 'the Blackshirts were victorious in Italy and that the Hitler shirts were victorious in Germany, as assuredly . . . the Blueshirts will be victorious in the Irish Free State.'

In more recent times Fine Gael has shown a reluctance to identify with its first leader. O'Duffy has been erased from its history, and rarely gets even a passing reference in official Fine Gael documents. Political opponents continue to use the term 'Blueshirt' as a term of abuse – although this now historic episode has little, if any, bearing on the party's activity in twenty first century Ireland.

Nevertheless, the party's controversial birth has not gone away. During the 2007 general election when Enda Kenny was delivering a campaign speech in Galway a passing motorist shouted, 'You fucking Blueshirt.' Kenny smiled and quickly responded. 'Thank you very much. I'm proud of it.' Accepting the term as another reference to Fine Gael, 70 years on, it was possible to ignore the Blueshirt legacy. But in the mid-1930s many Fine Gael politicians desperately wanted rid of the alliance, and so after a false start the party returned to the control of serious-minded, constitutional politicians.

Decline was the dominant feature of the party's story. Cumann na nGaedheal won almost 39 per cent of the vote in 1927 – by 1948 Fine Gael's support fell to just less than 20 per cent. The party was on the margins of Irish politics. One particular nadir came in December 1945 when five by-election contests were held but Fine Gael was only able to nominate a single candidate. Membership levels were low and party activity levels were lower still. Former Fine Gael Oireachtas member and academic Maurice Manning has described these years as 'the most dismal in Fine Gael's history.' After two decades in a leadership role, Cosgrave stood down in 1944. His successor Richard Mulcahy, another prominent figure in the revolutionary period, led Fine Gael until 1959. When he became leader Mulcahy warned about the need for action to counter 'the suggestion that Fine Gael had no purpose.' But, as the history of Fine Gael shows, the demise of political parties – and especially the three largest parties – while well written about, is, in fact, a rare occurrence in Ireland. The three main parties have over many years, and when faced with many different challenges, managed to adapt in order to survive.

So even in its weakened state in 1948, Fine Gael still had sufficient Dáil seats to form an anti-Fianna Fáil government. De Valera's party fell short of a majority in the Dáil and in the aftermath of the 1948 general election maintained its anti-coalition stance. After 16 years of continuous Fianna Fáil rule the opposition parties were able to form a multi-party arrangement. Fine Gael led this alternative government until 1951 when it was replaced by Fianna Fáil before another Fine Gael-led coalition came into office in 1954. This latter multi-party government survived until 1957 when Fianna Fáil again returned to office.

Mulcahy's hard-line stance against the anti-treaty side after independence made him unacceptable as Taoiseach to the other parties in the inter-party arrangement in 1948. John A. Costello – a senior Fine Gael figure – was nominated as Taoiseach. The first inter-party administration formally declared Ireland a Republic but splintered over the Mother and Child Scheme which offered free health benefits. Fine Gael adopted a conservative and traditionalist position over the latter and gained little from the former as confusion reigned about Costello's announcement while on a visit to Canada. The 1948-51 inter-party government broke up in disarray but it had some achievements, not least a hospital building programme and the fight against TB. Labour Party historian Niamh Puirseil has described the second inter-party government from 1954-57 as 'a contender for the worst administration in the history of the State.' Her conclusion was largely based on the government's failure to progress a coherent economic agenda.

The Irish economy was certainly in dire straits in the 1950s. Net migration averaged forty-one thousand a year during the decade. The longstanding protectionist policies of the previous 20 years had failed to deliver. Much credit for the move to an outward-looking strategy, which opened up the economy to foreign investment, has been attributed to Fianna Fáil's return to office in 1957. But the initial policy reappraisal actually got underway while Fine Gael was leading the second inter-party government. Academics David Doyle and John Hogan argue that 'the ideas associated with the outward-looking strategy that Ireland eventually adopted were first utilised by the coalition government of 1954-57.' In this regard, the Fine Gael-led administration decided in 1956 to allow the IDA to distribute grants to export-orientated industries and also introduced an export profits relief tax.

The two periods in office between 1948 and 1957 helped Fine

Gael to survive. The party was politically relevant and increased its vote from the low of 1948. The Labour Party was now an ally in forming an alternative government to Fianna Fáil. But Fine Gael still spent the following 16 years out of office. The prospects of convincing the electorate of the merits of an anti-Fianna Fáil government were not helped by the anti-coalition stance adopted by the Labour Party. There were concerns in Labour that its involvement in coalition arrangements hindered its ambition to build an organisation that would be a dominant force. Irish politics was in a period of transition. De Valera departed party politics for the presidency in 1959 and, in the same year, Mulcahy stood down as Fine Gael leader at the age of 73. For the next six years James Dillon led the party and in 1965 Liam Cosgrave – son of W. T. Cosgrave – became the fifth leader of Fine Gael.

Cosgrave was associated with the old guard but Fine Gael sought redefinition in the 1960s with an emphasis on social justice and redistribution. The so-called 'Just Society' programme was adopted in May 1964 and formed the basis for the party's manifesto at the 1965 general election. But there was ongoing tension over the policy platform with a more conservative leadership resistant to the ambitions of a more liberal grouping associated with younger members including Garret FitzGerald. A proposal at the 1968 Ard Fheis to describe the party as 'Fine Gael – Social Democratic Party' was opposed by the party leadership. Yet despite the internal divisions Fine Gael did move in a moderate social democratic direction. The policy platform helped to bring the party closer to the Labour Party which had not made the electoral gains hoped for by its anti-coalition stance. In 1973 Fine Gael and Labour offered themselves as an alternative option to a Fianna Fáil government. Cosgrave became the first leader of Fine Gael in the 40-year history of the party to hold the position of Taoiseach as Mulcahy had stood aside for Costello in the two inter-party governments. The coalition remained in office until June 1977 but had the misfortune to be in power during a global economic recession. Fianna Fáil offered a highly attractive set of policies in 1977 which delivered an electoral landslide. Fine Gael lost votes and seats, and Cosgrave resigned as party leader. Garret FitzGerald was unanimously chosen as his successor and the party entered the most successful phase in its electoral history – that is, until Enda Kenny became leader in 2002.

FitzGerald gave off the air of a distracted professor – he was an economist by training and lectured for a period in UCD – but he was also a tough politician with a populist touch. Fine Gael became more professional in this period, membership increased, organisational structures were overhauled and the party came within a handful of seats of becoming the largest political organisation in the State. At FitzGerald's first election as party leader in 1981 the Fine Gael vote reached its highest level since the 1920s when Cumann na nGaedheal formed single party administrations. This was the period of three general elections in 18 months – Fine Gael and the Labour Party formed a minority coalition from June 1981 to February 1982; a minority Fianna Fáil government was in place for eight months in 1982 only to be replaced in November 1982 by a second FitzGerald-led Fine Gael-Labour administration. The Fine Gael result in November 1982 was truly historic. The party won over 39 per cent of the vote – higher than previously achieved by either Fine Gael or Cumann na nGaedheal. The result left the party within five seats of Fianna Fáil.

FitzGerald was a hugely popular leader with the public from 1977 to the mid-1980s. He was 'Garret the Good' in contrast to Haughey who, even at that stage, was faced by questions about his integrity and unexplained wealth. The poor economic conditions meant FitzGerald was unable to embark upon any serious policy initiative in his first term as Taoiseach. 'We came down to earth very quickly,' he recalled. FitzGerald's second coalition government negotiated the Anglo-Irish Agreement with the British but was embroiled in a divisive abortion referendum and failed to introduce divorce in 1986. By the latter stages of the coalition's term, satisfaction with FitzGerald had declined sharply. The Fine Gael-Labour coalition had become increasingly unpopular in the face of an economic situation which continued to worsen as a divided government was unable to respond and faced a highly opportunistic opposition. The so-called constitutional crusade had been divisive – Fine Gael was split into warring factions – and the voters were more concerned about a lack of jobs and high taxation. By the time a general election was called in February 1987 FitzGerald had lost considerable public support and Fine Gael could only watch as the newly formed Progressive Democrats won favour with the electorate. Fine Gael ceded the ground made in previous elections. The party lost 19 seats and achieved its lowest vote in 30 years. Four leaders followed FitzGerald including Enda Kenny, but it was only in 2011 in quite dramatic circumstances that Fine Gael recovered beyond its 1987 defeat.

In eight successive general elections prior to 1987 Fine Gael exceeded 30 per cent of the first preference vote. In each election from 1987 to 2007 the party did not break the 30 per cent threshold under five different leaders – FitzGerald in 1987, Dukes in 1989, Bruton in 1992 and 1997, Noonan in 2002 and Kenny in 2007. Developments in the political landscape in Ireland had an adverse impact on Fine Gael. The arrival of the Progressive Democrats in December 1985, and the Fianna Fáil decision four years later to end its opposition to coalition governments, hurt Fine Gael badly. The Progressive Democrats were formed out of divisions in Fianna Fáil but the new party plundered Fine Gael's support base. The first set of opinion polls in 1986 showed the PDs achieving ratings as high as 25 per cent as Fine Gael support collapsed, especially among middle-class voters attracted by the new party's tax cutting agenda. The organisational revamp in the early years of FitzGerald's leadership had not been significant enough to withstand the arrival of a new entrant. The formation of the PDs increased competition for voters at the 1987 general election although two years later the new party came close to collapse. Fine Gael recovered some ground in 1989 but could not win back all of the middle-class voters lost to the PDs.

Fianna Fáil's ending of its anti-coalition stance in 1989 meant that the party was now open to the type of multi-party arrangements that were previously only possible with the involvement of Fine Gael. When Fianna Fáil did a deal with the Labour Party after the 1992 general election – having secured a coalition with the Progressive Democrats in 1989 – it seemed that the party had the security of permanent government with a multitude of potential governmental partners. The idea of a Fianna Fáil-Fine Gael coalition was not entertained. In this new political landscape Fine Gael looked set to become a party of permanent opposition. With Fianna Fáil in the business of forming coalition governments, the relevance of Fine Gael to voters had become a real issue. It was now possible to change the nature of government without removing Fianna Fáil from office, and the incentive to support the smaller of the two increasingly non-ideological and catch-all parties lessened.

Alan Dukes succeeded FitzGerald in 1987 after a leadership contest involving Peter Barry and John Bruton. Dukes had first been elected to the Dáil in 1981 and joined a small group of politicians who, on their first day in parliament, were appointed to cabinet. The FitzGerald inheritance was a parliamentary party that was deeply divided about its place on the political spectrum and a membership still bruised after the divisive constitutional referendums and the 1987 electoral defeat. Dukes committed the party to the 'Tallaght Strategy' which guaranteed support for the minority Fianna Fáil government so long as prudent economic policies were pursued. The strategy was a commendable national stance and eased the parliamentary concerns of Haughey's minority government but it was not clear what Fine Gael would gain. Dukes informed his frontbench of the new initiative of non-opposition just prior to its announcement. His critics were given further ammunition to snipe at his leadership. Many senior figures had simply refused to recognise his authority and several leading politicians showed a lack of interest in regrouping after the electoral defeat and the departure of FitzGerald. Under Dukes, Fine Gael made modest progress in the 1989 general election – the party won four additional seats with 29.3 per cent of the vote. Nonetheless, leaving aside the result two years previously, this was the worst Fine

Gael general election outcome since 1957. While the Progressive Democrats saw their vote decline, the party was still a threat to Fine Gael. Dukes was also the first Fine Gael leader to be confronted by the Fianna Fáil decision to abandon its 'core value' of opposition to involvement in coalition governments.

The new leader's position was further damaged by the 1990 presidential campaign – he promised a candidate of stature. The party faithful at that year's Ard Fheis chanted 'we want Garret' believing the former leader would fit the criteria set by Dukes. But FitzGerald was not interested and the party struggled to find a credible contender as the Labour Party backed Mary Robinson, who emerged as the leading anti-Fianna Fáil candidate. Austin Currie, an influential politician from Northern Ireland who moved south of the border to win a Dáil seat in 1989, was eventually nominated as the Fine Gael candidate even though a private party poll showed he was unelectable. When Currie was nominated, Fergus Finlay, a leading Labour Party strategist rang the bookies looking for odds on Robinson winning the election. He got 10/1 on a Robinson victory and immediately put IR£100 on his party's candidate.

The Fine Gael presidential campaign was a nightmare. 'It was like getting a tooth extracted over two months,' one party figure said. There was little activity in some constituencies. Supporters of the party leader believed leading members of the parliamentary party were actively colluding during the campaign to remove Dukes. The leader's judgement was ultimately called into question when Currie, in third place, received only 17 per cent of the vote. Before the final result was even declared, a motion of no confidence was tabled. Dukes was initially defiant but the day before the motion was due to be voted upon he stepped down. Another minister from the FitzGerald era, John Bruton, was elected unopposed as his successor.

Bruton claimed the turmoil of the leadership change had brought the party together. He spent what has been described as 'ten uneasy years' as Fine Gael leader. But Bruton too faced the same post-FitzGerald difficulties that had confronted Dukes, including a lack of internal unity and uncertainty about the party's political direction. His first electoral outing in November 1992 was another disaster for the party. Fine Gael's vote fell to 24 per cent – a lower level than that achieved by FitzGerald in 1987 or by Dukes in 1989. It was the party's lowest vote since the 1948 general election. Yet, if Fianna Fáil had still been adhering to its anti-coalition stance, Bruton should have become Taoiseach in 1992.

The parliamentary arithmetic after the November 1992 general election meant an anti-Fianna Fáil coalition was a possibility with Fine Gael and Labour agreeing a deal with either the Progressive Democrats or Democratic Left, or indeed both minor parties. But Fine Gael – the largest party in the proposed arrangement – was less keen about involving Democratic Left. The objections to Democratic Left were ideological and practical. The ideological issue was derived from the party's origins and concerns over the criminality allegations which had dogged its predecessor, the Workers' Party, as well as a view of its positioning on policy matters including State interventionism, and capital and corporation taxation. It was also reported that Fine Gael had concerns about parliamentary arithmetic. A government comprising Fine Gael, Labour and Democratic Left would have had 82 of the 166 seats in Dáil Éireann; in effect, a minority coalition administration. The alternative option of Fine Gael, Labour and the Progressive Democrats would have had a combined voting bloc of 88 seats. Aside from the stability issue offered by the latter option, Fine Gael had more in common with the Progressive Democrats, thus ensuring that their ideological outlook commanded a clear majority within the three-party government. Moreover, Bruton had taken a decision about a Fine Gael-Labour arrangement with Democratic Left during the general election campaign.

'It wasn't about any negativity towards the Democratic Left but in terms of my own appreciation of what I thought the Fine Gael base could take at that time. I didn't think they were ready for Fine Gael coalescing with the Democratic Left at that time.'

But the Labour Party had coalition options beyond Fine Gael, its traditional partner. The choice of Fianna Fáil offered a very secure parliament; the scale of the majority even left open the possibility of a two-term arrangement. The larger party was also highly accommodating on policy during government negotiations. Moreover, relations between Bruton and Dick Spring, the Labour leader, were still strained, arising from the difficulties in the 1982-87 FitzGerald-led government. The two men met in the Shelbourne Hotel and during a long discussion, Spring settled many scores left over from ministerial conflicts between Fine Gael and Labour in the 1982-87 coalition. As he left the meeting, Bruton knew a deal was unlikely. Spring ultimately opted for Fianna Fáil, and Fine Gael found itself for the first time scorned by the Labour Party when a coalition deal was a real possibility.

The future looked bleak for Fine Gael. Financial debts were increasing, and at one stage party staff were asked to delay cashing their pay cheques. 'If we were a private company we would have been put into liquidation,' Michael Lowry, a party TD and fundraiser, later recalled. There was increasing unhappiness with Bruton's leadership. He faced a no-confidence motion in February 1994 but stood firm and ultimately remained in his job despite resignations from his frontbench and indications that party heavyweights opposed his leadership. How long he would have remained as Fine Gael leader is open to question but a series of unexpected events in the latter half of 1994 fundamentally changed the political landscape and the short-term prospects for Bruton's leadership.

As discussed previously, the outcome of the 1992 general election led to the formation of a Fianna Fáil-Labour Party administration which had a substantial parliamentary majority. The arrangement, however, was not without internal tension and eventually came undone in the latter stages of 1994. The collapse of the Albert Reynolds-led coalition created a novel political scenario in Ireland. For the first time since the foundation of the State, a government was formed without recourse to a general election. A number of post-1992 by-election results had tilted the parliamentary numbers in favour of an alternative coalition combination involving

Democratic Left, Labour and Fine Gael. This three party arrangement had a Dáil majority so President Mary Robinson used her constitutional authority to facilitate the formation of a new government to replace the troubled Fianna Fáil-Labour Party coalition without a general election. The new government was, however, made possible by more than just a favourable total of seats in parliament. Since the general election in late 1992 Bruton had cooperated more closely on the opposition benches with Prionsias De Rossa, the leader of Democratic Left. As party whip Enda Kenny had been working regularly with Pat Rabbitte, a senior Democratic Left deputy. He convinced Bruton to invite Rabbitte and De Rossa for a working lunch. When the two Democratic Left politicians left, Kenny turned to Bruton and said, 'So now, do you still think these fellows have horns?'

Discussions were in fact held between the leaders of the three main opposition parties – Fine Gael, the Progressive Democrats and Democratic Left – and the leader of the Labour Party. 'I conversed with Proinsias individually and we had meetings of the four party leaders. I think there were at least two meetings where of all us were present,' John Bruton recalled. The Fine Gael leader favoured a four party arrangement – Fine Gael, Labour, PDs and Democratic Left – which would, in his own view, have created a centrist administration but his preference found little support: 'None of them really wanted a four party government because the smaller parties recognised that one of them would be sort of surplus to requirements. There was a preference on the part of the Labour Party for the Democratic Left to be in government.'

In selecting his ministerial team in the Rainbow coalition Bruton rewarded those TDs who had backed him in the leadership crisis earlier in 1994. There were cabinet seats for loyal supporters including Enda Kenny, Nora Owen and Michael Lowry, who would prove a controversial appointment. Michael Noonan was the only detractor appointed to the Fine Gael cabinet team. The unexpected term in government was good for Fine Gael. The party's IR£1.4m debt was wiped out although in the absence of full transparency rules in those years the source of these donations has never been revealed.

The three-party government moved cautiously on economic matters, but during its term the early days of the so-called Celtic Tiger were evident in a host of official statistics. Progress on the peace process in Northern Ireland was slow with Bruton and De Rossa joining forces to deliver a hostile reaction to Sinn Féin and showing a greater interest in appeasing the concerns of the unionist community. The breakdown of the IRA ceasefire early in 1996 was a huge blow. Bruton had other successes, however, including achieving what FitzGerald had failed to do with a successful divorce referendum in 1996. The three coalition partners ultimately agreed to contest the 1997 general election on a joint programme although each party also produced a separate policy manifesto. But having failed to deliver a populist pre-election budget, the Rainbow parties struggled during the campaign to win voters over to their taxation policies. Fianna Fáil and the Progressive Democrats were judged to have won the taxation debate during the election campaign. They were considered in media comment to have had more easily understood policies of cutting income tax rates set against the Rainbow's apparently more complicated preference for increases in tax allowances and credits. A combination of these factors led to an election outcome which allowed Fianna Fáil and the Progressive Democrats to form a minority coalition administration with the support of a number of like-minded independent TDs.

The three Rainbow parties lost seven seats between them although Fine Gael made some small progress on its 1992 outcome winning 28 per cent of the vote and nine additional seats. But the party was still, in electoral terms, too close to its poor showing in 1987, and for the fourth consecutive general election Fine Gael ended up on the opposition benches. The glory days of November 1982 and coming within five seats of Fianna Fáil were now a 15-year-old memory. The gap between Fine Gael and Fianna Fáil widened to 30 seats in 1987 – it was 22 in 1989; 23 in 1992 and 23 in 1997. 'A road of endless opposition seemed to stretch ahead of Fine Gael,' was how academics Michael Gallagher and Michael March summarised the party's plight.

The continuing poor performance of Fine Gael under Bruton led to a leadership change early in 2001. But Michael Noonan fared even worse than the leaders who headed the party since 1987. When the final seats were allocated in the 2002 general election Fine Gael had 50 fewer seats than Fianna Fáil. This outcome raised serious questions about the very future of Fine Gael.

A major study of Fine Gael members was undertaken in the autumn of 1999, and the information gathered indicated, in part, why traditional parties continue to dominate, regardless of the ebbs and flows of electoral fortune. The study undertaken by Michael Gallagher and Michael Marsh, and published in their book, *Days of Blue Loyalty*, was the first such analysis of any Irish political party. Fine Gael had about 1,000 branches and 20,000 members in 1999, down from a high of over 33,000 members in the early 1980s. The survey showed that the typical Fine Gael member was middle-aged, male, middle-class and owned his own house. He was also a regular church attender.

The average party member was between 45 and 54 years of age; over 70 per cent of all members were over 45 and only 13 per cent under 35. Over 70 per cent of members were male although age had an impact – of those who joined after 1995 only 58 per cent were male compared to 65 per cent of those joining between 1976 and 1995. Moreover, there were also significant urban-rural differences in gender – in urban areas 54 per cent of members were male but in rural areas 73 per cent were male.

In terms of occupation the largest proportion of members – 32 per cent – were farmers. Only 10 per cent were skilled working class. One in four members had either a degree or a teaching qualification – a figure which increased to 41 per cent among those under 35. Almost half of the members were self-employed. The remainder were evenly split between working in the public and private sectors. The vast majority of members described themselves as middle class – 56 per cent – while 14 per cent as upper or upper-middle and a further eight per cent as lower-middle class. Only one-fifth saw themselves as working class. 74 per cent of Fine Gael members belonged to at least one other organisation – 20 per cent were also members of a farmers' association, almost a quarter also belonged to the GAA while 15 per cent were members of a trade union. When asked about their newspaper of choice, 52 per cent said they read the *Irish Independent*, 19 per cent the *Irish Examiner* and 16 per cent *The Irish Times*.

Interestingly, most members were born into families with a tradition of party membership and which had supported Fine Gael. 62 per cent of respondents said that one or both of their parents belonged to Fine Gael. Indeed, 75 per cent of members in 1999 said their families had a tradition of supporting Fine Gael that went back to the foundation of the State. The survey showed that Fine Gael members were generally non-ideological although they tended to describe themselves as centre-right and as relatively liberal. This membership base offered a tremendous resource for Fine Gael even at a time when the party was in difficulty. FitzGerald had been the only leader to tap into the potential of the Fine Gael organisation. The party professionalised and an astute team of handlers was led by Peter Prendergast who had been appointed general secretary after the 1977 general election campaign. A major recruitment drive brought new members into the party. If anything, for the first time in its history, the party started to act like Fianna Fáil which since its foundation has been marked out by an impressive national organisational structure and membership reach. By way of contrast, Fine Gael's organisational history was marked by inactivity. There was never an attachment to a membership-based organisation. Historian Tom Garvin has written that Cumann na nGaedheal had 'a positive contempt for the whole business of grass-roots organisation'. The main attraction of the ill-fated liaison with the Blueshirts was that the latter grouping would undertake the toil of organising around the country. Over subsequent decades there were many references to the weakness in the organisation. Many TDs were part-time and were reluctant parliamentary participants, with little active involvement in the party organisation. Gallagher and Marsh noted that in the 1950s and 1960s organisational deficiencies were all too apparent and that 'the parliamentary party continued to exude an air of amateurishness.'

The slick, professional Fianna Fáil campaign at the 1977 general election, inspired by political activity in the United States, contrasted with Fine Gael's almost gentlemanly approach. Under FitzGerald, Fine Gael sought to close the gap. Regional organisers were appointed and a centralised group around FitzGerald transformed the party's fortunes. But the change ethos was driven by FitzGerald's team, and was never institutionalised in the party's structures. The changes were resented by many TDs who complained about what they saw as the excessive influence of unelected 'handlers'. The relative collapse of the Fine Gael vote with the arrival of the Progressive Democrats in the mid-1980s showed that even the FitzGerald era reorganisation was not sufficiently deep-rooted. The story of Irish politics since De Valera first entered government in 1932 has been dominated by the fact that Fine Gael has never been as consistently good as Fianna Fáil when it came to organisation and to elections – until 2011, that is.

During the 1990s Irish politics professionalised, with Fianna Fáil, in particular, benefiting from significant corporate donations which allowed the party to employ backroom staff, undertake extensive market research and tap into the expertise of experienced election experts from the UK and the USA. Fine Gael attempted to match this activity but the party was always several steps behind. Following his election as party leader, Enda Kenny actively took on this party weakness. The activity after 2002 was relentless – an ongoing leader's tour, regional conferences, local meetings, phased billboard marketing and populist policy campaigns backed by townhall gatherings and website activity. Noonan's policy of declining corporate donations was ended and Fine Gael put in place a highly successful 'planned giving' operation that funded Kenny's objective of transforming the Fine Gael organisation into a mirror image of its great rival, Fianna Fáil.

The annual national draw has been a lucrative source of revenue – taking in over €1 million every year. For example, the party sold 15,395 tickets at €80 per ticket in 2009, a decline on the 16,250 the previous year but still sufficient sales to generate €1.23 million. 'Given that this was an election year and has also seen a serious economic downturn, it is a tribute to the hardwork of all our party workers,' parliamentary party chairman Tom Hayes admitted. The 'fantastic' outcome was credited to the strategy pursued by Anne Strain, who had been appointed full-time fundraiser in the post-2002 reorganisation having previously held a similar role in the charity sector.

Like the other political parties, Fine Gael's fundraising is covered by the rules laid down in the Electoral Acts. The party has not, however, declared any donations to the Standards in Public Offices Commision since 2002 – not because Fine Gael received no donations but rather the party has operated within existing rules which only require declaration of any donations above €5,078 (the maximum amount a party can accept from the same person in the same calendar year is €6,348). This 'planning giving' policy,while entirely legal, explicitly protects the anonymity of donors – an issue which led the *Daily Mail* in February 2011 to claim, 'Fine Gael has secretly raised hundreds of thousands of euro from business donors including property developers, bankers and the racing industry.' The newspaper said that golf classics and other events in Ireland and abroad were organised at which 'companies and wealthy individuals were encouraged to provide sponsorship in return for teeing off with Enda Kenny and members of his frontbench.'

The funds had been used to run a highly professional political operation. 'While political parties receive some funds from the State, these funds cannot be used for election campaigns. Every euro counts. €5 pays for one election poster. Just €10 covers the cost of 250 canvass cards, €20 will buy one 8'x4' advertising board,' a Fine Gael fundraising brochure for the 2009 European and local elections explained to potential donors.

Electoral success made it easier to attract donations. The party had a budget of €2 million for the 2011 general election campaign. Total expenditure was less than in 2007 due to lower media costs, the use of different media platforms with more cost effective online campaigning and the party's financial strength in a market with excess capacity. The Fine Gael strategy was to spend half of its budget in the lead-in period before the Dáil was dissolved and half in the formal campaign itself. 'In the event that there is a snap election it will not be feasible to spend all of the finances that is available to us,' the confidential Fine Gael Election Blueprint report for the 2011 contest concluded.

4

Enter Enda Kenny

Michael Noonan announced his decision to resign as Fine Gael leader on 18 May 2002 – election count night – although the resignation had not been formally tendered. There was some uncertainty about how the party would proceed in picking up the pieces after its election defeat. Numerous names featured in media speculation, among them Enda Kenny who had lost out to Noonan in 2001. Others included Richard Bruton, brother of the former leader and a minister in the 1994-97 coalition; Gay Mitchell, a junior minister in the Rainbow coalition; Simon Coveney, a young TD from an established Fine Gael family in Cork; Phil Hogan, a TD for Carlow-Kilkenny and a former organisational strategist under John Bruton; and Denis Naughton, from Longford-Roscommon, another young TD and a frontbench member under Bruton.

But the question of who would lead Fine Gael was only one of several to be answered by the depleted parliamentary party when it met for the first time the week after the election results were known. At that meeting Noonan indicated that he would remain on in a temporary capcaity as long as his colleagues wished him to do so. The party rules dictated that following the resignation of a Fine Gael leader his or her successor must be elected within 30 days. The electoral body, at that time, was limited to members of the Fine Gael parliamentary party. In the summer of 2002 that meant 49 individuals – newly elected TDs, members of the outgoing Seanad and members of the European Parliament.

There was some initial doubt over the method of selecting a new leader. A motion had been passed at the party's Ard Fheis in February 2002 calling for a broadening of the electoral body for choosing Fine Gael leaders. It was a similar suggestion to that made a decade earlier by an internal party renewal commission. In 2002 Young Fine Gael was proposing an overhaul of the system by way of an electoral college with weighted voting strength divided between the parliamentary party (50% of votes), local public representatives (20%) and party members (30%).

A postal ballot of Fine Gael members on the rule changes – accepted at the February 2002 Ard Fheis – had been planned prior to the calling of the 2002 general election. The ballot was due to be concluded by early July but waiting for the decision would have left Noonan in a caretaker role until the autumn. Young Fine Gael favoured this strategy and called for the leadership election to be postponed to allow the wider party membership to have its say. One of the few members of the parliamentary party to publicly support a delay was Wicklow TD Billy Timmins. In a public statement Timmins said: 'The phrase "Marry in haste, repent at leisure" comes to mind.' But most senior Fine Gael figures were unhappy about changing the electoral system. Fewer still were thrilled with the idea that the selection of a successor to Noonan would be delayed. They feared a political vacuum that ultimately would be counterproductive for Fine Gael. Outgoing senator Maurice Manning observed, 'There is going to be the most competitive opposition in the history of the State. If Fine Gael is a bystander with no leader during the early formative life of this Dáil then we would risk having permanent damage inflicted upon us.' There was also some concern among some senior Fine Gael figures that a vote of the membership would assist the leadership ambitions of younger – but politically inexperienced – TDs like Naughton and Coveney. There had been media speculation that Fine Gael might 'skip a generation' in the choice of its new leader. In any event, the options for a new voting system or a delayed contest were quickly shelved once parliamentary party members had an opportunity to consult.

In the final days of May 2002 negotiating teams from Fianna Fáil and the Progressive Democrats met to put shape on a new programme for government. While these negotiations were underway the depleted Fine Gael parliamentary party met for a special two-day session at the City West Hotel on the outskirts of Dublin. Fine Gael chairman Padraic McCormack said the meeting was to give the party time to reflect on its future direction. 'We will not be rushed by anybody. That's why I deliberately scheduled a two-day meeting. People can play a game of golf if they like. There is no agenda as such, except that we want to decide how we will approach the leadership.' At the City West conclave there were some behind-the-scenes efforts to reach a decision by consensus. A number of senior figures believed this would help the party move beyond personality clashes and the general election debacle. Among those backing a consensus approach was the former party leader and former Taoiseach, John Bruton who told his colleagues that a consensus leader was 'advisable and indeed desirable.' He pointed to the fact that all of Fine Gael's leaders elected to the post of Taoiseach had been appointed in this way, and observed that 'while historical precedent does not prove anything, this is probably too much of a coincidence to be ignored.' Initial speculation that Bruton himself might re-emerge in the position as Fine Gael leader never gained momentum, and while Bruton did not rule out the possibility he did little to encourage the idea.

Former opponents in the party were encouraged to talk to each other in small group sessions while potential candidates answered questions about what direction they would take the party. A straw poll was held of those present to see if there was any consensus about a likely victor. The results were not released but Enda Kenny came out ahead of the others who allowed their names to go forward. The unusual exercise was to give potential candidates an indication of their level of support. The City West meeting decided that the parliamentary party would proceed with the election of a new Fine Gael leader despite continued pressure from some party members for a delay to allow the electoral system to be overhauled. The majority view was that Fine Gael should have a new leader in place for the first sitting of the new Dáil. The party's 49 TDs, Senators and MEPs agreed to meet at 2.30 p.m. on 5 June 2002. Nominations had to be submitted by the previous evening and any contest would be determined by proportional representation. In the end four names appeared on the ballot paper: Enda Kenny, Richard Bruton, Gay Mitchell, and Phil Hogan.

None of the four candidates was the ideal fit. Each candidate had a perceived drawback. None came close to what Fine Gael wanted – a version of Garret FitzGerald from 1977 when the party was given a sense of purpose, underwent a process of reorganisation and modernisation, came within a shout of replacing the old enemy Fianna Fáil as the largest party in the State and, most importantly, enjoyed the experience of being in power. Political journalist Mark Hennessy succinctly summarised the dilemma facing those making the choice of leader:

'Hogan has organisational skills and an ability to graft, but is weak on policy issues. Kenny is extremely bright and personable, but often less than committed. The intellectual superior of the four, Richard Bruton is the ultimate "policy wonk", happiest under a pile of paper, though he has so far seemed unable to communicate his hunger for the job. Mitchell, on the other hand, is loyal, sharp-witted, utterly political and could teach a few of his parliamentary party colleagues a lesson on the value of hard work. And he has a clear view of where the party should be positioned. However, his abrasive personality tends to cause divisions rather than harmony . . .'

The candidates featured together on a number of radio and television debates. But the leadership election was dominated by a background campaign as the four contenders tried to win support with personal approaches to their parliamentary party colleagues. Two features emerged from the short leadership contest. First, there was a deliberate attempt within Fine Gael to avoid the public rancour so evident in the heave that ended Bruton's tenure as party leader. The candidates avoided personalised attacks and few of the potential voters went public with their preferences in an attempt to weaken the chances of rival candidates. The second lasting impression was the lack of ideological expression in the public positions adopted by the candidates. They all focused on the need to heal differences within the party, on the necessity to rebuild the Fine Gael organisation and the importance of rejuvenating the morale of party members.

This position was evident in a series of newspaper interviews with the four candidates. Mitchell was the only candidate to attempt to debate the party's future in any sort of an ideological context: 'I have set out the meaning of Christian Democracy. You can't have equality of outcome as socialists and the Labour Party want. We can have solidarity and equality of opportunity.' Hogan identified with perceived areas of traditional Fine Gael strength including law and order. 'I believe in the rule of law and strong opposition to criminality and subversion and also I am committed to an Ireland that provides equality of opportunity for all its citizens and protects its environment and heritage.' Bruton said Fine Gael was seen 'as part of a complacent establishment rather than as a party that is driving change. To revive the party we have to become a campaigning party.' He spoke about the need to campaign on issues such as special needs, literacy and remedial teaching in education.

Kenny was the only one of the four to have contested the party leadership previously and, with Bruton, he also held the distinction of having served in cabinet. His position was helped by the fact that having challenged Noonan he had no association with the defeated regime. When asked why Fine Gael should elect him as leader, Kenny focused on the need to unite the party: 'My record has been one of co-operation, consensus and team work . . . I want to give the membership of the party a sense of ownership of the party, leading to a more unified and cohesive party.' Being dropped from the frontbench had given Kenny plenty of time to listen to party members. His message in the 2002 leadership contest was honed to exactly what the party wanted to hear. He said that due to 'far too much infighting, there has been a failure to modernise the party. There has also been a rise in the dissent vote, and Fine Gael has been perceived as an establishment party. We need cohesion and unity and that is where team-building and an accessible leader is important. Fine Gael has to have a clear message, clear policies with a hard edge.'

This theme of party unity, reorganisation and an accessible leader would come to define Fine Gael in subsequent years. These principles were placed at the heart of all party strategy. In an *Irish Times* interview Vincent Browne joked about Kenny's famous promise from the 2001 leadership contest. 'You said you would electrocute the party the last time you ran for the leadership, do you still promise to do that?' Kenny replied: 'I didn't say I would electrocute the party, I said I would electrify the party. I think the structures and organisation are outdated in many areas.' As in 2001 Kenny stressed his political and ministerial record as evidence that he could deliver consensus and effective team work. 'For instance when I became Minister for Tourism I was involved in the creation of an all-Ireland tourism organisation. I have been around to most constituencies over the years, I was chairman of the strategy committee for the 1997 election which saw us winning seven additional seats.'

The questions Kenny faced in 2002 were very similar to those in the 2001 contest although he was not confronted with the same level of hostility or antagonism. It was perhaps not so much that Kenny was taken more seriously the second time around but that after its massive electoral defeat, Fine Gael, with questions about its future existence, was not given the same level of national importance. The Mayo man addressed perceived concerns about his ability to undertake the slog required in rebuilding the party, and stressed the affability factor which Bertie Ahern was perceived to have given Fianna Fáil: 'I am recognised as a person of sociable nature. People find it easy to talk to me, and access to the leader is crucial to rebuilding the party. I was the bridge to Democratic Left from 1992 to 1994, which laid the basis for the Rainbow coalition.

As for the contention that I don't have the application for the job, I would not be around in Mayo politics for so long if I did not have the application.'

Throughout the 2002 leadership election Kenny was non-specific on policy issues – as he had been in the previous contest. When asked about the three major policy reforms he would advocate, he responded: 'I would like to think that policy would not be laid down by the leadership; it would be determined by the membership. I would set up a framework within which the policies would be drafted. We are in favour of a strong, free-enterprise society, but balanced with that we have to go on to think about the kind of society we want. When you look at the difficulties on the streets, the rising incidence of young male suicide, the growth of greed and individualism, we have to reform areas in labour law, taxation and planning to develop community life.'

There was very little in Kenny's comments that provided the public with a sense of what type of politics he represented. When interviews turned to policy matters his comments became highly generalised and aspirational. He was obviously attempting not to make mistakes that would damage his electoral prospects but such was the vagueness in his responses that he left open the charge that he had no fixed views at all. The standard response was to give a short reply and then mention that all policy decisions were a matter for the Fine Gael parliamentary party. He may also have been attempting to reinforce his position as a consensus leader but he very much gave the impression of a politician without ideology or political belief. For example when it was put to him that Noonan had suggested that asylum-seekers undergo health screenings, Kenny replied: 'The first issue here is a tightening up of the Schengen agreements on border controls. Once that is done it would be a matter for the parliamentary party.' When asked if he was in favour of removing the ban on corporate donations – adopted by Noonan as Fine Gael policy – Kenny stated: 'You cannot run a professional political party without money. But that would be a matter for the parliamentary party.'

Kenny's contributions during the 2002 leadership contest provided no real sense of where he stood politically. In fairness he would not have been unique in Irish politics in adopting such a stance. But there was little passion from the Mayo man about policy and no evidence of an ideological bent to his political disposition. The second area where Kenny faced continued questioning was about his application and work ethic. There were doubts in sections of Fine Gael – and among those who acknowledged his popularity – about his hunger for the leadership. Political journalists picked up on these concerns. 'Though immensely liked, Enda Kenny has rarely shown the application that will be needed during dark, lonely night-time journeys to constituency meetings in the middle of nowhere,' one political writer observed. Long-time political commentator Bruce Arnold noted that 'for more than a quarter of a century Enda Kenny has remained the agreeable voice in Fine Gael of Mayo, promising a career leap forward that has never materialised.'

Kenny focused on his acknowledged popularity – a trait more than welcomed by a party that had been battered and bruised at the recent general election. The parliamentary party was receptive to a message that promised better electoral days ahead. One leading figure in the leadership election, who was campaigning for another candidate, read the outcome with a week to polling – when asked the likely winner by some officials working in Leinster House he quietly told them that Kenny was excellent value with the bookies at six to one. The wager delivered an excellent return.

Michael Ring was obviously conscious of his captive audience when he proposed his constituency colleague at the parliamentary party meeting on 5 June 2002. Kenny, Ring said, may have been in the Dáil for 27 years but he still would 'look well on posters and had a nice fresh face'. Kenny had asked Olwyn Enright, the party's newly-elected Laois-Offaly TD, to second his nomination. The choice signalled his intention to include the party's intake of new deputies at the heart of a rebuilding exercise. Enright told the parliamentary party that Kenny had the drive, energy and enthusiasm for the job. The mood at the three-hour meeting was relaxed as the four candidates made their final pitch for the position. 'In the previous leadership contest you could literally cut the tension with a knife. This time it was very amicable. There was a number of jokes cracked during the speeches,' Denis Naughton recalled.

The results were not made public and differing outcomes of the voting process were reported in different newspapers. In fact, Bruton was ahead on the first count by a single vote with Kenny in second place. Bruton had 17 first preference votes, Kenny had 16 while Hogan had nine and Mitchell had seven. Mitchell was first eliminated with Kenny and Hogan each getting three transfers while Bruton received a single vote. On the second count Kenny now had 19 votes with Bruton on 18 and Hogan on 12. The elimination of Hogan decided the contest. His 12 transfers benefited Kenny – 10 went to the Mayo man with only two going to Bruton. On the third and final count – Kenny had 29 votes, Bruton 20. Sixteen months after being defeated by Noonan – and subsequently dropped from the party's frontbench – Enda Kenny was leader of Fine Gael.

His first action was to meet briefly with the defeated leadership candidates. He wanted them actively involved, and they were asked what role they wanted to play on his frontbench. The message was clear: the party could no longer afford rumps and disaffected factions. The tag of 'family at war' was being removed from the party. The first public remarks from the new leader were understandably upbeat. 'Fine Gael's political mourning is over. This party is getting up off the floor and we are determined to demonstrate all over Ireland that we are a political force to be reckoned with in the future.' But the task involved in revitalising Fine Gael was recognised: 'I am looking forward to the challenge. There is an immense task to be faced by Fine Gael. The road ahead is uphill. But I think we are equal to it. And the prize is great at the end.'

Kenny had certainly given away very little in the leadership contests in 2001 and in 2002. And within Fine Gael there was an acknowledgment that the party had elected a leader who did not have a prior public profile like others who had previously taken on the job. An internal Fine Gael report prepared later in 2002, and which became the blueprint for the rebuilding process, was blunt in its image of the new leader: 'A strategic communications plan needs to be built around a high-profile programme which fully establishes Enda Kenny's leadership skills and credentials. Most voters outside of Mayo would not have been familiar with Enda Kenny at the time of his election and few would have a well-developed appreciation of his qualities.'

Kenny's three immediate predecessors – Dukes, Bruton and Noonan – were respected, perhaps, but none of them had ever had a warm relationship with the public. Back in 2002 Fine Gael believed it now had 'Enda' – a political leader who the party hoped would be its very own Mr Nice Guy, and a match for Fianna Fáil's 'Bertie'. But that scenario never materialised. Kenny's personal satisfaction ratings were consistently mediocre – and often very poor – and he met with an ongoing hostile reaction from most media commentators and political journalists. The personality of the man who engaged people in one-to-one situations never came through in broadcast interviews, particularly on television, the most important means of political communication in contemporary politics.

The editorial in *The Irish Times* on the day Kenny was elected party leader was typical: 'Mr Kenny comes with a clean slate but he has yet to prove himself. He first entered politics in 1975 – two years before the Taoiseach, Mr Ahern – and has little to show for a full 27 years close to the top of Fine Gael. He was Minister for Tourism and Trade in the Rainbow Government between 1994 and 1997. He served as Minister of State for Youth Affairs between 1986 and 1987. He has held many frontbench positions in different portfolios. For all of his years in the Dáil, however, he cannot be remembered for one political initiative. He has not espoused any particular policy. He has never played a high-profile role. He has presided over the Fine Gael domination of the Mayo constituency in many elections up to the last. But friend and foe say that he is a nice man.'

Kenny was damned with faint praise. But back in 2002 there was genuine hope in Fine Gael that the party's new leader would woo voters with his likeability. It was a trait longtime political watchers in Leinster House also saw in Enda Kenny's father, Henry. Indeed, Henry Kenny was widely considered one of the most popular members of Dáil Éireann during a political career that lasted just over 21 years. He was among a group of new TDs who joined an expanded Fine Gael parliamentary party when in 1954 Fine Gael became the largest party in the second inter-party government. Kenny was a farmer and the principal of a national school just outside Castlebar. He was a well-known figure on County Mayo due to his exploits on the GAA pitch. According to several accounts he was one of the best midfielders of his era. 'He was beautiful to watch – those final catches and so stylish,' another Mayo player Sean Purcell said. Kenny was known as 'the man with the magic hands' and won Mayo senior championship medals with Castlebar Mitchels during the 1930s. It was a decade of unprecedented national football success for the county. Kenny was a member of the Mayo team that won the county's first All-Ireland senior championship title in 1936. They had a two-point advantage over champions Kerry in the All-Ireland semi-final before trouncing Laois in the final at Croke Park by 4-11 to 0-05. 'A forest of green and red flags greeted us and a deafening roar, "Come on Mayo" drove us on to victory,' one team member recalled. It was the type of victory that establishes players as local legends and allows some to later build successful political careers. The new All-Ireland champions received an ecstatic homecoming as torchlight processions welcomed the team with the Sam Maguire Cup through the streets of Castlebar and other Mayo towns. The team also won six national League titles in a row from 1934 to 1939 – a record that stands to this day. 'They were an incredibly close group, that team of the '30s, and they stayed in contact with each other long after they finished playing,' Henry's son John later recalled. On the day Enda Kenny was elected Taoiseach his sister Marie wore a gold chain around her neck with a miniature football attached and inscribed with the date '1937' – a memento given to each member of the All-Ireland team a year after their famous victory.

Henry Kenny's family was not involved in politics. The 1954 general election was his first time being a candidate. He was initially reluctant to allow his name to go forward but Fine Gael, conscious of his popularity, kept up the pressure. The party had not won a seat in Mayo South since 1943. The constituency was still a five-seater in 1944 when Fianna Fáil took three seats and the other two seats went to Clann na Talmhan, which represented western farmers. During the 1930s Fine Gael in several general elections took two seats in Mayo South but with the emergence of Clann na Talmhan, the party's vote collapsed. In 1938 Fine Gael won 38.1 per cent of the vote but with the new party and its leader Joe Blowick on the ticket by 1943 the Fine Gael vote fell to 16.2 per cent. Fine Gael was so weak in the area that the party did not nominate a candidate for a by-election in December 1945. The constituency was subsequently reduced in size to a four-seater, and in the general elections in 1948 and in 1951 Fianna Fáil and Clann na Talmhan held two seats each. Fine Gael's identification of Kenny was undoubtedly influenced by the successful Fianna Fáil ticket in 1951 which included Sean Flanagan who had also enjoyed football fame with the Mayo team. The selection of Henry Kenny was a clever move as Fine Gael sought to re-establish a presence in Mayo South.

The ballot paper in 1954 included Flanagan; Michael Moran, a future Fianna Fáil minister; and Joseph Blowick, leader of Clann na Talmhan and a minister in the inter-party governments. Kenny polled well, receiving nearly 5,000 first preferences as Fine Gael's vote increased to almost 23 per cent. He took a seat at the expense of Clann na Talmhan. As a new deputy Henry Kenny would not have expected ministerial office in 1954 but he could hardly have anticipated that it would be almost two decades before Fine Gael would again emerge from a general election to form a government.

During this long period as a backbencher Kenny was acknowledged as one of the most popular members not just in Fine Gael but also in Dáil Éireann. In February 2011 a letter from Columban missionary Aodh O'Halpin recalled an amusing episode following a chance meeting with Henry Kenny in Malinbeg, county Donegal in 1966. At that time O'Halpin was based in the Philippines. He had returned home on holiday – something missionaries could expect to enjoy every seven years. But as he prepared to leave Malinbeg for his foreign posting, O'Halpin turned his thoughts to getting a good bottle of poitín: 'a Godsend against the flu and colds, which we often caught because of climate change – from the wind and windy weather of Donegal to the beautiful sunshine in the Philippines.' Henry Kenny who was also in Malinbeg overheard the missionary asking a local woman about getting some poitín.

'For God's sake don't get any poitín from around here, it's not safe! I will get you a bottle when I get back to Mayo,' Kenny said. The Mayo man was true to his word – and he arranged for his party colleague Paddy Harte to safely get the illicit drink to O'Halpin.

The Columban missionary wrote to *The Irish Times* in early 2011 to recount his chance meeting with Enda Kenny's father. 'I met Paddy Harte about ten years ago and I asked him if he remembered Henry Kenny getting me the bottle of poitín from the hills of County Mayo. Paddy responded: 'I remember it well. He got no bottle of poitín from the hills of County Mayo. He went into the Garda barracks in Castlebar and said, 'I want your best bottle. . . for a missionary priest going back to the Philippines.'

Henry Kenny held his seat in South Mayo at each election from 1954 to 1969. He was elected on the first count in 1961 and again in 1965 when his 7,071 first preferences left him just 200 votes shy of Fianna Fáil minister Micheal Moran. The 1965 contest was a big success for Fine Gael in South Mayo. Blowick had retired and in the absence of Clann na Talmhan, Fine Gael won an extra seat. Boundary revisions meant that Henry Kenny contested in the new three-seat Mayo West constituency in 1969 where he topped the poll. His own vote slipped slightly in the 1973 general election but the party's vote increased and Fine Gael took two of the three available seats. It was one of the best results for Fine Gael in a landmark contest as Liam Cosgrave led the party into a coalition government with the Labour Party. There was a reward for Kenny who had been his party's spokesman for the board of works from 1969 to 1973. Cosgrave appointed the Mayo TD to the position of Parliamentary Secretary (Junior Minister) to the Minister for Finance. He was given responsibility for the Board of Works (today, the Office of Public Works).

Henry Kenny did not, however, get to serve out a full term as minister. He had been ill for some time before his death from cancer in September 1975. He was 62 years of age and was survived by his wife, Eithne, a native of County Donegal, and their five children. Enda was born in Castlebar in 1951. He was the middle child in a family of five, having two older brothers and a younger brother and sister. He was educated in a two-roomed primary school at Cornanool outside Castlebar and later at St Gerald's College. He completed his education at St Patrick's Teacher Training College in Dublin, where he was a gold medal-winning student and later attended University College Galway.

Kenny was three years old when his father was first elected to the Dáil in 1954. 'Politics was always in the house and in that way it becomes part of you,' he says. The family household revolved around a husband and a father who was absent from Mayo for much of the week. The demands of political life in Dublin were in many respects far more trying in this earlier era. There was no text messaging or internet access, and even telephones were in short supply. 'Children don't care where you are or give a damn about distance so long as you keep talking to them,' Enda Kenny said many years later about his own absences from home.

Henry Kenny left behind an established record for hard work in his constituency. Along with the weekly clinics in local towns, there were often lines of people outside the family home in Castlebar. Throughout their teenage years his children helped out at election times and they were also involved in constituency work. Enda Kenny recalls bags of sugar and water on the table in the family home as gum was prepared to stick up posters at election times.

The Kenny children would be assigned sections of the electoral register and in long hand they would write the names and addresses of voters onto envelopes stuffed with their father's election literature. The young Kenny made a regular trip to the local post office to buy stamps for the multitude of envelopes sent to constituents and official bodies.

When Henry Kenny became ill, Enda, who had recently taken up a teaching position about 20 miles from the family's Castlebar home, became more involved. He ran the network of clinics and ensured that the concerns and queries of constituents were followed up. Henry Kenny died after his battle with cancer on 25 September 1975.

'My father was 62 years when he died. And even though he was sick, you still don't believe it – your parent is your parent and you think they'll always be around. My father was a strong, fit man. He played football for Mayo. You don't expect people like that to just go away like that.'

In a generous obituary, political journalist James Downey wrote, 'The present Dáil has lost several of its most popular deputies, but none more popular than Mr Kenny. The government has lost a competent member of the administration; the House a deputy notable both for his good humour and his good manners. He had the quality, too rare, of being witty without being offensive, and admired for the courage with which he faced his fatal illness.'

In 1975, Enda Kenny had no great yearning for a career in politics. He was working as a teacher in a small rural school at Knockrooskey near Westport and was playing plenty of football with his local club Islandeady. But with Henry Kenny's death, the 24-year-old was identified as his political successor. The two youngest Kenny children were still at school while of the two eldest sons, one was still at university and the other was working for a bank outside Mayo. The middle child was asked to step forward. In a comment on the hereditary nature of Irish parliamentary seats – and foretelling the establishment of another political dynasty – one newspaper published a headline, 'And to my son, I leave the seat'.

An early by-election was favoured by the Fine Gael organisation in Mayo. Kenny travelled to Dublin to meet Liam Cosgrave in the Taoiseach's office in Government Buildings. 'We'd like you to stand,' Cosgrave said. The Fine Gael leader had got on very well with Henry Kenny and during the remainder of his parliamentary career he adopted an almost fatherly attitude to Enda. Some in Fine Gael believe this identification with the Cosgrave wing of the party cost Kenny advancement during the subsequent FitzGerald era.

The intention with an early by-election in Mayo West was to take up where his father left off. 'The field is already ploughed,' Enda Kenny told reporters ahead of the selection convention in Castlebar. He said he had learned the value of hard work from his father as well as the importance of keeping your word. 'He was a man who really had a great understanding of human nature. I think people in his years in the Dáil made an agreement and stuck by it.' He says the most important political lesson learned from his father 'is always to treat people equally.'

'My father had been a big influence. I campaigned in elections even as a young lad. You get to learn very quickly how things happen, to read signs from people, whether they are supporters or what are the issues in any one campaign. But there was no sense that my da was grooming me. You don't expect your father to die.'

The selection convention was a mere formality. The Taoiseach was on the platform to congratulate the candidate. Cosgrave told the delegates that there was a 'new note of hope' in the West. It was the first formal speech in a month-long by-election campaign. During the convention proceedings former Fine Gael minister Patrick Lindsay was a late arrival. Lindsay had been a TD in Mayo North, was a leading criminal lawyer and a well-recognised speaker at Fine Gael gatherings since the 1950s. But he had only recently been appointed Master of the High Court, a position that effectively placed him above party politics. Lindsay settled himself down, lit a big cigar and proceeded to write a short note which was duly passed up to Cosgrave who was sitting beside Kenny at the top table. 'I wish to speak – L,' the note read. Cosgrave wrote back, 'Is that wise? – C'. The convention was proceeding as a final note arrived from Lindsay, 'Wise or not, I am going to speak – L', which he duly did in urging the party faithful to back their by-election candidate.

'It was the last of the old-style by-elections,' Kenny recalled, 'I remember Liam Cosgrave leading a parade from the racecourse in Ballinrobe into the town, with people carrying lighting sods of turf.' On another occasion Kenny was the final speaker at a late-night rally. Seated behind him were Cosgrave and other Fine Gael grandees: 'And here was I, a young fellow of 24 with long hair,' Kenny says. When he finished his address, Cosgrave tapped the candidate on the shoulder, said he had spoken well and handed him a collection of notes. 'Now go and buy them some drink,' Cosgrave said, pointing to the party's supporters. The Taoiseach's instruction would not have met with approval from independent candidate Basil Morahan, who as the campaign started, wrote to his opponents requesting that they would not buy alcoholic drinks for anyone while they were canvassing. Morahan said that all the candidates should declare publicly that they would stay out of Dáil Éireann rather than get elected with the help of 'booze votes'. One journalist wrote that 'Basil, who is also against the misuse of the dole, certainly knows how to turn off the voters.'

The Fine Gael-Labour government had been in office for just over two years. The national economic situation was difficult but the by-election campaign was dominated by local issues that sound all too familiar even four decades later – a failure to decentralise the headquarters of the Department of Lands to Castlebar; the down-grading of the rail service from Westport to Dublin; hospital over-crowding and poor-quality local roads. The government unveiled the Western Development Board at the start of the campaign. Plans for the agency had been underway before the by-election situation arose but Fianna Fáil still criticised the announcement as a political stroke, a move that was considered a strategic mistake in a region crying out for investment.

Despite Basil Morahan's best efforts, the by-election was a

straight fight between Fine Gael and Fianna Fáil. The early commentary in the national media referred to a tight contest in what was described as a marginal constituency. At the general election in 1973 Fine Gael won two of the three seats but Fianna Fáil had slightly more first preference votes – 12,701 against 12,405. But once journalists started reporting from the constituency itself they became fully aware of the considerable sympathy for Henry Kenny which was translating into a huge response for his son, Enda. The single biggest factor in the by-election contest was the Kenny factor. Party workers were also convinced that their candidate would win. One Fine Gael party member met Brian Lenihan snr. in a pub during the campaign. There was some banter about the by-election result with Fine Gael supporters having challenged the senior Fianna Fáil politician to a wager; 'I knew that Enda would be elected because of Henry Kenny's popularity, and I bet my week's wages from the bacon factory that he would win. He won, and I collected my winnings from Brian.'

The campaign was unusual in that the Labour Party, which was not contesting the by-election, actively campaigned for the candidate of their partners in government. Kenny was as much a candidate of the national coalition as he was of Fine Gael. 'I remember Dr Conor Cruise O'Brien [a Labour minister] advising people to vote for "young Kenny" and also saying that they must put down the IRA,' Kenny said. Cruise O'Brien was a curious figure on the campaign trail. In his history of the Labour Party, John Horgan recalled Cruise O'Brien arriving in a Mayo pub 'wearing a white linen suit and looking for the world, as one observer put it, like a tea planter with amnesia.' Kenny recalls the impressive ministerial presence in the constituency: 'Every morning down at the Travellers Friend there was a collection of State cars lined up for petrol.'

Ahead of polling day it was generally considered that Fine Gael would win but few predicted the overwhelming nature of the victory. Kenny was elected on the first count with 52.8 per cent of the overall vote. He received 15,584 first preference votes to 12,448 for Michael Joe McGreal of Fianna Fáil and 1,481 for Independent candidate Basil Morahan. It would be 34 years before another Fine Gael by-election candidate would again win over 50 per cent of the first preference vote – George Lee in Dublin South in June 2009. Brian Cowen achieved this notable distinction as a Fianna Fáil candidate in his by-election success in Laois-Offaly in 1984.

'The sympathy vote for the son of the late Henry Kenny was, of course, the most powerful element in his victory. Everybody in West Mayo loved Henry Kenny and yesterday they demonstrated their love. The debts owing to Henry Kenny were many and yesterday the slate was wiped clean,' reporter Michael Finlan concluded. In defeat the Fianna Fáil candidate summed up the task he had faced against the goodwill factor for Kenny: 'I knew his father well. He was a good friend of mine and if I was not a candidate, I honestly feel I would have put a No. 1 in the box for Enda Kenny.'

In victory Kenny thanked his supporters and promised to ably represent his constituents. 'When I go to Kildare Street next week and walk up those steps, and walk into the hallowed halls, I hope I carry with me the hopes and aspirations of all the people of West Mayo.' Enda Kenny was 24-years old, and the youngest member of Dáil Éireann when he arrived in Leinster House on 18 November 1975. His father had died at the end of September. For some in Fine Gael he could never match his father's achievements. 'In those early years you're faced with the thing of, "Oh you'll never be the person your father was," or "Oh I supported your father for 20 years and you'll never measure up at all." Oh yes, they'd say it straight to me, but they were a different generation, and time moves on, and you let it wash off you and you make your own way.'

Thirty-six years later, Enda Kenny carved out his own place in Irish political history. 'My father walked in those gates 57 years ago next May (in 1954) and he would never have believed that one day his son would walk out those gates as Taoiseach,' Enda Kenny's brother Henry said. When he delivered his acceptance speech having just been elected as Taoiseach Enda Kenny's thoughts turned to his family, his wife Fionnuala O'Kelly, his mother Eithne – in her nineties and watching from Mayo – and his late father Henry. The new Taoiseach's voice faltered as he read: 'They walk with me every step of this heart-stopping journey. For me, for Fionnuala and the children, they represent the nobility, decency and very soul of the Irish people, and because they do, their spirit is with us . . .'

5
Playboy of the Western World

During his initial days as a Dáil deputy, Enda Kenny says he first realised the responsibility involved in entering the national political arena. He arrived as the Fine Gael-Labour coalition was grappling with a severe economic downturn, the security situation in Northern Ireland was a continuing worry while confidence in the gardaí was hit by 'heavy gang' revelations about brutality in obtaining confessions. Irish politics was also on the cusp of professionalising – great changes would come in subsequent years – but in the mid-1970s in Leinster House, members shared offices, two secretaries worked for all the Fine Gael TDs, letters were written in long hand, telephones were in short supply and deputies were limited in the number of calls they could make each day. Kenny recalls the government chief whip John Kelly walking through the bar in Buswells Hotel to round up deputies ahead of Dáil votes and at afternoon time finding some TDs stretched out asleep on the couches in their offices.

The Oireachtas was populated with the last of the veterans from the fight to establish Irish independence half a century previously. One of them, John L. O'Sullivan, a farmer from Clonakilty in west Cork, had been a senior figure in the 3rd Cork Brigade of the IRA during the War of Independence. He had been a founder member of Cumann na nGaedheal but had only contested his first Dáil election in 1937 for Fine Gael. He was unsuccessful on that occasion, and ran again without success in 1954, 1961 and in 1965. O'Sullivan eventually won a seat in 1969 – at the age of 68 – and held on in 1973. When the new Mayo West TD arrived in Leinster House, O'Sullivan was in his mid-70s and chairman of the Fine Gael parliamentary party. Kenny recalls that the republican veteran would remind party members that he had had breakfast with Michael Collins on the morning the republican leader was shot dead. Kenny was not long in Dáil Éireann when he received some words of advice from another veteran politician, Jim Tully, a Labour Party minister in the coalition government. 'Go down and sit in the chamber. Listen and observe, that's how you'll learn,' Tully said. Ironically, Kenny passed on the same advice to another new Fine Gael TD in 2009 – George Lee.

Kenny was just over a year in the Dáil when the 1977 general election was called. From this short stint as a government backbencher under Liam Cosgrave as Fine Gael leader he moved to the opposition side of the House. Garret FitzGerald was the new leader of the party which had suffered a big electoral defeat. Despite the national reversal Kenny topped the poll in Mayo West but Fianna Fáil took back the second seat it lost to Fine Gael in 1973. A new political figure also emerged for the first time in Mayo politics – Padraig Flynn, who took a seat for Fianna Fáil although he had some 4,000 fewer first preference votes than Kenny.

The young Fine Gael TD worked hard for his constituents. His Dáil contributions were typically weighted towards issues related to Mayo West. He spoke when it was revealed that there were limited promotion opportunities for the 160 civil servants who had moved to Castlebar in the first decentralisation initiative. 'If these officials have to go back to Dublin to fulfil their ambitions it will defeat the whole purpose of the decentralisation exercise,' he claimed. A Dáil sketch from *The Irish Times* in 1981 very much captured Kenny's involvement in parliamentary life: 'Enda Kenny tried a bit of local vote-catching when he pursued the Minister for Agriculture about the need to establish a brucellosis blood-sampling centre at

Castlebar, and Ray McSharry didn't even blush when he responded that an extension to the centre in his own constituency of Sligo would soon be capable of dealing with the whole of the north-west.'

Along with protecting his domestic political base Kenny gained some national profile although not for taking any significant political stance. He was a participant in the first series of the *Superstars* competition in early 1979 – broadcast by RTÉ. *Superstars* was in many ways an early reality television programme in which well known personalities from the worlds of politics, entertainment and sport competed to be overall winner and to represent Ireland in an international version of the programme. Kenny joined Bertie Ahern, Liam Lawlor and Ruairi Quinn as the political contestants. Ahern and Kenny would eventually joust as political leaders on opposite sides in Leinster House. 'I have known Bertie Ahern since 1977, and no more than myself, he had long hair at the time. We went over to London to participate in the first-ever soccer match against the House of Commons and a photographer of that year shows myself and Bertie Ahern side-by-side playing for Ireland,' Kenny later recalled. 'My relationship with him on a personal basis is very good, but I would prefer to think that my style of politics is different.' Kenny's involvement in sporting events made sense – he was one of the youngest TDs in Leinster House and he had been appointed Fine Gael's spokesman on youth affairs and sport in 1977. He held that position until 1980 when he was moved to spokesman on western development.

After the 1977 election defeat, Garret FitzGerald embarked upon a significant reorganisation programme. The new leader toured the country as members were recruited and candidates identified. There was huge excitement in Fine Gael ranks. When FitzGerald arrived at Castlebar railway station over 600 people turned up. Kenny was involved in this work programme especially with the newly-formed Young Fine Gael. Kenny and FitzGerald were two of the speakers at a series of regional conferences organised in 1978 to attract younger members into the party. The party still had some work to do to match Fianna Fáil's organisation. 'Fine Gael is still tentative, a little unsure and self-conscious in its overtures to the young by comparison with Fianna Fáil who wooed them in the last election with way-out T-shirts and soft-rock pop tunes,' reporter Michael Finlan wrote.

In Limerick city Kenny worked the queues outside a local cinema but the response from those waiting to go inside was not hugely enthusiastic. 'If we had the Boomtown Rats playing here today,' Kenny later told a Fine Gael conference, 'you wouldn't be able to get within an inch of the place.' He especially bemoaned the lack of interest in Northern Ireland that emerged from his questioning of the movie-goers. 'It seems that people in the South couldn't care less about the North,' he asserted.

Early in 1980 Kenny was a passenger on a four-seater aircraft along with FitzGerald and his wife Joan travelling from Carrickfin in County Donegal to Castlebar airport. A tyre burst on landing and the short journey became a news story. Yet, despite this involvement – and receiving frontbench positions – the young deputy was overlooked when FitzGerald led Fine Gael into government with the Labour Party in June 1981. 'I wasn't too pushy with him about an appointment,' Kenny says. He did not expect a cabinet post but there was some surprise when he was not appointed to one of the 12 available Minister of State positions. His frontbench responsibilities went elsewhere – Michael Keating was appointed minister with responsibility for youth and sport while Ted Nealon was given the western development ministry.

The first FitzGerald-led Fine Gael-Labour coalition was short-lived, collapsing after eight months in office. Charles Haughey's Fianna Fáil formed a minority government and with Fine Gael back on the opposition benches Kenny once again received the western development brief. The minority Fianna Fáil administration was out of office by the end of 1982 when a second general election in a single calendar year saw Fine Gael and the Labour Party secure sufficient seats for a parliamentary majority. But when government beckoned late in 1982 Kenny was for the second time omitted from FitzGerald's ministerial list. Promoted in opposition but overlooked in government – it was 'a curious distinction' according to the authors of the *Magill Book of Irish Politics*.

There was disgruntlement in Fine Gael ranks at FitzGerald's ministerial choices. Deputies who had worked hard in opposition were overlooked after the 1981 general election as Jim Dooge was catapulted into Foreign Affairs via a Seanad nomination and Alan Dukes was given the Agriculture portfolio on his first day in Dáil Éireann. Kenny also had to watch as Paddy O'Toole, from the neighbouring Mayo East constituency, was rewarded. O'Toole was first elected in 1977 and was given a frontbench position. When the Fine Gael-Labour coalition was formed in 1981, O'Toole was appointed Minister for the Gaeltacht in what was seen as compensation for ending support for the Knock Airport project. One constituency in Mayo prospered under FitzGerald but unfortunately for Enda Kenny it was not his part of the county.

Whatever about the choice of individuals for the Fine Gael cabinet posts, reasons of geography and party politics dictated most of the promotions to Minister of State positions. Kenny was among a group of Fine Gael TDs who could reasonably have expected promotion, but in 1981 and again in 1982 he was passed over. After FitzGerald filled his ministerial positions in late 1982, political reporter Denis Coughlan wrote: 'Enda Kenny was another disappointed deputy. He had worked hard for the party both at constituency and Dáil level, but it was felt that providing him with a car would not necessarily improve the party's chances of a second seat in Mayo West.' But veteran political commentator John Healy argued differently: 'Enda has held his corner against Fianna Fáil heavyweights, and if there was to be a chance given to him to reverse the two-one situation, the nod as a Minister of State would have been a help.'

His links to the Cosgrave regime were probably not unhelpful to his promotion prospects with a new regime running the party. But Kenny may also have harmed his own cause. 'He was a victim of his own disposition. Garret took to what you might call "serious people" which is not what you got from Enda's personality or from his lifestyle,' one party veteran says. Kenny was a single man until he turned 40 and, as he explained himself, 'I had a good long bachelor innings!'

By the time FitzGerald formed his second coalition government in November 1982 Kenny was an experienced parliamentarian. He was still being described as 'one of Fine Gael's young men with a future'. But around him in the mid-1980s Fine Gael TDs of his own age had been appointed to senior and junior ministerial office. Kenny was 33 years old in 1984 – John Bruton (cabinet minister) was 37; Dukes (cabinet minister) 39; Jim Mitchell (cabinet minister) 38 and George Birmingham (junior minister) 30. Kenny seemed out of step with the Fine Gael leadership. John Healy wrote about two groups in FitzGerald's Fine Gael – The Donnybrook Set and The Culchie Set. He had a view about which 'Set' Kenny belonged to.

Healy wondered about 'Enda, a young man who was used by Garret to nail down the youth vote only to find when the real, as distinct from the shadow, jobs were going Enda suffered of not being a member of The Donnybrook Set. Is it the accident of his birth in the politically retarded west which has stopped him from being picked? Garret is great when he's picking Shadow Ministers, Senior and Junior. Picking costs nothing then. Twice he picked Enda Kenny when it cost him nothing but a shadow nomination. But when the [political rewards are given out], the Kennys of the disadvantaged areas don't rate. The brains are east of the Shannon.'

Kenny merited but a single passing reference in Garret FitzGerald's memoirs. Within the Kenny team today there is a privately spoken annoyance with the former party leader. 'He doesn't rate Enda,' one senior strategist says, 'there has hardly been a mention of Enda Kenny or his achievements as party leader in Garret's newspaper columns.' The annoyance only increased with FitzGerald's declaration in September 2009 that an early general election was not in the national interest. The Healy thesis is acknowledged by Kenny's team. 'There is an intellectual snobbery there. Kenny is a bright man, well-educated but within certain sections of Fine Gael there is a certain south Dublin snobbery.'

Despite the disappointment at being overlooked on two occasions in short succession for ministerial office, Kenny kept his views to himself. There was, however, evidence of his frustration in late 1984 – he was just over nine years a TD when he described the Fine Gael-Labour coalition as 'tattered and even tainted in some ways'. There was implicit criticism of the performance of some ministers when he welcomed the party's decision to hold a series of regional conferences – he said they would attract members from outside Dublin and would bring ministers into contact with real opinion in local areas. Kenny's criticism, however, never touched upon FitzGerald personally or any individual Fine Gael minister. Regardless of his frustration there was continued loyalty to his party.

Resigned to the life on the backbenches, Kenny worked hard in his constituency and any job he was given was completed without fuss. He played a part – minor as it was – in the New Ireland Forum and was a diligent secretary of the Fine Gael parliamentary party. The Dáil record shows an unexceptional contributor although this is not unsurprising given his status in the mid-1980s as a government backbencher. But there is little evidence from these years to provide any sense of Kenny's political beliefs. His membership of the New Ireland Forum presented some limited opportunities to carve out a role although most of the serious work was undertaken by senior government members. He was a firm supporter of FitzGerald's policy of creating a society in the Republic which was more attractive to unionists. In one of his rare public comments on Northern Ireland he expressed the hope that unionists would adopt a more conciliatory attitude towards the Republic. He also acknowledged the need to recognise the separate traditions of nationalists and unionists including the British identity of the unionist community in Northern Ireland.

The Fine Gael delegation at the New Ireland Forum included a number of backbench TDs including Kenny; Maurice Manning, a

UCD lecturer and a TD for Dublin North East; and David Molony, a TD for Tipperary North. Kenny, Manning and Molony were quite a combination during this period. Any of the trio could have been ministers, and their exclusion from office led them to be called 'the government in exile' within Fine Gael. They became close friends, enjoyed an active social life and were regulars on the nightclub scene in Dublin. Mid-week nights when the Dáil is sitting are often the only free time available to TDs especially those who represent non-Dublin constituencies. Backbenchers, in particular, enjoy the freedom of being able to go out for a few drinks without the prospect of being approached by a constituent with a query or a problem.

Kenny and his group of political friends enjoyed their revelry which frequently went on into the small hours of the morning. Along with Manning and Molony, Kenny was part of a group that frequently included Austin Deasy, John Farrelly and Ivan Yates. 'When I knew him first we were both single, footloose and fancy-free TDs. We would go out to nightclubs together and he would be happy to stay in bed half the day. He wasn't ambitious,' Yates recalled. Kenny was outgoing, gregarious and highly entertaining with an endless stream of engaging stories and humorous mimics. He was known for his impersonations of rivals including Padraig Flynn. He entertained colleagues with recitations of speeches by US President John F. Kennedy. There were also trips abroad on parliamentary business and during one visit to New York a senior Northern Ireland politician who enjoyed Kenny's company nick-named him, 'the playboy of the western world'.

Kenny shared offices in Leinster House at various stages with colleagues including Nora Owen, John Farrelly, Ivan Yates and John Boland. A close friendship developed with John Bruton when the two men later shared an office. Before he became Fine Gael leader, many of Kenny's colleagues questioned his ambition for a senior role. Kenny says of this period in the 1980s, 'Ambition grows on you. You see ministers doing things and you say, "I would like to do that, to make any impact."' There were flashes of potential.

In June 1984 he spoke out against drug pushers who were described as the 'harbingers of humiliation, destruction and death . . . no bail should be granted to them . . . in other countries pushers may be hanged or shot or have parts of their bodies removed. People involved in these activities deserve no mercy.'

He also worked on a number of issues with Dublin North TD, Nora Owen. 'He is a great people person. He will sit and he will listen to people. And he will take on board what they say,' Owen later recalled. Kenny and Owen put their names to several public statements. In May 1983 Dean Victor Griffin of St Patrick's Cathedral in Dublin attacked the clientelist nature of Irish politics – which he said was to the detriment of a concentration on national issues – and the low standing of Dáil Éireann and its members with the public. Griffin's remarks generated considerable public debate. Kenny and Owen issued a joint statement. 'When has Dean Griffin faced endless queues of ordinary people who turn to their public representatives in time of need? Does he drive 40,000 miles a year in the service of those he represents? What proposals has he made to reform an obviously outdated Dáil system which is currently under review? As a leader in his community surely he could show come semblance of respect for the democratic system and for those who choose quite freely to elect their public representatives. If the Dean believes that the Dáil is being treated with derision and contempt, has his incitement improved matters? Let him, therefore, accept an open invitation to spend one day in observation of what our so-called part-time job entails.' When Vincent Browne also criticised the work of TDs, Kenny challenged the newspaper editor to spend a week in his constituency to see how hard rural TDs worked.

Kenny was never seen as one of the cheerleaders for Garret FitzGerald's constitutional crusade nor was he an overt champion of the liberal agenda. But there were episodes which showed that neither was he was a member of Fine Gael's conservative wing. Kenny along with Owen, Manning and Molony, all members of the New Ireland Forum, argued that if the 1986 divorce referendum failed then the commitment to an Ireland respecting different traditions would be seen as false. They claimed that rejection of the constitutional amendment would result in the border with Northern Ireland assuming the severity of a Berlin Wall – 'separating the troubled North from what will be seen as a partitionist, inward-looking and smug State dominated by the views of one Church.'

But there was no real sense that Kenny had a deeply held interest in the subject – he may have been a believer but he was never one for going out to convert others. His reputation was as an effective constituency TD who liked a few rounds of golf and a couple of pints after reaching the eighteenth hole. He gave the impression of not taking politics too seriously. He featured in media reports of a Dáil discussion of family planning legislation in 1985. The legislation proposed to increase the availability of condoms and a Fianna Fáil TD was explaining that he had 'the best of medical advice that condoms are only 70 per cent safe' and that 'teenagers will be using these condoms without knowing how to use them.' Parliamentary reporters noted the contribution was met with laughter from the public gallery and that Kenny on the Fine Gael benches was in hysterics.

A trawl of newspaper cuttings from the two constitutional referendums during the FitzGerald era throws up few references to Kenny. Today he describes himself as a 'pragmatic conservative' – a fair assessment of where middle ground Ireland rests on many contentious issues. In a 2007 interview with *Hot Press* magazine he was asked if he believed in God. 'Well, I am a Catholic and I am a Christian. I wouldn't be the best Catholic in the world – I am probably a better Christian than a Catholic. I will go to mass on Sunday mornings in Castlebar at 10 o'clock if I am around. I do believe there is something out there. Whether you go from spirituality to God, I think I will probably end up in somebody's lap sooner or later.'

As Fine Gael leader he has been utterly pragmatic about the positions his party adopted on potentially contentious issues. While being a member of the first party to publish civil partnership proposals, Kenny opposed legislation to allow gay couples to marry. 'We will have to wait and see how the registration of civil unions would operate in practise, first of all. I think they are going to have some serious cases where succession rates, property rates and taxation issues have to be dealt with. I don't favour same sex marriages.' He opposed abortion and has rejected any attempt for parliament to legislate to regularise the complex legal situation that exists in Ireland in relation to pregnancy termination arising from the 1992 'X' case judgement. 'I don't favour abortion. Obviously, I am aware that people travel to other countries for abortion. I would try to make as serious a case as possible in advising young people, informing young people, and educating young people about these matters.'

In a reshuffle in early 1986, Kenny finally got a ministerial promotion. There were serious concerns in Fine Gael about the emergence of the Progressive Democrats. An MRBI opinion poll in February 1986 showed Fine Gael had slipped to third place behind the Progressive Democrats and Fianna Fáil. From its dizzy heights in November 1982 when the party was within reach of Fianna Fáil, Fine Gael's support was now recorded at only 23 per cent. The PDs had targeted a disgruntled former Fine Gael member as a potential candidate in Mayo West. Kenny's appointment was as much about shoring up the party's position in the constituency as about overdue reward for a longstanding TD. Kenny was appointed Minister of State at the Department of Education and the Department of Labour with special responsibility for Youth Affairs. After just over a decade in Dáil Éireann, Kenny finally got a taste of ministerial office.

In the same reshuffle that saw Kenny promoted, Paddy Cooney was moved from the Department of Defence to be Minister for Education. Cooney arranged to meet his junior colleague. 'He said to me, "I'm placing you in charge of the school building programme,"' Kenny recalls, although the senior minister added that he was retaining responsibility for schools in his Longford constituency. The main difficulty for Kenny was a lack of money as the economic situation remained bleak. He did, however, start working on adult literary programmes and, having heard one parent's story, he overruled a department inspector in the case of a number of intellectually challenged children in a Dublin school where the official assessment was that the children should be taught in what was then described as a 'mentally handicapped' unit of another facility.

But there was insufficient time to make any sort of an impression in the new position. The coalition was in its final stage in office. Kenny held his junior position from February 1986 to March 1987. But the result of the 1987 general election offered little prospect of an early return to power for Fine Gael. Kenny backed his friend John Bruton in the leadership election which followed FitzGerald's sudden resignation. 'That decision caused mayhem and was the start of a very difficult period for Fine Gael,' he says. Kenny was appointed to the Fine Gael frontbench by the party's new leader Alan Dukes in 1987 and given responsibility for the Gaeltacht but just over a year later he was dropped. Kenny believes the decision was motivated by his opposition to disciplining John Donnellan, a critic of Dukes, over a remark he made that 'if it was raining soup then Alan Dukes would be out there with a fork'. Donnellan was a veteran Galway TD, and Kenny told Dukes the issue should be sorted out with some common sense rather than by an expulsion motion at the parliamentary party. Donnellan withdrew his remark but Dukes persisted with the penalty. Kenny was sitting beside Dukes at the meeting when the motion was tabled, and he raised his hand to vote against the leader's preferred choice of action.

There was media comment and party reaction to a number of other people demoted by Dukes in the reshuffle but no mention of Kenny. 'Pleasant character who endears himself to party elders. Ministerial calibre if he applies himself,' was the verdict of Who's Who in Irish Politics when it was published at the end of 1990. But in truth by the time Kenny marked his 40th birthday in April 1991 his political career had hardly taken off. He had topped the poll in five consecutive general elections from 1977 to 1987 and while he again polled comfortably at the 1989 general election he was beaten for the top position for the first time by Padraig Flynn, his main Fianna Fáil rival. Flynn had the advantage of senior ministerial rank since 1987 when Fianna Fáil returned to government, and he made the most of his position outpolling Kenny by over 3,400 first preferences at the 1992 general election. Kenny was still comfortably returned as a TD but he was no longer the main star in the Mayo West constituency while nationally he had failed to make a serious breakthrough.

Friends and close colleagues believe Kenny's attitude to politics changed following his marriage to Fionnuala O'Kelly in 1992. In a revealing comment at the time Kenny admitted that his new wife was more advanced in her career than he was. O'Kelly was a highflyer. She was a member of the Fianna Fáil backroom team which supported Charlie Haughey in opposition in the 1980s. When Haughey was elected Taoiseach in 1987 O'Kelly was appointed head of the Government Information Service where she continued to work closely with senior Fianna Fáil advisors including P. J. Mara and Martin Mansergh.

O'Kelly was was born in Clontarf in north Dublin and studied French and German at UCD before completing a postgraduate degree in French at the University of Nancy. The couple met in Leinster House. Kenny was speaking in the Dáil chamber when he looked up into the press gallery and 'saw a vision with flowing chestnut hair in a blue dress and I stopped and thought "Jesus!"' He says he winked at her. The political rivals continued their courtship discreetly although the relationship was not hidden. In the late 1980s with different media priorities, no serious attention was paid to the couple who did not feature in gossip columns or in news stories. O'Kelly left Fianna Fáil to become RTÉ's public relations manager at the end of the Irish Presidency of the European Union in June 1990. 'I remember going to CJH [Charles J. Haughey] at that time to tell him. He said, "Look if this has anything to do with young Kenny, there is no need to go,"' O'Kelly later recalled.

The couple were based in Dublin for most of the mid-1990s

travelling to Mayo at weekends. Friday evenings for O'Kelly consisted of collecting her now two small children from childcare and rushing to Heuston Station to get the train to Mayo to meet her husband who had already travelled from Dáil Éireann. Kenny and O'Kelly kept irregular hours with their respective careers. The pressures increased after the formation of the Rainbow coalition at the end of 1994. Kenny's ministry in the department of tourism and trade involved a great deal of foreign travel. His agenda took him regularly to the United States, to India and throughout Asia. He was at an investment conference in Pittsburgh in October 1996 when back in Ireland his wife gave birth to their third child. During her maternity leave O'Kelly asked how they could maintain the weekly commute between their home in Sandymount in Dublin and their weekend base in Castlebar. When her maternity leave ended, O'Kelly took a career break but never returned to work with the national broadcaster.

The demands and pressures eventually forced a decision on career options and also the location of the family home. The choices were partly influenced by quality of life issues related to the excessive travelling between Castlebar and Dublin, and also partly because their eldest child was about to start primary school. They decided to make Castlebar their permanent home. 'When the children were of school-going age we moved west, like all good people,' Kenny said, 'Fionnuala made a big move to leave Dublin and her work, to give it all up and go down to the West where she didn't have any connections other than myself, and take on the business of rearing a family and getting involved in the political scene down there.'

O'Kelly had invested considerable effort in building a hugely successful career. While she missed the social aspects of her job she threw herself into family life in Castlebar with three small children – Aoibhinn was born in 1993, Ferdia in 1995 and Naoise in 1996.

'For everyone, life changes completely once children come along,' Kenny said. 'They make you understand relationships better and the meaning of life and, for myself, I think I benefited from being a bit older. I think I know better how to give them character and a sense of humanity.' Every summer at the end of August the family travel to a house in Killarney owned by O'Kelly's father who had a successful civil service career. 'I enjoy those holidays and have visited Skellig Michael and the Blaskets. I'd put these holidays as my best experiences. I've gone with my family every summer since they were little kids,' Kenny remarked.

The couple made a deliberate decision to keep their children away from the public gaze. And neither did O'Kelly take on a frontline political role. When she moved to Castlebar she played no active part in the local Fine Gael organisation or in her husband's clinics with the exception of elections when her family members would arrive to manage the household to free her for canvassing and other election duties. She maintained a relatively low profile after Kenny became leader of Fine Gael although she has been visible at party conferences, has done a small number of joint media interviews with her husband and was on hand at the start of the 2007 general election campaign. Her visibility automatically increased following her husband's election as Taoiseach in February 2011. But even in the tough years in opposition she has not been afraid to intervene. Six months before the 2007 contest, O'Kelly was the guest speaker at a Fine Gael fundraising lunch. She warned that there was a danger of Ireland becoming a 'one-party State' if Fianna Fáil secured a third successive term in office. 'It is really a question of people needing an alternative. It is an inevitable consequence of people being in government too long that they become arrogant. If they are questioned in the Dáil, they take it as a slight. We are coming to a time when most senior civil servants cannot remember working for any minister other than a Fianna Fáil one.' The intervention created a media stir especially given her Fianna Fáil background, and is mentioned by friends as evidence of her keen grasp of party politics.

Kenny's political activism – especially after he became Fine Gael leader – took him away from the Castlebar for up to six days a week. There were times when O'Kelly drove with the three children across Ireland just to meet up with her husband. This remarkably secure family setup allowed Kenny to pursue his political career. He has joked that his wife picks the ties that he wears but there is no doubt that O'Kelly has had a significant influence since his career started to finally progress in the 1990s. 'My wife and I can have conversations about everything and about nothing. It is real husband-and-wife companionship, and wherever we go we are happy,' Kenny said. O'Kelly's politics were shaped by her work with Fianna Fáil – as one Fine Gael veteran put it, 'she has a Fianna Fáil view of politics that there is no point being involved simply to make up the numbers.' Close colleagues say that marriage changed Kenny's ambition. 'Fionnuala is a very serious person. She put shape on Enda,' is the assessment of one family friend. 'I believe his marriage to Fionnuala greatly strengthened him. She is a real politician herself and she filled him with ambition. He is a late developer,' Ivan Yates said. On his election as Taoiseach in February 2011 Kenny thanked Micheal Martin for his congratulatory comments and kind words for his family and for Fionnuala, who the Fianna Fáil leader recalled had once worked for his party. 'Were she still with you, you might be in a much stronger position today,' Kenny joked to universal laughter in the Dáil chamber.

Kenny's first real opportunity to prosper as a national politician eventually came when Bruton replaced Dukes as Fine Gael leader in late 1990. Kenny and Bruton were young TDs elected during Liam's Cosgrave leadership – Bruton was first elected in 1969, Kenny arrived in Leinster House six years later. They became good friends although they were an unlikely combination as Bruton was serious and ambitious while Kenny showed little public inclination in climbing the political career ladder. Kenny was one of Bruton's strongest supporters as Fine Gael leader. Bruton appointed the Mayo man to his frontbench position as Fine Gael party whip. He was ideally suited to the position which required considerable liaising with his government counterpart about the weekly schedule of parliamentary business. A kitchen-cabinet of sorts developed around Bruton which included Kenny, Lowry, Owen, Yates and

Hogan. It was an uneasy time in Fine Gael. But the tightly knit team of Bruton loyalists successfully defeated a heave in 1994, and they were rewarded some months later when, unexpectedly, Fine Gael formed a coalition administration with the Labour Party and Democratic Left. Kenny was appointed Minister for Tourism and Trade in the new administration. It was not a senior ministry but the mid-1990s was the beginning of the economic boom – trade figures started to grow strongly and the tourism sector, in particular, experienced considerable expansion. The department also benefited from access to €350m in European Union funds which were available for investment in tourism projects. As a result, throughout his two and a half years as a cabinet minister, Kenny was primarily associated with good news.

He was a near-perfect choice for the department, especially the tourism brief which required an outgoing personality and a politician who saw the job as selling Ireland. Within days of his appointment Kenny was in Paris for the unveiling of Eddie Jordan's new Formula One car. A shamrock on the side of the car and on the drivers' suits was prominent evidence of Irish government financial support for the Jordan team. But Kenny was a new minister who wanted to make his own mark. 'I don't think that the appropriate exposure was achieved by the Government's involvement in this project last year. So I will be contacting our embassies or consulates in the various grand prix host countries to remedy that situation.' A group of French car racing reporters were impressed by the attendance of a government minister. 'I'm delighted to be here because this Formula One team portrays the Ireland we're trying to promote on a world-wide scale – a young, dynamic nation identifiable with all that is best in modern technology,' Kenny declared. The new minister was obviously taken by the Formula One team. The following July he hosted a party in their honour at the Irish embassy in London ahead of the British grand prix. 'It was very nice of the Minister to recognise our efforts in building Ireland's image,' Jordan said.

The officials who worked with Kenny in the Department of

Tourism and Trade recall a hardworking minister. The mood among staff was very good, so good that some officials labelled the department 'happy valley' in this period. Early in his term as minister, Kenny was at a Northern Ireland trade investment conference in Washington with British minister Baroness Jean Denton and Ron Brown, the US secretary of commerce. As he was announced at the podium, Kenny turned to his civil servants, and jokingly said in reference to his Fianna Fáil rival in Mayo, 'Eat your heart out, Pee Flynn.' The event was a success in a difficult time in the stalled peace process in Northern Ireland, and afterwards Kenny approached the officials from Dublin who were in the company of their counterparts from Northern Ireland. 'Thanks for all your work,' the minister said before departing. The civil servants from Belfast remarked that such pleasantness was not always forthcoming from British government ministers.

There were a number of successful initiatives associated with Kenny's time as a government minister. He strengthened existing policy to develop the potential of golf tourism. Funding was provided for several major events held in Ireland including the European Open. Plans to bring the Ryder Cup tournament between Europe and the United States to Ireland commenced during this time. Kenny also backed moves towards an all-Ireland campaign to promote the island as a tourism destination. An expanded St Patrick's Day festival in Dublin was introduced while Kenny also sold the idea of enticing the Tour de France organisers to hold one of their stages in Ireland. The idea was not without precedent. When Stephen Roche won the tournament in 1987 the race had started in Berlin. In early 1995 Kenny attended a dinner after an Irish rugby international at which a presentation was made to Stephen Roche and Sean Kelly by the director of the Tour de France. Over drinks somebody mentioned the idea of the tour coming to Ireland. 'Would that be possible?' Kenny asked. A proposal was subsequently prepared, and Kenny fully backed the plan which ultimately delivered huge international publicity for Ireland and generated an estimated €30m in tourism revenue.

Kenny's department put through little legislation which was not unusual given that the nature of the work in tourism and trade was heavily weighted towards external promotion. At regular cross-department advisory meetings of the government programme managers, there was frequent joking about the 'the department of fun' when the agenda reached – and quickly finished with – Kenny's portfolio. But despite the soft image associated with the department, officials say Kenny was no soft touch. When plans to host the 1998 world equestrian games in Ireland hit difficulties in the spring of 1996, Kenny stood his ground that no further government funding would be available. There was also controversy over the decision to abandon a competition for a new national conference centre in favour of entering exclusive negotiations with the RDS. Fianna Fáil was very critical of the decision to delay work on the project. The party claimed tourism was on the 'margins of government policy'. But Kenny easily knocked back these assertions. Visitor numbers hit 4.6m in 1996 and were estimated to reach 5m people in 1997. Over 110,00 people were employed in the sector while the value of tourism to the economy was put at about IR£1.5bn.

During the Irish presidency of the European Union in the latter half of 1996, Kenny co-chaired the World Trade Talks with external economic relations commissioner Leon Brittan, a former Conservative Party minister in the Thatcher governments in the United Kingdom. Although they were unlikely bedfellows, the men developed a good working relationship. Progress was achieved at a World Trade Organisation summit in Singapore in December 1996. The meetings were long and detailed. There were arguments about the acceptability of child labour, farm subsidies and opening European markets for agriculture and other products. Kenny says the talks were 'a revelation' as they really brought home to him the nature of the European Union and the inter-dependency of the relationship between the different member States. 'I was struck by the fact that all the other countries in Europe were outside the discussion room waiting for the person to come back out and explain that this is where we stand for Europe.' Kenny's role during the Irish Presidency was very much like his tenure as a minister – he kept out of trouble, got on with the job and oversaw a successful council of ministers meeting with his EU counterparts which included bringing the entire delegation for drinks to a pub on Baggot Street in Dublin.

The tourism and trade portfolio required considerable foreign travel. The contrast with the bleak years on the opposition benches was considerable. Kenny was in New York in March 1995 – his first St Patrick's Day as minister – there was breakfast with the city's mayor Rudi Guiliani and other functions with a host of dignitaries. There is no doubt but that Kenny put in the hours as a government minister. But possibly because he was not in a senior portfolio he never succeeded during this period in fully dispelling the view that he never pushed himself to his limit. The lingering doubts about his application remained and resurfaced during the leadership contests in 2001 and 2002. He had many successes in the two and a half years that the Rainbow coalition was in office but there were no major policy initiatives or radical innovations. Ultimately, he proved to be a safe pair of hands. The Mayo man loved being a minister, and for the first time his political career had a real focus. Those who know him best believe a latent ambition emerged in this period. 'For the first time he was seriously challenged and he enjoyed it,' one close friend says.

By the time the 1997 general election took place, boundary revisions had collapsed Mayo East and Mayo West – two three-seaters – into a single five-seat constituency. Bruton was welcomed by a crowd of 300 people at a Fine Gael rally in Castlebar. Kenny took a swipe at his Fianna Fáil opponents. 'The Kennys were in the Dáil when the Flynns were still making hats on Main Street,' he declared, and as for the other Fianna Fáil candidates, 'I don't see them getting a State bicycle, let alone a car.' The crowd lapped up Kenny's rabble-rousing entertainment. Several media commentaries mentioned the possibility that the tourism and trade minister might be in trouble. During his frequent absences abroad on ministerial business his backbench Fine Gael colleagues had the advantage of working the ground in the constituency. Michael Ring had emerged as a grassroots champion, and he topped the poll with just over 10,000 votes. But Fine Gael still won three seats – Kenny polled over 8,500 first preferences while Jim Higgins was the other successful party candidate.

Kenny may not have had the same local presence due to his ministerial commitments but as a minister he knew the value of looking after his homebase. When the Rainbow coalition was in power there were tangible benefits for the Mayo constituency. Westport and Achill were included in a new tax relief scheme to support 'traditional seaside resorts.' Kenny took credit for the political windfall although, as one newspaper noted, 'Westport is a lovely place to visit but not exactly bucket-and-spade country.' Not that Kenny was concerned. He had sat on the sidelines for too long watching Padraig Flynn assume the political mantle of 'King of Mayo' that he enjoyed delivering for his constituency when it was his turn to sit at cabinet. Some IR£20m in EU money was pumped into the western region with a major development of the river Moy. There were other benefits including a new aqua-centre in Westport and a holiday village in Castlebar. There were expansion plans for the airport at Knock, an announcement only came weeks before the 1997 general election but caused some discomfort later when the project was not progressed by the new government.

With Fine Gael out of office, the post-1997 period was a time for regrouping after the hectic pace of ministerial office. Kenny had his first sustained period in Castlebar since his wife and three young children had moved permanently to County Mayo. 'There was some sense of normality to my life,' he says. There was also more time for golf, cycling and other sporting interests. He is well travelled, does a lot of hill walking in Ireland and abroad, and once walked over 100 miles south of the Rockies on an American holiday. But his favourite sporting moment was achieved playing in a charity golf event when he paired with American professional Mark O'Meara. And as they approached the 18th hole, walking down in front of a gallery of over 1,000 people, Kenny used a nine iron to tee off and his ball landed some 40 feet from the hole on the final green. The Fine Gael politician lined his putt, and with O'Meara watching, the ball was sunk into the hole. 'You're the man,' O'Meara said with a high five for his golfing partner. 'The pinnacle of my golfing career.' Kenny says.

This range of interests means he is far more grounded than many other politicians. He is a fan of Bruce Springsteen, and it is difficult to envisage any of his contemporaries having a conversation about the merits of various Springsteen albums. 'I was down in the Point to see the Seeger Sessions – he blew the roof off. Eighteen musicians. It was absolutely brilliant. It was like New Orleans gone wild. "Born in the USA" or "Come on up for the Rising" just gets me in here (points to his heart),' Kenny told one interviewer. This engagement is not contrived. He comes across as genuine. Friends believe having three young children has kept Kenny young.

After Fine Gael returned to opposition following the 1997 election, Kenny had a number of frontbench roles. But he made little impact first in Arts and the Gaeltacht and later in Education. 'He wasn't madly applying himself,' one party official says. The decision to contest the 2001 leadership was met with considerable amazement from friends and derision from detractors. But politics is not a straightforward career and just over a year later Kenny was leader of Fine Gael. John F. Kennedy is one of his political heroes, and one of Kenny's party pieces is to quote from memory – and with a Boston accent – some of Kennedy's speeches. 'Definitely dinner-party material,' one newspaper concluded in the mid-1990s. But when Enda Kenny was elected Fine Gael leader in 2002 the question was asked: 'Definitely Taoiseach material?'

6

Defining Fine Gael

Enda Kenny was less than two years Fine Gael leader when he delivered his first address at a party Ard Fheis. During the wide-ranging speech, Kenny promised, 'leadership not salesmanship'. The phrase was a sideways swipe at the ethos underpinning Bertie Ahern's tenure as Taoiseach since 1997 and also a clever play on P.J. Mara's famous 'It's showtime' remark at the start of the 2002 general election campaign. But a sales pitch was very much at the heart of Kenny's leadership. He was selling the proposition that Fine Gael could again lead a coalition government. The party was on the floor – the new leader had to convince the electorate that there was a place for Fine Gael on the Irish political landscape. With the benefit of hindsight it may be grandiose to say that this process of achieving relevancy was underpinned by a sophisticated plan of action. Party strategist Frank Flannery oversaw a review committee which provided a blueprint of sorts for organisational renewal. But the main challenge was to turn Fine Gael into an organisation that was no longer content to play the role of lead opposition party, and that enjoyed government whenever the opportunity happened to arise. The objective was to transform Fine Gael from second place – and more often than not, second place losers – into winners. And that meant effectively transforming Fine Gael into Fianna Fáil.

The party system in the Irish Republic has been dominated, almost exclusively, by three parties – Fianna Fáil, Fine Gael and Labour. The party system has frequently been labelled the 'two and a half party sytem' given the presence of two larger parties – Fianna Fáil and Fine Gael – alongside the smaller Labour Party. A number of newer parties have periodically emerged to challenge the established order – some participating in multi-party governmental arrangements with one or more of the big three including Clann na Poblachta, Clann na Talmhan, the Progressive Democrats, Democratic Left and the Green Party. But these new entrants have had a poor record in challenging the traditional dominance of the three traditional parties – even when the larger parties have suffered significant electoral losses as Fine Gael did in 2002 and Fianna Fáil did in 2011.

None of these smaller parties survived sufficiently long to establish a lasting presence on the political landscape – and even the Green Party suffered a national wipeout after its spell in government from 2007 to 2011. They all struggled when faced with a multitude of challenges such as membership, organisation and leadership. They have also failed to deal with the larger parties 'stealing their clothes' by adapting programmes and positions to preserve their predominance. The durability of the main parties is impressive – even when faced with a decline in their first preference vote, Fianna Fáil, Fine Gael and the Labour Party have adapted to changes and challenges so that they continue to win more or less the same percentage of Dáil seats.

Fianna Fáil and Fine Gael – and to a lesser degree the Labour Party – are essentially catch-all parties with a flexibility to reach accommodation with societal changes to build broad coalitions of support. Academic Sean McGraw has argued that, 'this catch-all character of the major parties has reinforced the pragmatic nature of Irish politics'. In general, catch-all parties dilute their ideological individuality in order to maximise their appeal to centre-orientated middle class voters. They compete for votes not on significant policy difference but rather on competency and personality, with competency equating with economic management and personality defined by the likeability of a party leader.

The narrowing of party difference has been evident in the main areas of political debate in Irish society over the last two decades – Northern Ireland, the economy and the liberal/moral agenda. And this uniquely Irish convergence was played out as the global political scene was transformed in a post-Berlin Wall environment with a merging of economic ideology and a blurring in the differences in political orientation between most mainstream parties which had their origins in twentieth-century left and right politics. During this period of political convergence from the late 1980s onwards Fine Gael was confined to the opposition benches in Leinster House, unsure about the personality traits the party wanted in a leader to succeed Garret FitzGerald and struggling to convey any sense of policy competency to the voters. Only when Enda Kenny was elected party leader did Fine Gael adjust to this new political world.

Kenny's political career provided few clues about what type of party leader he would be but his entire career in public life had in fact run in parallel to the transformation of Irish society. The nature of the family, the role of women and the position of the Catholic Church were just some of the areas subjected to radical change from the 1960s onwards. Kenny arrived in Leinster House in late 1975 at the early stages of this process of transition. Over the following two decades Irish society was marked by bitter battles over divorce, abortion and, to a lesser degree, contraception. Writing in 1992, Basil Chubb captured the transformation that was underway: 'In the second half of the century, the traditional, stable attitudes associated with nationalism and with the lingering pre-industrial society, together with the values and lifestyle inculcated by an austere and authoritarian church, began to be eroded. Changed circumstances and new influences increasingly undermined these three foundation pillars on which that stable society had rested.' These changes did not challenge the stability of the two-and-a-half party system although it has taken Fine Gael longer than Fianna Fáil to adapt to the new realities.

There were two significant blocs in Irish society representing both the liberal and conservative positions. The traditional lobby's influence was waning but it still held significant sway. But, by the early 1990s Ireland experienced considerable societal change. Whereas there was still a distinctive conservative appearance to Irish society, within a few years evidence of greater liberalism was to become clearly available. Many factors aided this transformation into a far more liberal and secular society. There had been a dramatic shift in Irish demography over the preceeding decades. The marriage rate had declined while marital fertility had fallen with a rise in non-marital births. The number of non-marital births moved from three per cent of all births in the mid-1960s to 19.5 per cent in 1993. Membership of the European Union helped to push equality up the domestic legislative agenda as the number of married women in the labour force increasd significantly. These changes must also be considered in the context of a transformation in the position of the Catholic Church in Ireland. Church attendance was in decline – during the 1980s the numbers attending church/mass more than weekly declined by one-fifth. The authority of the Catholic Church was significantly damaged in the 1990s following a series of controversies involving clerical child abuse and high profile clerics being exposed as having fathered children. Evidence of more independent public thinking can be seen in the debates about contraception, abortion and divorce. The liberalisation of contraception legislation was a gradual process from the 1970s onwards. Initial limited reform caused some political controversy. The importation and sale of contraceptives was prohibited until 1979. The legislation in this area lagged public opinion but by the early 1990s political attitudes to contraception had changed.

The main political parties can be placed on a variety of different points on a spectrum encompassing liberal to conservative values. An analysis of potential voting patterns during the 1992 general election – when three abortion referendums were held on the same day as the Dáil poll – allows for a clear determinant of party positions. The analysis is based on combined responses to three opinion polls undertaken approximately seven days before balloting in the actual general election and referendums. According to academics

Michael Marsh and Richard Sinnott: 'the striking feature of the [data] . . . is the identity of the views of Fianna Fáil and Fine Gael supporters (both being 57 per cent liberal and 43 per cent conservative) and the considerable contrast between these and supporters of Labour, the PDs, Democratic Left and the Workers' Party, who also share a virtually identical and more liberal view (70 per cent liberal and 30 per cent conservative).'

Fianna Fáil had traditionally been the more conservative of the main parties although the party did have a small liberal wing. The party supported moves to insert an anti-abortion clause in the constitution in the early 1980s, opposed moves to further liberalise the family planning laws and campaigned against the divorce referendum in 1985. There was, however, a shift in the Fianna Fáil position on these so-called moral issues in the 1990s in line with changing values in the wider population. Fine Gael had similar divisions to Fianna Fáil on many of the so-called moral issues which were to the fore in political discussions from the 1970s onwards. Liam Cosgrave as Taoiseach in the 1973-77 Fine Gael-Labour coalition actually voted against a proposal from his own government to make contraception more widely available. Under the leadership of Garret FitzGerald the party adopted a far more liberal positioning – including campaigning for the introduction of divorce – and was to the fore in promoting progressive policies reflecting the direction in which the public was moving. But Bruton was a more conservative leader than either FitzGerald or Dukes. Fine Gael's image – according to the 1992 opinion poll data – became more conservative in the 1990s despite their involvement in the campaign to introduce divorce in Ireland.

But it was not just in the area of liberal-conservative policies that the two main parties had converged in their thinking. Traditional policy demarcations in the two other key domestic policy areas which dominated public discourse from the 1970s onwards – Northern Ireland and economic management – also narrowed between Fianna Fáil and Fine Gael. In pre-Celtic Tiger Ireland, five parties participated in a number of different governmental arrangements – Fianna Fáil, Fine Gael, the Labour Party, Democratic Left and the Progressive Democrats. The economic policies of these respective governments were driven by the national economic environment which throughout the 1980s continued to be bleak. Each of the main parties in Leinster House advocated measures to restore stability to the public finances. Room for significant national movement was limited. Fianna Fáil in the early 1980s signalled a willingness to tackle excessive public spending but the party did not match its actions to the words of party leader Charles Haughey who went on national television to preach fiscal austerity. The 1982-87 Fine Gael-Labour administration was undermined by the different priorities of the two coalition partners, which resulted in continuous internal tension and insufficient action to deal with the growing fiscal crisis. A continuous austerity programme was only implemented in the late 1980s, in part because the position had been reached that politically and economically there was no more room for procrastination. The Tallaght strategy adopted by Alan Dukes backed fiscal retrenchment but the move delivered no political or electoral benefit for Fine Gael.

The formation of the Progressive Democrats had an especially strong impact on the national economic debate and as such the policies of the different parties. The new organisation backed substantial taxation reductions and an increased role for the private sector. The Labour Party was a more willing advocate for State interventionism and higher taxation to fund public services than any of the other main parties, all of which supported Ireland's membership of the European Union. During the 1990s the points of difference of economic policy narrowed even further – Fine Gael and Fianna Fáil put broadly similar economic manifestos to the voters in the various general elections in recent years. In the post-1997 period, economic competency was rewarded with electoral success – Fianna Fáil under Ahern coasted on the successes of the so-called Celtic Tiger. Fine Gael worked within the same economic framework as the incumbent government but out of office it was not in a position to receive any gain from the economic success story and a number of ill-considered policy proposals under the Noonan regime left the party open to ridicule and robbed Fine Gael of the mantle of competency. Following the 2002 general election Richard Bruton as his party's finance spokesperson warned repeatedly about the dangers of Ahern's policies to economic well-being but it was a hard message to sell with all the main indicators still registering positive after a decade of success. In the aftermath of the post-2008 collapse of the Irish economy and the international banking crisis Fianna Fáil shed its image as the party of competency, a change was hugely relevant for Fine Gael's electoral performance in the 2011 general election.

The narrowing of party difference has also been evident in relation to policy on Northern Ireland. The three main political parties in Dáil Éireann share the common goal of Irish unity. There have, however, been significant differences in their respective approaches to ending partition. Fianna Fáil has certainly had a much stronger attachment to the objective of Irish unity than either Fine Gael or the Labour Party. The contemporary conflict challenged the attitudes of all the politicial parties in the Republic but they responded in different ways. One significant point of difference was evident in the stances adopted by the three main parties in relation to the New Ireland Forum (NIF) – a FitzGerald government-sponsored initiative to find a common nationalist approach which reported in May 1984. The NIF provided three alternative options for a new Ireland: a unitary State, a federal/co-federal State comprising Northern Ireland and the Republic of Ireland, or joint authority with the British and Irish governments having equal responsibility for the administration of Northern Ireland. Fine Gael was prepared to negotiate around the three options. But on the day the report was published the Fianna Fáil leader Charles Haughey declared that the only solution was 'a unitary State with a new constitution,' while rejecting the idea that the consent of the majority in Northern Ireland was a precondition for Irish unity. In his memoir, *All in a Life*, Garret FitzGerald observed: 'The role of Fine Gael and, since the end of the 1960s, the Labour Party is, I believe, quite different [from Fianna Fáil], namely to pose an alternative, pluralist concept of Irishness that would have room for unionists as well as nationalists.'

During the peace process era in the 1990s Fine Gael was far more hostile to the republican movement than Fianna Fáil. The party was harder on the issue of decomissioning of IRA weapons as well as accepting the bona fides of the Sinn Féin leadership. Fine Gael did not accept the Fianna Fáil line that Irish governments should give greater consideration to nationalists in Northern Ireland. A number of remarks reported in a major study of Fine Gael's membership illustrated some of the points of difference from a Fine Gael point of view: 'Fianna Fáil are only able to see one side of the equation as regards Northern Ireland (nationalist). Fine Gael has always put forward a more equal approach and have always been more stern in their condemnation of terrorism . . . [and] Fine Gael treat Northern Ireland even-handedly.' The party made strong efforts to include unionist viewpoints in its policy stances. As explained by John Bruton: 'It was essential to bring the unionist viewpoint to the table and to show unionists in Northern Ireland that public opinion in the Republic was interested in their welfare too . . . So I was very determined that unionism would be taken into account, and Sinn Féin had a bit of difficulty with the idea . . .'

But the hardline attitude to the republican leadership may have hurt Fine Gael. The public in the South was more generous in its attitude to Gerry Adams and his colleagues than Bruton's Fine Gael even if they were unwilling to back Sinn Féin candidates in a serious way in elections in the Republic. They gave credit for the peace process efforts but in truth wanted both traditions in Northern Ireland to resolve their difficulties, work together and not impinge upon politics south of the border. So not only was the Fine Gael antagonism to Sinn Féin too harsh, but the party's embrace of unionism was never going to win votes in the Republic.

The publication of the Belfast Agreement in April 1998 removed many of the major policy differences on Northern Ireland that remained between the main parties. From 1998 onwards it has been easier to conclude that Fianna Fáil, Fine Gael and the Labour Party were committed to a broadly similar framework in relation to Northern Ireland. The parties accepted the central role of Anglo-Irish contacts and the importance of relations between Dublin and London. They also supported the principle that an internal political settlement should be driven by the parties in Northern Ireland and that North-South cooperation was vital to offering reassurance to the nationalist community. In campaigning for a positive outcome to the referendum on the Belfast Agreement in May 1998 the main parties in the Irish Republic co-operated in supporting the terms of deal and, in many ways, few substantial policy differences remained between them.

One approach used to determine what differences exist between the political parties drew on expert assessment where academics and other political experts were invited to plot the differences between the parties. The results of expert surveys in 1992 and 1997 provide a useful assessment of Fine Gael's positioning in a number of key policy areas. In the area of economic policy – taxation and public spending – the results confirm the conventional wisdom of a policy spectrum that ran from the PDs, clearly to the right, through Fianna Fáil and Fine Gael in the centre through the centre-left position of Labour, to the Greens and Sinn Féin to the left. On European and foreign policy there was only a small difference in the positioning of Fianna Fáil and Fine Gael with both parties recoding pro-outward looking stances while on Northern Ireland Fine Gael recorded a strong pro-British presence in Northern Ireland. None of the headings showed any substantial difference between the policy positioning of Fine Gael and Fianna Fáil. Interestingly, the Fine Gael members who participated in the 1999 survey accepted that there were few great policy differences between their party and Fianna Fáil. The main area of difference was identified as integrity. 'Fine Gael are honest, Fianna Fáil are completely dishonest,' was one member's explanation.

But honesty or integrity as a point of difference is obviously not of sufficient concern for most voters. Even in the face of the revelations about Bertie Ahern's finances which first emerged in September 2006 Fine Gael was unable to capitalise sufficiently to break out of its post-1987 electoral range. In this blurring of political difference Fine Gael has fared worse than Fianna Fáil as it has remained in the shadow of the larger party. In government Fianna Fáil was able to display competency in running the country. The public apparently did not know what Fine Gael, as the smaller of the two main catch-all parties, was actually for. A very high proportion of respondents to a 2002 survey had no image at all of Fine Gael. One respondent remarked: 'They can't decide between themselves what they stand for so how am I supposed to know?'

This telling observation went to the core of the Fine Gael problem. Fianna Fáil had never been shy about stressing its historical achievements to provide current political definition and advantage over its opponents. The party found it easy to remind voters that under De Valera it wrote the 1937 constitution; under Lemass it published the White Paper on Economic Development and under successive leaders at the end of the twentieth century it delivered an unprecedented economic boom and lasting peace in Northern Ireland.

Fine Gael never made such a good sales pitch for its achievements. Consolidating democracy and establishing the Irish State in the 1920s may not have contemporary resonance but it ranks alongside – and possibly higher than – writing a new constitution in 1937. The party was in government in the 1950s when the first decisions were taken to adopt a new outward-looking economic policy while it was in office in the mid-1990s when the so-called Celtic Tiger was born. For a party that has been in office so little over the last 80 years Fine Gael has a bank of serious political achievements. But there was a pattern of coming one step after events – entering opposition in 1932 for an extended 16-year period when Fianna Fáil pursued Michael Collin's policy of using freedom to achieve more freedom; returning to opposition in 1957 for another 16-year period as Fianna Fáil capitalised on a new policy of outward economic development; arriving into opposition in 1997 for what became 14 consecutive years, as Fianna Fáil spent – and misspent – the largesse of economic prosperity.

Only once in a general election from 1932 to 2007 – under FitzGerald in November 1982 – did Fine Gael come close to replacing Fianna Fáil as the largest party in the State. But the November 1982 result was not sustained, and Fine Gael faced a real struggle for relevancy after 1987 when the party left government demoralised after a stinging electoral defeat. But it was not just the departure of FitzGerald that hurt the party; after all when FitzGerald stood down he was a leader rejected by the electorate and who had led an unloved government. The arrival of the Progressive Democrats and Fianna Fáil's embrace of coalition left Fine Gael rattled and unsure how to respond.

A 2004 study of the decline of Fine Gael's vote suggested that there was evidence that the party's performance could be explained by the gain and loss of a core group of middle-class floating voters. This group were attracted by the FitzGerald agenda but fed up with the economic record of his 1982-87 government they switched allegiance to the Progressive Democrats in 1987. With Fianna Fáil available to lead coalition administrations of very different party combinations, the floating voters have been unconvinced about Fine Gael's relevance to government formation. In more recent times these powerful floating voters backed Labour in 1992 and Ahern's Fianna Fáil in electoral contests. 'Given the volatile nature of this vote, Fine Gael may be able to re-attract this support in the future,' academics Eoin O'Malley and Matthew Kerby speculated. In the party's Election Blueprint for the 2011 contest, Fine Gael strategists identified this key support base as 'Negative Equity Man' and the 'Middle Class Liberals'.

It has taken the party two decades to formulate its response to the new environment of political convergence and middle class voter flux. During that time Fine Gael debated moving closer to the Labour Party or, alternatively, aligning itself with the Progressive Democrats. But under Enda Kenny, Fine Gael adopted a different strategy – Kenny accepted that ideology meant nothing in modern politics. He had no interest in left or right. The key middle class voters were apolitical. They were attracted by competency and personality. 'What will you do for us?' they asked. Kenny and his senior advisors concluded that Fianna Fáil's great electoral strength was based on delivering to these voters a combination of competency and personality. Ahern had won in 1997 based on his popular appeal. Noonan had been defeated in 2002 due to the tag of incompetency and a lack of the likeabilty factor. Fine Gael no longer pretended that it had anything radically different to offer over Fianna Fáil other than competency and personality. The decision recognised that in recent times the traditional domestic policy demarcations between the main parties in Leinster House have vanished. Kenny's Fine Gael would be built on competency in a limited number of populist policy areas, matched with the personal qualities of the new leader who would seek a profile by engaging in near-permanent campaign. The strategy had worked for Fianna Fáil so why not for Fine Gael? Kenny spelled it out very clearly: 'If you can't beat them, then join them at their own game.'

7

Rebuilding

In the aftermath of the 2002 general election Fine Gael was no longer the largest group on the opposition side in Leinster House – holding only 31 of the 77 non-government seats. The gap with Fianna Fáil was significant. Fine Gael now had some 50 seats less than its traditional rival. 'The party's present condition verges on terminal. It lacks everything: vigour, credibility, a secure place in the political line-up,' an *Irish Independent* editorial observed. Rebuilding was one considerable challenge – which many doubted was possible – the other was the search for a place on the political spectrum. But the latter was not a new issue. Back in 1943 Joseph Blowick, the leader of Clann na Talmhan concluded: 'Fine Gael are virtually dead and any attempt on their part to give that party a few extra years is doomed to failure.' Half a century later, in the early 1990s, an internal Fine Gael commission observed: 'There can be little doubt that Fine Gael is in a state of crisis.'

A decade later, little had changed about that conclusion although after the 2002 meltdown the party was in much deeper trouble. There was advice from many quarters for the new leader, Enda Kenny. His Mayo constituency colleague Michael Ring said, 'Fine Gael has got to stop behaving like a party in government when we are a party in opposition. Let's tell the people who we represent and who we will not represent, so that we end up representing somebody.' Kenny had given away little about his own political beliefs but for the new party leader questions about ideology were academic and of secondary importance when the practicalities required action to rebuild the party organisation.

The ideal requirements for a successful political party include large size, united membership, dynamic approach and internal democratic structures. According to Jean Blondel in his 1978 study *Political Parties*, larger parties have more influence and tend to be more effective while united parties avoid unnecessary disruption. He also argued that dynamic parties avoid the public perception that they are 'do nothing' organisations while internal democracy ensures greater responsiveness to party rank and file. The four requirements contribute to the ideal position but they are not always easily achievable. Fine Gael met the size requirement but in the aftermath of the resignation of Garrett FitzGerald in 1987 the party was marked by ongoing divisions and, increasingly, failed to capture the public imagination. Some in Fine Gael argued that FitzGerald resigned too quickly after the 1987 election defeat and that the wrong leader emerged from the subsequent leadership contest. The party was not united under Alan Dukes and his two successors also had to contend with internecine warring factions.

One of the consequences of the electoral defeat in 2002 was the exit of leading figures associated with Noonan and Bruton in the previous leadership battles. Some in the party questioned whether Fine Gael was even worth fighting over given the scale of the losses. The four leadership candidates met immediately after Kenny secured victory. There was agreement that they either worked together or else they would oversee the slow terminal decline of their party. Kenny worked hard to end the divisions and to create a good internal working environment. From the outset of his leadership, decisions were motivated by a desire to include all members of the parliamentary party. 'We are going forward as a unified team with diligence and coherence to build a strong Opposition in the next Dáil and, from there, to form the next government,' he promised. A significant achievement over the next few years was the restoration of internal peace within the party. And over time Kenny also generated a certain energy within Fine Gael.

One of new leader's first moves was to restore Frank Flannery to the centre of Fine Gael's organisational operations. Flannery had been one of the advisory group involved in the FitzGerald era but the Galway man had not been centrally involved after Dukes took over as party leader and neither had he a role for the initial stages of the Bruton leadership. He was not a member of Bruton's renewal commission but prior to the 1997 general election he was asked to assist with the party's strategy in the Dublin constituencies. Flannery's influence increased after the party returned to the opposition benches; he was a director of elections for the 1999 local campaign and when Bruton was removed as Fine Gael leader in early 2001 Flannery had just started work on a strategy plan for the subsequent general election campaign. As part of the latter planning, in a presentation to the Fine Gael parliamentary party he stressed the importance of displaying a united public front. Any hope for unity was eliminated with the 2001 Noonan-led heave. As the victor in that contest, Noonan removed or sidelined officials and activists associated with the Bruton leadership. Flannery's role during the 2002 general election was confined to being a media commentator. 'I was one of the few voices on election night trying to keep it up for Fine Gael as the party experienced one disaster after another,' he says.

Kenny and Flannery were not particularly close prior to the 2002 leadership contest. Flannery was, in fact friendly, with another candidate, Phil Hogan. But he recognised that the choice of Noonan's successor was 'a key event' in giving Fine Gael a serious future. Flannery met with Kenny for a drink at Sheridan's Bar in Milltown in County Galway. The two men talked about the massive challenge required to rebuild the party organisation. Flannery believed Kenny 'would be a breath of fresh air'. In the Mayo politician, Flannery says, he saw 'a genuinely popular leader, even a populist one, and I felt that what Fine Gael needed was somebody who people would warm to.' The day after the two men met for a drink in Milltown, Kenny declared his candidacy for the leadership contest.

Flannery was more than just a political junkie. He had a strategist sense of electoral politics, and a deep knowledge of the constituencies that helped him become a leading figure in the reorganisation efforts. Kenny liked what Flannery had to say: 'Here was somebody who was prepared to say "let's rebuild the organisation and let's get on with it."' Flannery had made his name as boss of the Rehab Group, a successful voluntary organisation which championed the cause of people with disabilities. By the time Flannery retired as chief executive in December 2006, Rehab delivered services to 60,000 people in 200 centres in Ireland, England and Scotland. The organisation had 3,000 staff and an annual turnover of €160m.

Flannery's role was in a voluntary capacity – although he would assume an officer position after the 2007 general election – and one of his first tasks in 2002 was to head up a strategic review group to advise on Fine Gael's future. For some time a poor relationship existed between Fine Gael headquarters and the Leinster House operation, and under the Noonan leadership the party's structures and chain of internal command had become highly dysfunctional. The review group met staff and activists to assess what had gone so badly wrong in the 2002 election and what changes were needed to ensure that the party would start to grow and become electorally relevant.

While Flannery's review group was consulting and preparing its blueprint, steps were taken to introduce the new leader to the party grassroots. A series of regional meetings became part of the party's recovery process. At these well-attended meetings almost 4,000 Fine Gael activists were introduced to Kenny who performed well and, in many cases, dispelled internal doubts about his ability and application. Some in the party saw him as old-fashioned, inexperienced and a rural politician. But the feedback when members met Kenny, and heard him speak, was far more positive.

These initial engagements in 2002 showed party officials that Kenny's strength was being out and about, and that whatever people's initial reservations, he had a personal charm that won over doubters. The new leader was blunt: the work involved would require an enormous commitment in terms of hours and effort but he believed Fine Gael had a future. 'We don't need to have a yellow streak or an inferiority complex,' Kenny said.

The gatherings were organised into workshops and the talk was about what had gone wrong in the recent general election and what should be changed if the party was to have a future. Kenny met a huge degree of defeatism. There was considerable anger and criticism of the party's performance at national level. The party was described as being slow to react to events, as being irrelevant, and sometimes invisible, in media coverage.

Each of the participants was asked to look at Fine Gael in terms of its strengths and weaknesses as well as the threats and opportunities it was facing. The party's strengths were seen as its new leader, party history, Young Fine Gael and involvement in European Union politics. By way of contrast, the party's weaknesses included the post-2002 election situation that many constituencies had no Fine Gael TD, the age and gender profile of party membership, disunity and a lack of party solidarity, and a vague identity. The feedback from these regional meetings was that the threats facing Fine Gael included fragmentation of the party system with small parties and independents, poor local organisation, apathy and a lack of appeal to young people. The opportunities included the 2004 local elections, a new young frontbench, an enthusiastic membership base and the chance to open membership up to young people. The meetings focused on the party's core values and the impact on politics from the changing nature of Irish society. The feedback was similar at all the sessions. Integrity and honesty were identified as Fine Gael's important characteristics. There was an acceptance that new ways of organising in constituencies were required especially to attract more women and young people into the party.

The feedback from the regional meetings worked its way into the Flannery report which was delivered in September 2002 with a stark message. The party risked disappearing from the political scene. 'Every year, long-established companies, institutions and so on disappear without trace. In many ways, we have been blinkered. We have all been strung out for a generation encouraging social and economic change, presiding over the greatest social revolution in Ireland's history, watching all the old certainties disappear. Somehow, it never seemed to occur to us in the traditional political institutions that we would also be swept along in the same wave. Do we somehow think that we are different, insulated from the socio-economic forces that determine everything else, enjoying a permanence that nothing else enjoys? The truth is that whilst Ireland has changed beyond recognition over the last generation, Fine Gael has stood still.' The party's electoral record from 1982 to 2002 showed 'a picture of progressive decline' and if the trend continued Fine Gael 'could come under threat of becoming irrelevant – even extinct.'

In the post-2002 general election atmosphere in Fine Gael, there was a view that the scale of the seat losses would be the start of a process of terminal decline – unless the party acted quickly to wrap itself in relevance. 'Fine Gael needs to foster a culture of critical realism where counter-intuitive initiatives deliver real solutions rather than symbolic gestures,' the strategy report declared, although the task of determining where the party stood politically was not spelt out. Aside from delivering a stark message – if one was needed – the strategy report was about organisation, and the lessons that had to be learned from its traditional rival: 'Fianna Fáil long ago recognised that politics are increasingly personality/people-driven and are not as policy-driven as in former years.'

Fine Gael was compared to an old-fashioned product on a supermarket shelf. 'An outdated product, with poor packaging, survives in the supermarket environment because there is a traditional, yet shrinking, constituency who buy it because they are individuals who are unaffected by consumer climates, because their father or mother swore by it, because old habits die hard and because they have always bought it. It really is apparently good for you but tragically fewer and fewer people are even aware of that.' Fine Gael was – the report concluded – similar to that unfashionable product:

'The current image of Fine Gael is wholesome, healthy, traditional and boring. It seems to belong to another age.'

'The presentation, image, identity and focus of any political party in the new political age is inextricably linked with its leader. A lousy party can succeed with a brilliant leader – the opposite does not work.' Fianna Fáil, the report stated, understood this reality: personality over policy. 'The leader of a political party, in the new political age, is a principle conduit of his party to the market place. His image helps to define, shape, colour and highlight what the party is about. In a profound sense of public perception, he is the party.' Fine Gael had to arrive at this position if the party was going to progress. Flannery set a two-year objective to get Kenny's name recognised by the public and associated with a positive image for the party.

The thrust of the Flannery report would define Fine Gael under Enda Kenny – reinvention was the theme but the intention was clear: in a post-ideological political environment Fine Gael would only succeed if the party was transformed into a version of Fianna Fáil; the future was 'in combining the best facets of Fianna Fáil populism with a rejuvenated expression of the great ideals which Fine Gael stands for.'

Flannery and other key Fine Gael strategists had long looked with envy at the Fianna Fáil electoral machine. They now had an opportunity to tackle the reasons why in the early years of the twenty-first century Fine Gael continued to lag behind its long-time rival. 'Fine Gael's way is not about offering an alternative to Fianna Fáil but about offering an alternative and better version of the modern political organisation which is needed to win votes in today's Ireland.' The strategy report promised that the 'bedrock' ethos and values of Fine Gael were not being dropped. But the past was another country, and while due acknowledgement was given to the party's history, in truth, Kenny was only interested in the future. 'Forget about history, traditions, places in history, famous old faces, and political records. Forget about traditional constituencies, old faithful lobbies, and old allegiances. In the world of 21st-century politics, the voters out there could not care less.'

Kenny had little difficulty with the recommendations made by Flannery, including a streamlined and more efficient Leinster House operation and a reorganisation of party structures in the Dublin region. Over the first 12 months of Kenny's leadership a core team of advisors was put in place alongside Flannery and Hogan as well as outside advisers like Mark Mortell, a one-time Fine Gael councillor in County Wicklow and successful business-man whom Kenny had appointed chairman of Bord Fáilte in 1997.

Like Flannery, Mortell had been banished by Noonan. But his marketing background and knowledge of electoral politics made him an invaluable member of Kenny's team of unpaid advisors. He took a seven-week leave of absense to work on Fine Gael's 2007 campaign and after several requests he moved into a full-time posi-tion with the party in September 2010.

The Flannery Report in 2002 concluded that the existing man-agement structures were inadequate and inappropriate for a mod-ern political party. Changes to internal management processes and systems were instigated and new positions created in a radical over-haul which added about €400,000 to the party's annual expendi-ture. Kenny ended a ban on donations introduced by his predecessor, and as mentioned previously the successful operation headed by national fundraiser Anne Strain – who was recruited in 2002 – meant that Fine Gael became a very well-resourced organi-sation. Other new staff were appointed included Gerry Naughton, who had a 20-year civil service career until he joined the Institute of Chartered Accountants as communications director late in 1997. Naughton had worked in the Irish Embassy in London in the mid-1980s and also as private secretary to numerous ministers including John Kelly, Frank Cluskey, Des O'Malley, Padraig Flynn and John Bruton. When the Fianna Fáil-Labour coalition was formed in 1992, Naughton became an advisor to Charlie McCreevy in the Department of Tourism and Trade. When the Rainbow coalition was formed, Kenny had wanted to keep Naughton but Fine Gael took a party decision only to employ non-civil servants in programme manager positions. Naughton remained in the department until the end of 1995 working on a number of different projects for the new minister before moving to the Department of Finance. He had had little contact with Kenny until September 2002 when the implementation of the Flannery Report required the recruitment of a new chief of staff in the party leader's office. Naughton accepted the job offer but not before the position was re-titled political director. 'Michael Collins was Fine Gael's last chief of staff and he was shot dead at Beal na mBlath,' Naughton joked with his new boss.

Naughton was not a Fine Gael activist but his civil service career had given him an understanding of how politicians operated, and this knowledge was extremely useful as he hit the ground running in his new role. Although Mark Kenneally, who was chief de cabinet under Noonan, remained in place, Naughton as political director in effect operated like the party's chief executive officer. A huge overhaul of the party was required. Shortly after arriving into Leinster House Naughton conceded to a colleague that working for Fine Gael was 'like arriving in a war zone.' A second key position was filled when Ciarán Conlon was recruited to head up the party's media operation. Conlon had worked as a researcher with the Dublin Chamber of Commerce before entering the public relations sector. He had been involved in devising the successful media strategy for the Progressive Democrats in the 2002 general election. But he faced a vastly different challenge with a demoralised Fine Gael. Just days after starting his new job an opinion poll showed Fine Gael's support hitting a new low. 'Are they blaming you?' Conlon's mother anxiously asked her son.

Conlon and Naughton established a good working relationship and provided an axis from the Leinster House operation to the party's headquarters in Mount Street where the work of general secretary Tom Curran and Dublin organiser Terry Murphy was complimented by the strategic input from Flannery and Hogan. Internal relations had been extremely poor under Noonan's divisive leadership. Naughton moved to improve communications. Weekly meetings were held between staff in Kenny's office and senior personnel based in Mount Street. A strong team spirit emerged, and faced with continuing questions about Fine Gael's relevancy the party's professional staff adopted the zeal of converts in promoting Kenny. But they faced an uphill battle to get media attention where the response was not so much hostile as dismissive – Fine Gael was a byword for defeat and decline, and the party was not considered relevant to political developments. Kenny was not rated – especially when compared with Ahern – and the party was considered a policy-free zone. But the Kenny team remained upbeat and believed that the worst possible scenario was a small increase in party support which with a more positive distribution of Dáil seats would deliver ten or more extra TDs. It would not be enough to get into government but it would be progress, nonetheless, from the 2002 disaster under Noonan.

Alan Dukes was asked to head up an internal party policy commission, and its recommendations were fed back to the party. Small internal units were established with policy staff and press officers assigned to specific frontbench members. But key policy decisions increasingly emanated from Kenny's kitchen cabinet. Naughton became the sounding board for all policy proposals before they made their way to Kenny. Conlon oversaw what the party said, and how it was said. This inner circle was responsible for a series of populist policies on consumer prices and anti-social behaviour. The preference was to agree on policies that matched the results of focus group research and the feedback from Kenny's regional meetings – the subsequent national campaigns were marked by condensed messages which delivered good media soundbites. There was a reluctance to embrace issues which would not deliver mainstream political gain. 'Don't waste time on minority issues' was the mantra. The opposition party only had a fraction of the resources available to the government so out of necessity there had to be a concentration on a narrower range of issues. But party officials were also reminded of a story about a frontbench meeting when John Bruton was party leader. There was a discussion about an issue which one frontbench member argued would be popular with the public, to which Bruton was said to have interjected, 'it doesn't matter if its popular – is it right?'

The Kenny team accepted that the big debates over economic dogma, Northern Ireland and the liberal agenda were largely concluded. The issues which galvanised Fine Gael in the recent past – and had given the party a distinct identity – had diminished in their significance in 21st-century Ireland. The Noonan leadership had been disastrous as the party was seen as inconsistent and lacking in clear and specific policy positions. Lessons were learned. The philosophy was now to use focus group research to determine what public concerns were – especially those of middle class voters – and then to respond accordingly with policies tailored to deal with those concerns. Kenny's Fine Gael was interested in simple messages that were unambiguous and truthful. Attention spans had decreased. There was less tolerance for what were perceived as boring political debates. But competency was essential regardless of what policy was being pushed.

Kenny delegated responsibility to his staff and to frontbench colleagues who, once given a brief, were allowed considerable freedom to get on with their work. The approach was in complete contrast to previous leaders like Bruton who had a tendency to micro-manage and Noonan who centralised all authority. The atmosphere within the party was better than it had been for several years. Kenny set out to include rather than exclude parliamentary party members from internal debate although given the small number of TDs at that time most key decisions were taken by a tightly knit group around Kenny including Hogan, Flannery, Conlon and Naughton. This level of party control held by Kenny and his team of advisors became a source of ongoing tension after the 2007 general election.

The leader's personality helped but he also displayed a natural quality towards inclusiveness underpinned by a singular objective of overhauling the party. His task, as he saw it, was to 'use the best talents in the party to the best effect'. Kenny was not a politician for immersing himself in detail – regardless of whether the subject was organisational or policy-related – although he maintained the final say on all decisions. From the outset, he approached the leadership position as a chairman rather than as a chief executive. Party advisors argue that their man has an astute political touch and has got few decisions wrong. 'He has an uncanny sense of what is right or wrong for the party. He is the classic safe pair of hands,' Flannery says.

Officials who were dealing with Kenny at close quarters for the first time were impressed. They talked about his common touch, informal but direct approach to management and ongoing font of stories. The new leader also surprised colleagues with the work ethic and the sense of urgency that he brought to the party leadership. They saw new qualities, long questioned about the Mayo politician: a stamina and a hunger for the continuous grind involved in rebuilding. Kenny was working long days, often six days a week. The schedule frequently meant leaving Castlebar for Dublin late on a Monday night, spending Tuesday to Thursday lunchtime in Dublin with Thursday afternoons and Friday and sometimes part of Saturdays dominated by constituency visits all over the country. His job was to get party activists reengaged and to restore a degree of self-belief. He knew that without their involvement and belief, Fine Gael had little prospect of persuading the wider electorate that it had a future role. Kenny's personality helped. Those close to him describe a man with a positive outlook on life: 'He gets up in good humour every day. If he didn't he would have been worn down by the gruelling work of meeting after meeting.'

There were, however, some early mistakes. In early September 2002 Kenny attended a reception in Buswells Hotel in central Dublin. The room was full of politicians and journalists. It had been a tough day for many in Fine Gael with the news of the sudden death of former Tipperary North TD, David Molony. When Kenny spoke at the function he recalled his late friend and recounted an anecdote from a trip he had taken with Molony and Maurice Manning to Portugal some years previously. In the mid-

1980s the three politicians were in a bar when they noticed a cocktail on the menu called a Lumumba. They thought the drink many have been named after Patrice Lumumba, an African nationalist leader who was the first democratically elected leader of the Congo and who had been assassinated in 1961. According to Kenny, Manning asked the Moroccan barman about the drink, to be told that the cocktail was named after 'some nigger who died dans la guerre.' The three men were highly amused by the idea of a Moroccan dismissing a famous African leader as a 'nigger', a word none of the three white politicians would have dreamed of using.

Kenny mentioned several times that he did not want to see the story appear in a newspaper but several days later his anecdote generated considerable controversy when it featured in a number of Sunday newspapers. Various groups including the Labour Party, the Irish Refugee Council and the Irish Council for Civil Liberties were critical of the Fine Gael leader when told about the anecdote.

The episode said as much about media news values and the spread of political correctness as it did about Kenny. The story was not intended as racist but the subtlety was lost. The new Fine Gael leader swiftly apologised. 'Some of the people in whose company I used this have gone to great lengths to explain that the word was used in recounting a true incident in the past. However, the fact is that I used the word, and no context excuses it. I failed to exemplify my own standards and the standards of a party absolutely committed to diversity. I am sorry.' Nobody in Fine Gael came forward in defence of Kenny. The general view was that a man putting himself forward as an alternative Taoiseach should not be telling politically incorrect jokes particularly with the media present. 'You can tell risqué jokes that might be racist or sexist or homophobic to your friends who know you are not racist or sexist or homophobic but you really shouldn't risk doing it in front of journalists,' one Fine Gael politician said privately. The episode damaged morale within the party. 'It was a serious mistake when many people were writing us off, and now we were asking, "will Enda Kenny last? Or are we really facing slow terminal decline?"' one party official admits.

There was further embarrassment several months later when the band booked for the Fine Gael Christmas party played several republican ballads including one with a raucous chorus chant of 'ooh, ah, up the 'RA'. The songs surprised many of the several hundred guests who attended the event. John Perry, the Sligo-Leitrim TD who hired the band Sons of Erin, quickly made his way to the main stage during the performance which ended before Kenny arrived at the party. Perry was quick to accept sole responsibility for the embarrassing episode. 'The party leadership had no input into the decision or awareness of who was playing,' he said.

The media picked up on these episodes to reinforce what became a running narrative that Fine Gael was finished and that Kenny was not up to the job of leading a national political paty. Nevertheless, Kenny kept his focus on the rebuilding process and raising his profile. 'I always knew it would take a couple of years of hard graft as a leader plus going through an election before you get recognised, known and judged by the people,' he says. Only weeks after the demoralising 2002 defeat Kenny started planning for the next Dáil contest. In a cynical but politically astute move Fine Gael used the 2002 Seanad elections as a base to build future Dáil seats. It was not a new approach. The Upper House was long considered by the main parties as a place to either blood potential TDs – to provide national profile and to build a local base – or to allow those defeated in a general election the space to rebuild a political career before the next Dáil contest. This was not the role for which the Seanad was established but it had been a successful strategy for Fianna Fáil over several elections. Fine Gael had never been so ruthless – in the 1997-2002 period the party had a group of grandees in the Seanad, some in effect gentlemen politicians who never had any intention of seeking a Dáil seat or, if they did, their prospects of success were slim.

Kenny now adopted the Fianna Fáil strategy. Outgoing Fine Gael senators who had no prospect of winning Dáil seats were cast aside as party headquarters were instructed to favour defeated high-profile candidates from the recent general election who would challenge for Dáil seats at the next general election. From a list of 50 names Fine Gael selected only 12 individuals. The list was targeted at winning Dáil seats and included former TDs Brian Hayes (Dublin South West), Ulick Burke (Galway East) and Jim Higgins (Mayo). The other official party candidates included unsuccessful candidates in the recent general election including Noel Coonan (Tipperary North), John Bailey (Dun Laoghaire), Fergal Browne (Carlow-Kilkenny), Sheila Terry (Dublin West), Joe McHugh (Donegal North East) and Nicky McFadden (Westmeath). The only non-general election candidate on the list was John Mullin who had been the party's director of elections in Dublin North West.

A number of sitting senators had opted for retirement while four other outgoing senators who wanted to continue – Madeleine Taylor Quinn, John Connor, Dino Cregan and Ernie Caffrey – were dropped from Fine Gael's official line-up. All four secured nominations from outside bodies but ultimately none was elected. Others cut adrift by Kenny's policy included outgoing senators Mary Jackman and Fintan Coogan (neither was returned in 2002) while, after some confusion, the internal nomination process also led to the removal of Maurice Manning, a respected party veteran, from national political life.

Kenny had been involved in the party's candidate selection process for the relatively successful 1999 local elections so he had a certain familiarity with the Fine Gael councillor base. Several councillors from the 1999 intake were also encouraged to seek nominations from outside organisations as were former TDs including Paul Bradford and Frances Fitzgerald. The determination to favour candidates with Dáil potential was pursued ruthlessly. Kenny met local councillors to ask that they use their votes to secure the election of future TDs. He stressed their role in reviving the party. The strategy paid dividend, only two of the successful Fine Gael senators were not planning to be Dáil candidates at the following general election. Outgoing Killarney based-senator Paul Coghlan showed what a canny political operator he was in holding off a strong challenge from Deirdre Clune who had lost her Dáil seat in Cork South Central while Paddy Burke from Castlebar in County Mayo had the support of the new party leader.

A raft of defeated general election candidates were returned to national political life via the Seanad elections in 2002. Fine Gael now had national political representation in constituencies where its Dáil presence had been wiped out only a few weeks previously. And the depleted Fine Gael parliamentary party suddenly took on a different profile with the arrival via the Seanad of Brian Hayes, Noel Coonan, Paul Bradford, Ulick Burke, Jim Higgins, Sheila Terry, Michael Finucane (Limerick West), Feargal Browne, John Paul Phelan (Carlow-Kilkenny), James Bannon (Longford-Roscommon), Frank Feighan (Longford-Roscommon) and Joe McHugh (Donegal North East). The strategy left the party in a strong position to challenge for extra Dáil seats in several constituencies where it had suffered losses in 2002 and had no Dáil representation. 'Fine Gael public representatives have applied their voting power in a strategic way that will see most, if not all, of these senators taking new Dáil seats in the next general election,' Kenny declared. Five years later, Coonan, Hayes, Burke, Bannon and McHugh were among the new intake of Fine Gael TDs.

The 2002 general election analysis lasted for almost six months. At a one-day conference in February 2003 the party sought to bring closure to the election inquiry. 'The post-mortem is over. We've analysed the whole lot, warts and all,' Kenny declared. The new party leader still faced two challenges – to make Fine Gael relevant again and to develop his own national profile. The European and local elections in June 2004 were the means to achieve both objectives. A membership recruitment drive in early 2003 was one of the first components of the strategy for these electoral contests. Party membership at the time was estimated at 20,000 – the same level as recorded by the *Days of Blue Loyalty* study in 1999 which, if true, would have represented a remarkable achievement after the four disastrous years in opposition which followed the Gallagher and March membership survey. Kenny wanted more women and young people as members but particular attention was also paid to lapsed members. The exercise was not just about attracting members – the party needed to find candidates for the 2004 local elections. 'I'm looking for people with conviction and ambition to join and to stand for the party in every constituency, every local authority and every ward in Ireland,' Kenny said.

The importance of the Dublin region was obvious – the party's decline in the capital was even more dramatic than elsewhere. At the November 1982 general election Fine Gael won just over 41 per cent of the vote in Dublin, taking 22 seats in constituencies in the capital. By 2002 that vote had fallen to 14.5 per cent and Fine Gael had only three TDs in Dublin. The party had no Oireachtas representation in seven of the 12 constituencies in the capital. There were also weaknesses in the party's local council representation in Dublin – Fine Gael held 27 of the 130 seats in the four Dublin councils while there was no Fine Gael councillor in eight electoral areas, and of these, five were on Dublin City Council. The local party organisations were in rag-order: meetings were poorly attended while the average number of branches in Dublin constituencies was seven but one constituency had only three local branches.

The Flannery Report – which described Dublin as 'a special case' – recommended a number of measures to deal with this huge problem. Former junior minister George Birmingham agreed to head up a Dublin Regional Taskforce which started work in early 2003. Former candidates and potential candidates were involved in discussions about reorganisation, recruiting members and winning back support in the capital. An audit of each constituency was undertaken to assess the local party's financial position, membership numbers and activity levels while the 2002 general election campaign was reviewed.

Staff in national headquarters were assigned specifically to the reorganisation effort in Dublin where Gay Mitchell played a lead role. Similar exercises were undertaken in Munster, Leinster and Connaught-Ulster. The work in these three regions was also focused on dealing with the problems in Dublin. A database of members and supporters was created to identify people now living in Dublin who came from known Fine Gael families outside the capital. 'There are loads of people in Dublin whose fathers were the chairman of the local branch back at home, who are totally anonymous to Fine Gael in the housing estates. It is amazing the number who disappear. We are calling meetings, asking people to try and think who from the area is living in Dublin to put together contact details,' Jim Higgins, who was heading up the reorganisation effort in Connaught-Ulster, said.

The individuals identified as living in Dublin and from Fine Gael backgrounds received a letter from Kenny. They were invited to party meetings and to become involved in the reorganisation work or simply to support the party in the capital without necessarily becoming involved in branch activities. Over the following months, as initial planning for the local election campaign commenced, sitting TDs were given responsibility for specific areas in Dublin where the party was without a national representative, and when local candidates were selected they were paired with members of the parliamentary party who, in effect, operated as political mentors.

Little of this time-consuming reorganisational work was ever going to generate a short-term boost to the party's national fortunes. Kenny under Fine Gael found it hard to make any impression and, according to a succession of opinion polls, the new leader and his party did not benefit from the poor ratings of the Fianna Fáil-Progressive Democrat coalition after the 2002 general election. Support for the government declined dramatically as the post-election environment was dominated by public expenditure cutbacks and the publication of the Flood Tribunal report into political and business corruption in the planning process in the Dublin region. Between May and October 2002 Ahern's personal satisfaction rating fell by 26 percentage points. But despite this government weakness, Kenny's election as Fine Gael leader had done nothing to help the main opposition party. In an October 2002

Irish Times opinion poll, support for Fine Gael was at 19 per cent – a decline of four points on the previous poll. It was the party's worst showing in over two years. Fine Gael core support in the Dublin region was now recorded at a mere 8 per cent – a level which put it behind Fianna Fáil (30 per cent core support), Labour (14 per cent) and Sinn Féin (9 per cent), and equal to the Dublin core support of the Green Party.

Kenny struggled to make an impact. In October 2002 his personal satisfaction rating was at 32 per cent with 23 per cent dissatisfied with his performance while a significant 45 per cent had no opinion. He was hardly a household name. 'Enda Kenny has yet to make his personal mark on a national basis, with 4 in 10 of all electors still not prepared to venture an opinion as to how they would vote his performance,' pollster Ian McShane wrote after another poor showing in February 2003.

On his first day in the Dáil chamber as Fine Gael leader, Kenny told Ahern he would oppose and expose the government where he could and where it was necessary, and that there would be support where he considered their actions good and right. But his early Dáil performances were inconsistent, frequently hesitant and often underwhelming. There was too much contrived indignation and anger – and the impact was often lost when a nervous-looking smile crossed his face. His questions were overlong, and he persisted in asking too many questions. Ahern was frequently left off the hook. 'Now, Ceann Comhairle, which one [question] did I miss?' the Taoiseach once asked.

Shortly after Kenny became leader he attended a funeral where he was approached by many party activists. 'People came up and shook me by the hand and said, "Give them stick, put the boot in, and go for the jugular" – all at the same time!' Everywhere he went the advice was free-flowing but often contradictory. Sometimes it seemed as if Kenny was not sure what strategy to use when dealing with the mercurial but popular Fianna Fáil leader who was skilful in parrying opposition criticism with false displays of agreement.

The Fianna Fáil attitude was to ignore Fine Gael, which may

have been underpinned by a belief that its rival was so broken after its electoral meltdown that any sort of serious comeback was impossible. Ahern had seen off Bruton and Noonan as Fine Gael leaders, and there was the sense that he did not rate his latest opponent who initially struggled to land any punches. 'Either he was too tentative and oblique, or he indulged in wild hyperbole – and his embarrassed smile indicated that he knew why the government benches were jeering at him,' commentator Olivia O'Leary wrote in one Dáil sketch. Ahern treated Kenny with disdain in the Dáil chamber. Their initial exchanges were characterised by the Taoiseach openly dismissing the contributions of his inexperienced counterpart. In his autobiography, Ahern dismissively described Kenny as 'a straightforward and decent person' who never 'managed to lay a glove on me.'

Kenny's public performances were generally well received when scripted. His delivery skills were good. But his media performances were weak. In radio and television interviews he came across as uncomfortable and wooden. Like in the Dáil chamber, he did not seem composed when moving away from a script. It was as if there were two Enda Kennys leading Fine Gael – there was the politician reborn, and growing in stature within his party from the positive feedback from Fine Gael members and members of the public who he met touring the county; and then there was the politician seen by television viewers and heard by radio listeners who was hesitant, lacking in authority and seemed to have a poor command of detail. Kenny did not hide from the work required not just to make Fine Gael relevant but also to convince the public about his own credentials. 'I would say that the public are not yet fully impressed. That is my challenge. I will give them every opportunity to be impressed. I hope I can rise to that challenge,' Kenny said.

Fine Gael staff repeatedly argued that a strong Dáil performance did not guarantee electoral success and they pointed out as examples both Pat Rabbitte (as Labour leader, 2002-07) and Michael McDowell (as PD leader, 2006-07). Over time Kenny's Dáil performances improved and, although he never came across as a natural in the chamber, he brought greater authority and confidence to his contributions. During one exchange with Ahern over wasteful public spending the Taoiseach remarked, 'I know the sums sometimes come as a problem to Deputy Kenny' to which Kenny quickly replied, 'At least I did not falsify my degree – a reference to Ahern's incorrect claim that he had a qualification from the London School of Economics. The retort signalled – Olivia O'Leary said in one of her radio sketches – that 'iron had entered his soul.' But for the Fine Gael leader there was a long way still to go but, in truth, Kenny never achieved any sort of consistency in his public performances.

The opinion poll results for the government remained poor but the largest opposition party for a long time saw no uplift in its own fortunes. Kenny's deputy leader, Richard Bruton was forced into defending further appalling figures in May 2003 – a poll commissioned in the immediate aftermath of the Labour Party conference pushed Labour ahead of Fine Gael into second place in the party rankings. Support for Fine Gael was now at 20 per cent; satisfaction with Kenny was at 26 per cent. 'Of course, we are disappointed that we aren't doing better in the polls,' Bruton admitted. Picking the party up from the 2002 general election defeat was proving a slow exercise. 'There is an expectation that it will take time and Enda has been putting his work into building that strong team for the longer term. The problem is that turning an oil tanker after a defeat of the nature that we have had takes time, and the energy of the party has had to go into rebuilding and strengthening the team around Enda Kenny.'

The frontbench appointed by Kenny in June 2002 was a mixture of experience and youth. The electoral whitewash had seen many individuals from what could be described as the party's officer corp lose their seats. Kenny had to pick a team from his 30 colleagues, and many were only promoted because there was no other alternative available. Former leader John Bruton was given a place without a portfolio while Kenny indicated that when Michael Noonan was ready to resume a frontline role he would be included.

The three other leadership contenders were given prominent positions. Richard Bruton was appointed deputy leader and given the high-profile finance brief with Phil Hogan at Enterprise, Trade and Employment and Gay Mitchell at Foreign Affairs. Two newly elected TDs were brought onto the frontbench – Olwyn Enright in Education and John Deasy in Justice. The elevation of Enright and Deasy showed Kenny was prepared to take some risks but that he was also willing to give those perceived to have political ability an opportunity to shine. The frontbench weakness became even more apparent later in the Dáil term when Bruton resigned on his appointment as EU Ambassador in Washington, and Mitchell and Simon Coveney, who had started to make an impact in the Communications brief, were more focused on their European Parliament duties.

One of the only positives for Fine Gael from the 2002 general election had been the election of several new young TDs. In a parliament generally dominated by greying men over the half-century mark, the Fine Gael corridors were filled with the makings of a new generation. Born in 1967, John Deasy was the eldest of this grouping. Several others were children of the 1970s. Paul Keogh from Wexford was born in 1972, Laois-Offaly's Olwyn Enright was born in 1974 while Damien English from Meath was born in 1978. Other young members included Denis Naughton, (born in 1973) and Simon Coveney (1972), while there were also young faces in the Seanad including Brian Hayes (1969), Joe McHugh (1971), Fergal Browne (1973) and John Paul Phelan from County Kilkenny (1978) who was the youngest member of the 23rd Seanad.

Collectively this grouping offered the potential to transform Fine Gael into a party that was relevant to the new cosmopolitan and multicultural Ireland. Their presence in the Fine Gael ranks left open the possibility of the party being genuinely different to their main political opponents in both appearance and approach. Kenny was never going to bring Fine Gael into government on his own back. Early in the post-2002 political cycle there was an expectation that Fine Gael faced a two-election timeframe to return to where the party was before the Noonan meltdown. A more favourable seat-to-vote distribution than at the 2002 election would see Fine Gael gain maybe 10 extra seats on that dismal performance. But, to have any chance of being in government, Kenny needed well over 50 TDs in his next parliamentary party. Bruton had 54 seats in 1997 and still ended up serving out his political career on the opposition benches. Ahern had had two superb electoral results in 1997 and 2002. But for all his exceptionally strong personal popularity ratings, Ahern still needed the support of political heavyweights like McCreevy in 2002 – and Cowen in 2007 – to get Fianna Fáil over the finishing line.

With so much senior Fine Gael talent lost in 2002 Kenny desperately needed his young deputies to fill that void. But the party's young guns in Dáil Éireann struggled to make a national impact. Kenny was aware he led an inexperienced team. 'Some did not have any experience of taking a brief, of being able to focus on issues. There has been a learning experience there,' he said. But the Fine Gael leader was prepared to tolerate mistakes so long as the individual was working hard and willing to learn, and when they were successful he devolved authority and considerable latitude to trusted colleagues.

Deasy was the most high profile of the new young recruits. The Waterford politician was given a huge role in the rebuilding process when Kenny asked him to shadow Michael McDowell in the Justice brief. The opportunity to be a serious player meant Deasy had a chance at becoming a political figure of some statute and if a Fine Gael revival did get underway he was likely to be a key figure in a future Kenny-led government. But instead Deasy become the source of ongoing difficulties although the manner in which the Waterford TD was dealt with by Kenny revealed something about his approach to leadership.

Deasy struggled against McDowell which was not unexpected given the superior experience of the PD politician. But Deasy did not help his case – he was often ill-prepared and he had a tendency to talk out of line. As early as December 2002 he was challenging his own party's decision to accept the release from prison of Dessie O'Hare, the notorious INLA kidnapper. O'Hare was serving a 40-year sentence in connection with the kidnapping of dentist, John O'Grady. Under the terms of the Belfast Agreement O'Hare was judged to qualify for early release, a decision which Kenny reluctantly accepted. Deasy, however, had other ideas. 'This guy should remain in prison. I don't think 14 years is long enough. Fine Gael's stand on this one should be very definite,' Deasy asserted. Kenny was forced to issue a statement clarifying Fine Gael's position: 'We might not like this but if we start to pick and choose [from the Belfast Agreement] then we run counter to the courts and make a mockery of the entire package.'

Following a disappointing set of opinion poll results in the first few months of 2003 Deasy took it upon himself to criticise the performance of some of his colleagues and to publicly advise the party leader about the composition of his frontbench. 'People cannot expect Enda Kenny to do everything. It is time to bring Michael Noonan back and to give frontbench roles to David Stanton and Jim O'Keeffe . . . Fine Gael must be a party with clear convictions. I would like to know why some members of the parliamentary party are in politics in the first place.' Kenny remained tight-lipped but only a few weeks later he was forced to speak with Deasy when the Waterford politician broke ranks to vote with the government on immigration legislation. Sinn Féin taunted Kenny that his party was incapable of providing real opposition.

There was very little sympathy for Deasy among his parliamentary colleagues who judged his interventions as extremely unhelpful to the efforts in restoring party credibility and embarrassing for the new leader who had invested considerable responsibility in the new TD. But Kenny chose not to sack his increasingly erratic frontbench justice spokesperson as would have been the norm for disobeying the party whip. Deasy was given a final warning to stick to party policy. But even as he was apologising and Kenny was saying the matter was closed, a magazine interview was published in which

Deasy said of Fine Gael: 'We're too fond of seeing both sides of every argument. And, as a result, I don't think the electorate understands where Fine Gael is coming from.'

What was emerging about Kenny's leadership style was a strong desire to avoid unnecessary division – his view was that Fine Gael had seen too much infighting in previous years. He opted not to make a public fuss when a number of Fine Gael deputies including Michael Noonan and Jim O'Keeffe challenged his decision to oppose government policy allowing the US military to continue using Shannon Airport. The approach was repeatedly to place the individual issue in the context of the bigger picture – how did the episode and any leadership response impact on getting Fine Gael back into government? In that regard, considerable patience and latitude was given to Deasy, in particular. But the Waterford TD eventually pushed too far when he broke the smoking ban in the Dáil bar in April 2004. Party officials initially attempted to keep the story under wraps but once the media started enquiring, Kenny was left with little choice but to dismiss Deasy from the party's frontbench.

The incident was the culmination of almost two years of difficulties with Deasy. But it also showed another aspect of Kenny's approach to leadership – he was willing to forgive past sins and forget previous personal transgressions. Everyone under his leadership started with a clean slate but those who messed up on his watch were not given a second chance. Deasy was trusted with considerable responsibility but he did not deliver, and Kenny did not again consider him for a senior position. Similarly, John Perry was allowed his mistake in booking the republican balladeers for the 2002 Christmas party but even his considerable loyalty to Kenny offered no protection from an ineffective performance as chairman of the influential Public Accounts Committee (PAC). In a reshuffle in the autumn of 2004 Noonan returned to the party's frontbench – he had no portfolio but was given the PAC chairmanship. (Personal circumstances meant Noonan withdrew in 2007 but returned in dramatic circumstances in 2010). Perry was initially given the low-key marine role but after the 2007 general election he was dropped from the frontbench altogether. He remained loyal through the heave in June 2010 and was reward with a return to a frontline role and a junior minister position when Fine Gael entered government in March 2011.

The initial restoration of Noonan to a frontline role was in 2004, in Kenny's mind, simply taking a decision that was for the good of Fine Gael. He was not going to dwell on the manner in which Noonan dropped him from the party's frontbench after the 2001 leadership contest. In a similar vein, during the second Nice Treaty referendum in 2002 there were some questions about Kenny's decision to allow three former leaders – FitzGerald, Dukes and Bruton – to front the Fine Gael campaign. But Kenny's rationale was that the decision made sense for Fine Gael. Once more party was placed first.

In the same reshuffle which saw his supporter John Perry dropped in favour of his old political foe Michael Noonan, Kenny had to face down his Mayo constituency colleague, Michael Ring, who objected to being moved from Social and Family Affairs to the Marine. 'Gutted, hurt and disappointed' was Ring's reaction to what he saw as a demotion. Ring had been one of the few politicians to publicly support Dana Rosemary Scallon's bid for a presidential nomination in 2004 when Kenny had been absolutely clear that he wanted to avoid a contest. 'It is evident that Enda Kenny is punishing Michael Ring,' Scallon said as she rowed into the Fine Gael controversy. Ring said he would take time out to reconsider his future: 'I felt Fine Gael owed a lot more to me than that.' But, while hardworking, Ring had not landed many punches on Minister Mary Coughlan whom he was shadowing in the Social and Family Affairs brief. Kenny was unfazed by Ring's public remarks and kept him on the party's backbenches until after the 2007 general election.

Kenny was brutally pragmatic in dealing with all of these internal party issues. He kept his focus firmly on the local and European elections in June 2004. Those contests were going to be the test of his rebuilding exercise. But first the leadership group around the Fine Gael leader had to deal with one tricky issue – a potential presidential election in the autumn of 2004 which they saw as offering Fine Gael only unnecessary financial expense, another defeat at the ballot box and distraction from its core objective of blooding new Dáil candidates at the local elections. A presidential election was far down the priority list for the Fine Gael leader. 'My focus is to get candidates for the locals and the European. It [a presidential contest] does not rank in the same category at all as the locals or the preparations for the general election,' Kenny admitted.

As she entered the final year of a seven-year term which began in 1997 Mary McAleese had not publicly said she wanted a second term. But rather than play a game of wait and see, Kenny decided to announce the Fine Gael attitude to a presidential contest – the party was not interested in getting involved. He confirmed that Fine Gael would back McAleese for a second term as president if she opted, as was her right, to nominate herself as a non-party candidate. 'I just think that if President McAleese does decide to nominate herself she has done a very good job for the country and in those set of circumstances I would certainly go back to the parliamentary party and say, "This has changed the usual business."'

Although unspoken, Kenny's decision was also based on the reality that Fine Gael had little chance of winning a presidential election, especially if McAleese was a candidate, and regardless of whether she was a non-party or a Fianna Fáil nominated candidate. Since she was elected to Áras an Uachtaráin in 1997 McAleese had achieved opinion poll satisfaction ratings consistently above 80 per cent. Even allowing for slippage in that rate in an electoral contest it would have been hard not to see her winning a second term with a handsome margin over any rivals. Kenny had also witnessed at close hand the impact of the two previous presidential contests on Fine Gael leaders. The ill-fated Austin Currie campaign in 1990 when the Fine Gael candidate was placed third ultimately cost Dukes his job as party leader. Seven years later, Mary Banotti had run a better campaign but the outcome ultimately did little for Bruton's position as party leader.

Kenny's decision was criticised in the media. 'Fine Gael stumbles over its stance on presidency' was one headline while there was an uncomfortable appearance on RTÉ's Questions & Answers programme when the Fine Gael leader was left looking weak for not wanting a presidential contest. The Labour Party seized on the opportunity to gain ground at perceived Fine Gael weakness. 'There should be a contest and Labour should run a candidate,' a party spokesman said. Former minister Michael D. Higgins was widely seen as the Labour Party's likely candidate. Kenny had based his strategy on the premise that McAleese would be unopposed. He was now faced with the awkward prospect of Fine Gael and Fianna Fáil backing McAleese as the other opposition parties possibly rallied around a Labour Party-nominated candidate. But the Kenny strategy was based on sensible political pragmatism – McAleese was unbeatable – and an early opinion poll backed his judgement. In the event of a presidential election, three quarters of voters – with majorities across all parties – would give their first preference to McAleese. Only 10 per cent of voters would back Higgins – and in a damning statistic some 69 per cent of Labour voters said they would back McAleese over Higgins. An attempt by Dana Rosemary Scallon to run as an independent candidate was effectively blocked by Kenny when he instructed Fine Gael councillors not to support her nomination.

The Labour Party played its hand too firmly and too early while the media commentators had misread the situation. Kenny was now out of the loop in terms of any presidential contest while Labour had the embarrassment of dealing with questions about its preference for an election and its potential candidate right up until September 2004 when it signalled its intention not to oppose McAleese who declared for a second term which she subsequently secured without an electoral contest. The presidential election decision – to effectively back a Fianna Fáil candidate – caused some party figures to reassess their view of their new leader. 'It showed there was more substance than was previously thought. He took a decision to conserve the party's energy and he stuck to it,' one official recalls. Kenny spent over a week climbing Mount Kilimanjaro in Tanzania in September 2003.Along with eight others, the Fine Gael leader battled altitude sickness and freezing temperatures in scaling the 19,335ft summit to raise funds for several charities in County Mayo. By the time he returned to Ireland for the start of the new parliamentary year his honeymoon period had ended. 'We have come quite a distance from where we were when we regrouped after the last general election,' he said. But the opinion poll ratings were still unimpressive. Support for Fine Gael had hardly shifted from the level which delivered the 2002 general election meltdown. Kenny's personal satisfaction ratings were rising slowly but the upswing was narrowly based with increased positive sentiment in rural areas, amongst the farming community and in those aged over 50 years. These were hardly the voters to secure success for Fine Gael especially in the Dublin region. Looking back on the opinion poll results achieved up to early in 2004, Frank Flannery admits that if they had been repeated in the local elections: 'we were looking at a disaster'.

Kenny's first significant set-piece event as party leader came in December 2003 when he addressed the party's national conference in Galway. Just before he went onto the main stage Kenny realised the importance of the televised speech: 'I said to myself, "This is an opportunity." And if you mess it up people will say, "He hasn't got it and the party has not measured up."' The speech focused on trust in politics and a list of undelivered promises made by Fianna Fáil at the 2002 general election as well as crime and health. The party pushed out a hard-hitting agenda. 'We had to generate alternative attention for the party,' one official admits, 'the objective was to take the attention away from an exclusive focus on where we were in the opinion polls.' Kenny was happy with his performance. 'I think the reaction resonated with Fine Gael people, and non-Fine Gael people. They said this outfit is capable of competing and has a vision for the country that is different.'

8
The Comeback Begins

Fine Gael continued to struggle in the national opinion polls under Enda Kenny while the Labour Party was registering reasonably high ratings. One very fortunately-timed survey in the immediate aftermath of Labour's annual conference in May 2003 provided Pat Rabbitte's party with a high positive bounce. There was media comment about a race having officially commenced for the role of the main opposition party – Fine Gael and Kenny were viewed as the likely losers. Rabbitte was more effective in the Dáil chamber and was a better media performer. Labour Party figures were privately scathing about Kenny and his capacity to revive Fine Gael. They believed Rabbitte would emerge as the real leader of the opposition in a similar way to the position secured by Dick Spring over John Bruton in the 1989-92 period.

But Kenny's revival strategy required Labour Party assistance. Without a pre-election deal with the Labour Party the job of selling the idea of Fine Gael as the lead party in an anti-Fianna Fáil coalition would be impossible. Dukes in 1989, Bruton in 1992 and Noonan in 2002 had all struggled to sell the credibility of Fine Gael in government without a pre-election arrangement with the Labour Party. Fine Gael wanted a vote transfer pact with Labour – and the Green Party – for the 2004 European and local elections. 'Voters want to see evidence of an electoral pact that they can examine and say, 'Is this what I am being asked to buy?' Kenny explained. Rabbitte had signalled that he would not support a future coalition arrangement with Fianna Fáil which, in reality, meant he was open to government with Fine Gael. Against this backdrop, Frank Flannery was able to open contacts with Rabbitte – the two men had been involved in student politics together, and Rabbitte was best man at Flannery's wedding.

There was also some co-operation between the parties on issues in the Dáil. But Rabbitte's party remained unconvinced about Kenny and they feared being too closely associated with a poor Fine Gael showing in the local and European elections. Nevertheless, the Fine Gael leader took the first step towards offering the electorate the option of an alternative to Fianna Fáil at his party's 2004 Ard Fheis. Fine Gael voters were asked to continue their preferences for Labour Party and Green Party candidates. 'Let us build our part-nership. Let us offer people choice,' he said. He also spoke about the success of the 1994-97 Rainbow government 'in which myself and Pat Rabbitte worked closely.' But Rabbitte declined to recipro-cate the offer on a voting pact. He eventually called on his party's voters to transfer 'against the government' rather than explicitly asking them to confine their preferences to Fine Gael and the Green Party.

Fine Gael set sufficiently low targets for the 2004 elections. The objective was 25 per cent of the vote in the locals – an advance on the 22.5 per cent achieved in the 2002 general election – but actu-ally down on the performance at the previous local elections in 1999 when Fine Gael won 28 per cent of the first preference vote. The party had had a decent day out in 1999 – its 28 per cent share of the vote delivered 32 per cent of the available seats. The party's performance on the previous local contest was up 1.7 per cent with a seven-seat gain. An added complication in 2002 was the end of the dual mandate which meant many high profile national TDs and Senators were precluded from contesting the local elections. The new policy had implications for all the main parties but the scale of the challenge for Kenny was evident in the 1999 locals when 34 Fine Gael TDs contested and all but one was successful.

Kenny repeatedly made it clear that his responsibility started from the date of his leadership. 'When I was honoured with the leadership of Fine Gael after the last general election we were at 22 per cent in the polls. That is the base that I am starting from . . . That is my base. That is what I was left with and what I got to work with and I am working off that.' The expected 1999 results were repeatedly downplayed. While local feedback was fairly positive, senior party strategists were readying themselves for the possible loss of some council seats. Flannery briefed reporters that the party would win in the region of 260 to 290 seats. The range left open the possibility of seat losses as the 1999 contest had given Fine Gael 273 seats. Kenny said: 'What I want out of the local elections are candidates who can win Dáil seats. That is what this is about, ultimately. Quantity is, of course, critical, but even more so in quality.' The party targeted 12 to 15 potential candidates to emerge out of the locals for Dáil seats in the Dublin region. At the close of nominations Fine Gael had 55 candidates in Dublin – 29 were standing in an election for the first time. Despite a reduction in the overall number of European parliament seats from 15 to 13, Fine Gael also maintained its objective was to retain its four MEP seats. 'We will do very well to hold what we have,' Kenny asserted.

Like the Seanad Éireann elections in 2002, the electoral contests in 2004 were approached with a singular objective – find electable Dáil candidates for the next general election. Kenny had displayed a determination in removing high-profile party senators with little prospect of, or little interest in, becoming a TD. The strategy had been a success: 'we have never had such a nakedly ambitious group in the Seanad. That place is just humming to do the business,' the party leader said. The same sentiment was now evident in the selection process for the local elections. Outgoing local councillors were given the message very clearly by Kenny: 'We want no messers, no quota squatters. I want competition in every district. I am going to give women and young people the opportunity where possible to stand. I have said that publicly. They know that. When faced with the challenge, I am going to make the decision.' Frank Flannery stressed the importance of the mid-term elections to the party's future prospects. 'We have picked a huge number of local election candidates and we have a good European Parliament team. It is essential that we win. If we do that we can change the whole atmosphere around politics this summer that will carry in the party and the public as a whole.'

The electoral contests were the first opportunity to test almost two years of hard work in rebuilding the Fine Gael organisation. 'The conventions we have held for the local and the European elections have been huge. The potential is there, and I feel that the organisation has the bit between its teeth and recognises that there is a serious challenge here and it's within our grasp to achieve that,' Kenny said. He knew that political parties did not disappear overnight – but following the meltdown in the 2002 general election a poor outing in the local and European contests would shatter morale and significantly set back any realistic chance of clawing back national support under his leadership. There was widespread commentary in the national media that Fine Gael would lose seats as the by now well-established media narrative continued to dominate coverage of Kenny and his party. 'It would be a miracle akin to the Lord's loaves and fishes if Fine Gael holds onto its 1999 seat total,' was the verdict of one political correspondent. But Fine Gael strategists insisted otherwise. 'We will hold onto seats on borough and county councils and we will increase our seats on town councils,' Phil Hogan, who had become a significant party figure, predicted.

Over €150,000 was spent in a pre-election publicity campaign focused on raising Kenny's profile. The national billboard campaign ran in the fortnight before the party's Ard Fheis – the first for the leader. Using photographs of Kenny the posters at 230 sites contained two messages – 'Its time for the truth in politics' and 'I'll put YOU first'. Kenny in a crisp white shirt was pictured behind his desk in Leinster House almost in 'JFK' mode which provoked much media ridicule. The strategists wanted to project the image of Kenny in work mode, a man in charge who was willing to listen. 'There is a strong focus on leadership. Fine

Gael is entering a very active period,' Flannery said.

The billboard campaign developed the themes of 'truth' and 'trust' which had been the main focus of Kenny's speech at the national conference gathering in Galway the previous December. Fine Gael concentrated on the undelivered promises from the 2002 general election and repeatedly returned to issues of ethics linked to Ahern including placing long-time controversial TD Liam Lawlor on the Oireachtas Ethics Committee; appointing Ray Burke as Minister for Foreign Affairs when serious questions remained about money received from businessmen; and putting Denis Foley, the holder of an offshore account onto the Public Accounts Committee. Kenny said: 'Truth is where politics begins and ends. But politics and government have been seriously debased by the current administration, its separation from the truth and the way it constantly pursues its own narrow political interest over the people's interest. I want to get the message home to people that honest politics, politics with a conscience, does change lives for the better.'

The 2004 Fine Gael Ard Fheis was used as a pre-election rally. Some 6,000 delegates attended the event at the City West Hotel on the outskirts of Dublin. It was the party's first Ard Fheis since February 2002 and the first for Kenny since his election as leader. Like the other parties, which all held national conferences in the same period, the gathering focused primarily on the imminent elections. The highlight of the event was the televised leader's address broadcast for half an hour on RTÉ television on the Saturday evening. There was no room for real or open debate at any of these weekend-long conferences. Motions were well vetted by party officials to prevent public dissent. The individuals who got access to the main podium – especially during the televised two-hour session on the Saturday morning – were tightly controlled. In the case of Fine Gael the national executive proposed that all technical motions to change internal party rules were postponed until a later conference. The objective was to use the sessions to promote new candidates and to attack Ahern's government.

Kenny called on voters to use the local and European elections as a referendum on the Fianna Fáil-PD coalition. In his Friday night speech – which traditionally opens these conferences but is not broadcast live – Kenny delivered a hard-hitting assessment of 'a vulgar Fianna Fáil-PD government who have made treachery an art form.' There was time to list Ahern's difficulties with ethical issues associated with several of his leading colleagues. 'Shame on him. Shame on his Fianna Fáil ethics. Shame on the contempt he and the Tánaiste [Mary Harney] show daily for the Irish people.' The mood at the City West gathering was incredibly upbeat for a party written-off two years previously, which had endured a long series of mediocre opinion poll results and which was now facing into an uncertain electoral contest in a matter of weeks. 'It was more like Croke Park on Leinster Final day than a Fine Gael Ard Fheis,' journalist Frank McNally wrote. The venue was packed and the young age profile of many local election candidates was noticeable. The Artane Boys Band provided the warm-up for the Saturday evening leaders speech. Richard Bruton and Simon Coveney whipped the crowd up before the proceedings went live on television for Kenny's address.

The temperature in the low-ceiling conference venue was high with many delegates using booklets to fan themselves against the heat before giving Kenny a standing ovation as he arrived on the podium. His speech was widely seen as competent but low-key. If anything he had delivered a stronger performance – and an even more aggressive message – the previous evening in his opening remarks. The party leader also suffered under the heat, sweating visibly. As the speech concluded, and the live transmission ended, a birthday cake was brought onto the stage for Kenny who was celebrating his 53rd birthday. But the general assessment of the leader and his prospects continued to be mixed. At the end of April and throughout the month of May Fine Gael sought to build momentum. Kenny kick-started the election campaign with a 48-hour tour with visits to Cork, Clare, Mayo, Donegal, Sligo and Waterford. Any spare time was used to phone party candidates, all of whom received the same message: 'keep up the graft'.

The party had picked an experienced and very strong team of candidates for the European Parliament contest. When senior strategists first discussed the European elections they conceded there was the prospect that the party could lose its four seats. The position was not helped by the reduction in the number of Irish MEPs from 15 to 13. At the start of 2004 the party had no candidate in the South (Munster) constituency and was in a difficult position in Dublin with the retirement of Mary Banotti and the reduction of the capital from a four- to a three-seater. Sitting MEP Avril Doyle was considered to be vulnerable in the East (Leinster) without a strong candidate in the north-east section of the constituency while there were 'nerves' about the North-West (Connaught-Ulster).

Extensive party polling showed that if former leader John Bruton ran in Dublin he would easily take a seat. The results also showed that Alan Dukes or Nora Owen could win a seat but other potential candidates including Alan Shatter and Francis Fitzgerald were a risk. With Bruton and Dukes declining to run, Kenny turned to Gay Mitchell who had performed well in the private polls. Mitchell took convincing. He had a solid Dáil seat and significant national profile. But Kenny persisted, even spending several hours in Mitchell's home making the case for a Euro bid. In Mitchell the party got a seasoned politician who would at the very least mount a serious challenge for a seat and at a minimum deliver a respectable vote in the capital. Senator Jim Higgins was a good bet in the North-West which covered most of the Connaught-Ulster constituencies although the presence of independent candidates Dana Rosemary Scallon and Marian Harkin – and a strong Sinn Féin profile – complicated the contest. After some initial reservations, Simon Coveney, who had established himself as one of the leading figures from the younger generation of Fine Gael Dáil deputies, allowed his name to go forward in the South constituency. Coveney's prospects were helped by the decision of Independent MEP Pat Cox to bow out of electoral politics. As a sitting MEP Avril Doyle was reasonably well placed in the East constituency but the contest was given added spice by a Fine Gael coup in convincing well-known agricultural journalist Mairead McGuinness to run for the party. Fine Gael badly needed to hold onto its four European seats, and the strong line-up of candidates was evidence that little was being left to chance.

McGuinness's decision was a massive boost for party morale. She had a family link to Fine Gael but she was first approached by Tom Parlon to run for the Progressive Democrats in the East constituency. Senior Fine Gael strategists heard about the high level meetings with PD figures and intervened to offer the journalist a place on the party ticket. Fine Gael may have been down on its luck but the party had a core vote in the East constituency which the Progressive Democrats even in government could not deliver. Doyle and McGuinness ran highly visible campaigns, and they became one of the media stories of the 2004 contest. McGuinness had a strong public profile from her newspaper and television career. Doyle was the sitting MEP with considerable political experience. But relations between the two camps were very poor, especially as most people believed there was only one Fine Gael seat in the constituency. There were ongoing disputes during the campaign even down to a petty row about which candidate got to sit beside Kenny at certain public functions. In an unusual move the party decided not to divide the constituency between the candidates – a decision which only intensified the rivalry and increased their respective poster count throughout the entire region. In tiny lettering Doyle's poster contained a call on her voters to continue their preference for her party running mate; McGuinness had no reference at all to her colleague. 'It's not something I've raised but traditional Fine Gael people are upset that hers don't mention continued preferences,' Doyle said in one of the numerous spats during the campaign.

The internal battle at least ensured that Fine Gael did not have to worry about its seat in the East constituency. 'A bit of friction sometimes brings out the best in people,' Kenny remarked. Privately some Fine Gael strategists speculated that the rivalry could push up their vote to deliver two seats but few gave the positive scenario much credibility. 'If it was a four-seater, there might be a chance, because Mairead is a very good candidate. But in a three-seater, frankly, we have to be realistic,' Doyle stated. There were early signs that the Fine Gael strategy from its national billboard campaign to high profile campaign tour was paying dividend for its leader. Satisfaction with Kenny hit 34 per cent in a May 2004 TNS mrbi opinion poll – his highest level since becoming party leader. But the scale of the task facing Kenny and his party was also evident in other survey results. Ahern's satisfaction rating was at 43 per cent, Rabbitte at 46 per cent, Adams at 42 per cent while support for Fine Gael was at 24 per cent.

The opinion poll results, however, underestimated Fine Gael support. As the votes were counted in the local and European contests it become clear that the party had confounded the media pundits and its political opponents. 'Fine Gael is back,' one newspaper headline later declared. The party's share of the national vote hit 27 per cent – a five-point gain since the 2002 general election and only a single point off the 1999 local election outcome. For a party on the verge of going out of business only two years previously the results were impressive. The party gained 16 seats on the 1999 outcome to bring its councillor total to 293. The Fine Gael performance contrasted with Fianna Fáil's poor day which was marked by the loss of 80 seats and represented the party's worst set of election results in 80 years. Media reportage about Fine Gael was peppered with words such as 'resurgence' and 'momentum'. It was the type of positive reaction the party had not enjoyed in many years.

While the votes were still being counted it was already evident that Fine Gael would meet all its targets – increasing its vote over the 2002 general election outcome, holding the local council seats won in 1999, blooding new Dáil candidates and retaining its European Parliament representation. The party now had councillors in every constituency with real potential to be Dáil candidates. The outcome in the Dublin region was hugely significant where a roadmap to recovery in the capital was now visible with new councillors like Leo Varadkar, Lucinda Creighton and Paschal Donohoe. There was even more good news in Dublin from the European Parliament elections. Gay Mitchell topped the poll with just over 90,000 first preferences. Mitchell's 21.5 per cent saw him elected on the first count. It was an unprecedented vote for the party in Dublin. Mitchell was joined in the European Parliament by Jim Higgins who emerged from a highly competitive field to win in the North West and Simon Coveney who, with almost 119,000 first preferences, was only 2,000 short of the quota in the South constituency. And there was even more good news as the final counts were concluded.

The possibility that Kenny might be a 'lucky leader' emerged in the unlikely setting of the Puddenhill Equestrian Centre in County Meath where the European Parliament count in the East constituency continued slowly. The voters had cast their ballots throughout Friday but the final result only came in the early hours of Tuesday morning. The party had already secured a seat in each of the other three constituencies – and when the first count in the East was formally announced McGuinness joined Mitchell, Higgins and Coveney on the Fine Gael winners podium. McGuinness was marginally over the quota of 113,295 first preferences but outgoing MEP Avril Doyle with 69,511 first preferences was still in with a chance of a winning a seat. The Fianna Fáil vote had fallen significantly and Doyle held on to deliver a second Fine Gael seat in the three-seat constituency. 'We've waited 20 years for this. You have to savour these moments,' Phil Hogan declared. The party had pulled off a real coup – it now had the largest Irish party representation in the European Parliament with five seats against four for Fianna Fáil and single seat each of the Labour Party and Sinn Féin. Two independents filled the other seats.

'We turned a corner today,' Kenny said. But the results were not just about Fine Gael surpassing all predictions – Kenny himself had delivered. For two years he had asked that the party be judged on the local and European parliament contests. Poor opinion poll results and inconsistent Dáil performances were acknowledged but the Kenny mantra – frequently dismissed – remained the same: the reorganisation effort would come good in June 2004. He also displayed an impressive energy for the daily campaign grind covering some 12,000 kilometres in a national tour that matched Bertie Ahern's. Fine Gael was in the process of being transformed into a campaigning party like it had not experienced since the glory days of Garret FitzGerald's initial period as party leader. With a new professionalism and a ruthlessness in dealing with the party organisation and the issues it identified with, Kenny was truly transforming Fine Gael into a version of Fianna Fáil. Nowhere was this more evident than in the targeting of non-Fine Gael members as potential election candidates.

McGuinness's victory had a significance that went beyond her dramatic success. Her recruitment was evidence that when suitable candidates were not available from within the party ranks, Fine Gael would actively look elsewhere for alternative options. Parachuting candidates onto election tickets was nothing new in Irish politics. All the main parties had recruited well-known figures as election candidates. Kenny's father, Henry, came to the notice of Fine Gael in the 1950s primarily because of his high local standing as a Mayo GAA star. Gaelic football and hurling players were the most obvious constituency for the parties, and on-pitch victories helped individuals like John Wilson and Jack Lynch in Fianna Fáil, and Jimmy Dennihan for Fine Gael, to carve out successful political careers. Former farmers leaders had always been another source for new candidates while leading members from the media world like David Thornley, Ted Nealon and Orla Guerin had long been enticed into party politics.

After 2002 Fine Gael aggressively pursued non-party figures as election candidates, including Mayo football manager John O'Mahoney who won a seat in Mayo in the 2007 general election. In the European Parliament elections in 2009 former GAA president Seán Kelly – a school teacher originally from County Kerry and a first cousin of Fionnuala O'Kelly – was elected in the South constituency while RTÉ broadcaster George Lee was victorious in the 2009 by-election in Dublin South. Others welcomed in the party ranks but without electoral success in 2007 included businessman Brody Sweeney in Dublin North East and Meath GAA player Graham Geraghty.

The policy stalled somewhat with the adrupt departure of Lee from national politics after only eight months as a Dáil deputy. Nevertheless, throughout Kenny's leadership, Fine Gael has also been open to recruits with previous political allegiances including Timmy Conway who left the Progressive Democrats in June 2003, while from the end of 2007 as the PDs moved towards dissolution a collection of the party's local representatives joined Fine Gael as did the short-term final PD leader, senator Ciaran Cannon. Wexford TD Liam Twomey joined from the ranks of independents in 2004 as did Derek Keating, a poll topping Lucan-based councillor in 2008. In early 2009 County Cork local councillor Deirdre Forde joined from Fianna Fáil. It was difficult to find a common thread joining together this collection of new recruits beyond the offer of a place on a party ticket and the possibility of electoral success. There was certainly no ideological common dominator. Kenny had, in effect, succeeded in recreating Fine Gael with a centrist, pragmatic and populist image which allowed all-comers to join the party.

With barely two years as Fine Gael leader it was evident that Kenny was a quintessential political pragmatist, and in victory in 2004 he preached realism. 'It's half-time. It is game on,' he remarked. Flannery also offered a reality check. The party still only had 31 TDs. The local election results helped but Dáil seats still had to be won, especially in Dublin. 'It isn't nearly enough. We have a lot of work to do,' Flannery reminded the party. The momentum of the 2004 local and European elections was maintained prior to the start of the new parliamentary year when independent TD Liam Twomey agreed to join Fine Gael. Twomey had won a seat at the expense of Fine Gael in the 2002 general election. A medical doctor, he had campaigned on a platform of improving health services. 'This is a vote of confidence in this party,' Kenny said. In a frontbench reshuffle some weeks later Twomey was given the frontbench health position.

The addition of the Wexford TD brought the party's Dáil seat tally to 32. But the small size of the parliamentary party was no longer an impediment. The results of the European and local elections altered the political psychology within the party – Fine Gael had regained some confidence and believed it was in a position to progress a strategy of offering an alternative government to one led by Fianna Fáil. The 2004 electoral success obviously caused the public to look again at the Fine Gael alternative. Between the June and October MRBI opinion polls, satisfaction with Kenny increased by a significant 13 points – 46 per cent were now happy with his performance. It was the highest personal approval rating achieved by any Fine Gael leader in five years. Fine Gael was still at 24 per cent but the party and its leader were now the focus of discussion about an alternative coalition to Fianna Fáil whereas from 2002 to 2004 the narrative was about electoral wipe-out and the possibility of terminal decline. When asked about which coalition arrangement they would prefer to be the next government an equal number of respondents – 31 per cent – opted for a Fianna Fáil-Progressive Democrat administration as a Fine Gael-Labour-Green government. The improved electoral and opinion poll performances were sufficient for Fine Gael to present itself with credibility as the core of an alternative coalition. There was also satisfaction in seeing the Labour Party standing still in the local elections while in the European Parliament contest the party only retained its single seat despite pre-poll predictions of winning three seats.

The deal with the Labour Party actually came quickly after the 2004 elections especially given that the party had only a few weeks previously been unwilling to directly signal to its supporters to give their lower order vote preferences to Fine Gael. And the deal came with little cost to Fine Gael – there was no mention of a rotating Taoiseach position or debate about which party would be the dominant player in the nascent arrangement. If Fine Gael and the Labour Party formed a government after the next election Kenny would be Taoiseach and Fine Gael would lead the administration.

The basis for future partnership was formed in the unlikely location of Mullingar in County Westmeath. The 2004 local election results had given the two opposition parties a majority of the seats on Westmeath County Council for the very first time. The two parties reached agreement on a deal to improve local services in the midlands county. Similar deals were agreed in other council areas so the Mullingar alliance was not hugely significant in itself. But the deal was singled out because it was a first-time arrangement. Local TDs – Willie Penrose of Labour and Fine Gael's Paul McGrath – suggested Kenny and Rabbitte attend the signing of the local deal. But the Fine Gael side were surprised when Rabbitte went further and signalled that the arrangement was the beginning of a national push for power between the two parties. Kenny and Rabbitte signed the so-called 'Mullingar Accord' on local co-operation which they said was 'a good indicator' of how they could work together nationally. 'The message from the recent local and European elections was clear that the Irish people are demanding a change of government. It is the responsibility of the opposition to build an alternative government that puts the interest of the people first,' Kenny said, adding that the deal in Mullingar was 'symbolic of what we can achieve if we work together.'

What Mullingar delivered for Fine Gael was relevance and credibility – the party was able to give the impression of being the leader-in-waiting of an alternative government. Fine Gael could now sell the idea of Kenny as the alternative Taoiseach. The numbers game still left a huge amount of work to be completed – the combined seat total of the two parties was a long way short of a Dáil majority. Even on a good day there was the possibility of needing the involvement of another party, most likely the Greens. But the participation of the Green Party was left ambiguous. The Greens had not been invited to the Mullingar gathering – the explanation given by Fine Gael figures was that the party had no representation on the local council. But the Green Party made it clear that it would not be joining a pre-election alliance although its first preference was to see Fianna Fáil removed from office. Trevor Sargent's party was not, however, going to be taken for granted as Fine Gael and Labour sought to make up the numbers towards a parliamentary majority. 'I don't want any position in a government that will just be rearranging the deckchairs on the Titanic,' Sargent warned. But the Green Party leader left open the possibility of a deal once there had been discussions among the party leaders. 'I like Enda. He is someone who listens. He doesn't have airs and graces associated with some people in politics,' Sargent said.

That a Fine Gael-Labour coalition would need the involvement of the Green Party was left open in analysis prepared by Flannery who believed that a Dáil majority was possible with Fine Gael winning 55 seats, Labour 25 and the Green Party five. In a pragmatic move Kenny started to pay greater attention to Green Party announcements although he acknowledged that there were significant policy differences and some resistance from Fine Gael's rural base. He talked about the potential of 'creative ideas in the area of promoting alternative energy' and how some Fine Gael policies were 'parallel' to those being pursued by the Greens. But Kenny courted controversy with later remarks that 'some people would be of the view that the Greens are all hare-brained, and that many of their policies would lead to the destruction of so much that we have taken for granted in Ireland.' The comments did not please Green Party personnel but, in general, Fine Gael sought to maintain cordial relations with a potential future partner, and there was also increased parliamentary cooperation between the parties with a number of combined Dáil motions.

Fianna Fáil did not stand still in the aftermath of its drubbing in the 2004 local elections. The government sought to recast its image with a more caring hue, a move facilitated by the departure of Finance Minister Charlie McCreevy to the European Commission in Brussels and a December 2004 budget with increased funding for disability and social projects as well as additional support for first-time house buyers. The strategy paid some dividend as opinion poll satisfaction ratings for the Fianna Fáil-PD government started to improve during 2005 and return to the levels enjoyed around the 2002 general election. As they started to focus on the next general election the two coalition parties were also able to look forward to a strengthening economy, increased consumer confidence and the maturity of its generous SSIA savings initiative.

Kenny's satisfaction ratings were now well above the low figures which he had endured during the first two years of his leadership. For example, a TNS mrbi survey in January 2005 recorded that 44 per cent of respondents were satisfied with the Fine Gael leader. Momentum was now important. The party forced the pace in pressurising the government to support early by-elections in Kildare North and Meath to fill vacancies created by the departure of Bruton to Washington and McCreevy to Brussels. Fine Gael strategists knew they had to win at least one of the contests. The party's cause was helped by a formal election transfer pact with Labour for the two by-elections which were scheduled for early March 2005. Kenny and Rabbitte also sought to solidify their relationship with joint appearances on the canvass trail. The by-elections were an important testing ground for a pre-general election deal. 'We started this business last year with what the media termed the "Mullingar Accord". We have a co-operative venture in the two by-elections,' Kenny said.

Fine Gael selected local publican Shane McEntee in Meath and local councillor Darren Scully in Kildare North. Fianna Fáil was well placed in both constituencies but especially in Meath where the party took almost 45 per cent of the vote in the 2002 general election which opened up the possibility of a first government by-election win since Noel Treacy had been elected in Galway East in 1982. Government by-election successes had been more frequent in earlier decades – Kenny's win in 1975 was, however, one of the last victories for an incumbent government party. In Kildare North Fianna Fáil's chance of retaining the McCreevy seat was challenged by a strong local Labour Party organisation and long-time candidate Catherine Murphy who was contesting as an independent having previously been a member of the Workers' Party, Democratic Left and, most recently, the Labour Party.

Kenny called on voters to use the contests to 'continue the process of changing the government' which he said had begun the previous June. Fine Gael focused on themes which would form the core of its subsequent general election campaign. 'The current government has been in power too long, and we are seeing the results now – arrogance, broken promises and problems that go unresolved,' Kenny said. There was extreme annoyance at an opinion poll reported in one local newspaper which indicated that the Fine Gael candidate would poll poorly. But McEntee took almost 17,000 first preferences – just over 34 per cent of the total poll – as Fine Gael retained the Dáil seat vacated by former Taoiseach John Bruton. It was the first time since 1927 that a Fianna Fáil candidate had not topped the poll in a Dáil contest in Meath. The outcome was, Kenny said, a 'very sweet victory.' Scully polled well in Kildare North but was never in contention for the seat which ultimately went to Catherine Murphy.

Kenny and Rabbitte claimed success for their voting pact. In Kildare North, most of the transfers from the eliminated Labour Party candidate (39.2 per cent) went to Scully. The level would probably have been higher but for the presence of Murphy who attracted just over 31 per cent of the available transfers from her former Labour Party colleague. Assessing the pact arrangement in Meath was more complicated as the Labour Party and Sinn Féin candidates were both eliminated simultaneously and their combined votes for transfer were distributed on the final count with 43 per cent to McEntee of Fine Gael and 27 per cent to the Fianna Fáil candidate. Kenny said he hoped the pact would continue for the general election. The two party leaders met in the aftermath of the by-election results. The alliance between the two parties had effectively been settled although the Labour Party required formal approval from its members which came later in 2005.

Despite agreement on a pre-election pact there were policy differences between the two parties. The gap was most noticeable in the area of taxation. Richard Bruton said Fine Gael would not increase income or corporation taxes nor would it support the introduction of taxes on wealth or property. Labour also ruled out income tax and corporation tax increases but favoured increasing the tax take on the capital gains of wealthy individuals. Both sides knew they needed a coherent platform. But they were reluctant to agree too much joint policy detail to the detriment of their respective individual platforms. 'On the major issues that affect Irish society today we will agree a statement,' Kenny said. There were several exploratory meetings between the two parties in the summer of 2005. It became clear from these early discussions that there was not going to be an agreed joint programme for government in advance of the general election. Instead, the two parties would agree a statement of intent setting out the broad policy orientation of an alternative government. The two parties agreed they would campaign on their own platforms to maximise their own seats with a vote transfer pact in place. Kenny sought to confront talk about policy differences: 'We can point to the past record of Labour and Fine Gael in government, and where there were differences of opinion – and there were – they were resolved by collective responsibility.'

During 2005 as talk increased about a Fine Gael revival, Kenny's party came under greater media scrutiny about its policy plans. The two government parties also paid more attention to Fine Gael – they warned voters about taking a chance on a Kenny-led alternative. The long campaign to the 2007 general election got underway, and with over 18 months to polling day, Fianna Fáil and the PDs started to attack. Michael McDowell warned about a 'slump coalition' while Bertie Ahern predicted that a Kenny-led administration would engineer Ireland's entry into the third world 'in jig time.' Fianna Fáil minister Micheál Martin was even blunter: 'Instead of any real substance we have had several joint appearances by the two leaders. We have been treated to props, walkabouts, photo shoots and lunch dates. All we have been given is empty outings, devoid of content or any attempt to explain or reconcile their obvious differences. They point blank refuse to publish constructive policies with any serious details or costings. They are trying to win power without proper programmes. They are united only by opportunism.'

'We are all under scrutiny,' Kenny warned his parliamentary party colleagues in September 2005. But he was also enjoying the fact that Fine Gael was being taken more seriously by media commentators and by its political opponents. 'The very fact that government ministers are commenting on how Fine Gael are doing in the polls shows something between anxiety and electoral terror, because they know the people are waiting for them.' Kenny rejected criticism that his party had been slow to produce any policies. He pointed to the successful campaigns on consumer prices and anti-social behaviour. 'When the party put forward practical, positive solutions it got a response,' he said. Kenny was also clever in using the line – by now somewhat well-worn – that much of his time since becoming leader had been devoted to rebuilding the party. There was a growing internal confidence in Fine Gael that it had ended the first phase of its rebuilding process – and now with the Labour Party onside, Kenny's party could start the second phase of convincing the public that there was substance at the core of its proposed alternative alliance. Kenny promised 'tangible ideas'. The party planned a series of policy announcements over several months rather than the publication of a single document which Fianna Fáil would pick over.

Not everything went Fine Gael's way. There were gaffes – Kenny was left embarrassed when he used his own experience of being mugged to illustrate the breakdown in law and order in Ireland. It subsequently emerged that the incident had occurred some years previously – and in Kenya. There were also some policy inconsistencies. The party backed retaining the restrictive Groceries Order, a position which clashed with its 'rip-off Ireland' campaign against high prices. Kenny was also heavily criticised for indecisive remarks early in 2006 about the government's programme to decentralise 10,000 civil servants out of Dublin to 53 towns around the country.

Fine Gael had put the government under pressure over a policy increasingly looking like an ill-considered political stunt leading to fragmented policymaking and generating huge costs. But when asked about the staff to be moved to Knock in County Mayo, Kenny said the plans should proceed. He was seen as having put local constituency considerations ahead of the national interest. In general, however, these mistakes were not permanently damaging.

Fine Gael was building steadily towards the 2007 general election. Having restructured the party, restored electoral credibility and cemented an alliance with the Labour Party, Fine Gael started to set out its policy stances. Several policy documents were published at a party conference in Millstreet in County Cork in November 2005. The documents focused on areas where the party had attacked the government over the previous twelve months including primary healthcare, renewable energy, childcare, the food industry and anti-social behaviour. But in his televised address, Kenny targeted the perceived areas of government weakness – their length of time in office, projects that wasted public money and broken election promises. He also returned to a running theme about Ahern's failure to uphold high standards of accountability. 'Nothing is anyone's fault in this government,' Kenny asserted. The Fine Gael agenda started to be dominated by understandable and clearly presentable policies in three key areas – health, crime and value for money which included the misuse of public funds. The party was making progress – its focus on consumer prices paid off and gained further traction in the aftermath of a popular RTÉ television series *Rip-Off Republic* fronted by Eddie Hobbs. Damage was done to the government's credibility over significant cost overruns on public projects and wasteful use of public money on projects like electronic voting and the HSE's PPARS software payroll system.

The November 2005 conference – where, embarrassingly, 200 empty seats were visible on television – was also aimed at addressing the lack of national profile of many senior Fine Gael figures. The strategy was to use the gathering to push forward members of the frontbench team including Fergus O'Dowd, Liam Twomey, Denis

Naughton, Olivia Mitchell and Olwyn Enright. The conference theme was 'New Team, New Ideas'. But the lack of depth in the Fine Gael ministerial team-in-waiting was all too evident. Aside from Kenny – who had successfully established a national profile – Fine Gael's most recognisable faces were Richard Bruton, Gay Mitchell and Phil Hogan. Mitchell's domestic prominence had been reduced following his election to the European Parliament in June 2004.

Bruton had started to command a greater public profile. A serious policy-driven politician with a great command of detail, he offered an ideal compliment to Kenny. He had pushed for a Fine Gael decision to call for a postponement of public sector pay awards in 2003 which, while criticised by the government and the trade unions, met with positive public feedback. Bruton was given considerable latitude in his finance portfolio and as time revealed he was well ahead of most commentators in highlighting the weak economic decision-making at the heart of Ahern's 2002-2007 administration. There was sufficient evidence from numerous opinion poll surveys that many voters were weary of the Fianna Fáil-PD coalition but there was not enough evidence that they were confident about the alternative governmental option led by Kenny.

Satisfaction with Kenny had stalled in the early 40s in terms of percentage points, which was still lower than the level achieved by his main rivals. A Red C opinion poll for the Sunday Business Post at the end of April 2006 put Fine Gael support at 23 per cent, one point above the 2002 general election level. But the Fine Gael leader refused to accept that his party was losing ground. 'The game is on and it's all there to play for, and I don't underestimate the scale of the challenge,' he said. In early summer of 2006 Fine Gael undertook a six-week national billboard campaign to coincide with the party's Ard Fheis which outlined hard-hitting populist proposals on crime including electronic tagging for bail applicants.

The party's objective as with previous campaigns was to maintain momentum. The campaign, trading under the slogan 'Ireland Deserves Better', focused on health, crime and waste of public money which continued to emerge from focus group research as the topics that were most exercising the electorate. 'Ireland deserves better than rising crime and falling detention rates,' Kenny said. 'It also deserves a government that uses taxpayers' money wisely and well. And, most certainly, it deserves better than a health system that regularly sees hundreds of people stranded in hospital for days on end.' The initial billboard advertisements featured photographs of 'ordinary' voters with short text quotes indicating their concern about the three themes identified in the party's research. The quotes were taken directly from public meetings and were intended to highlight areas of government weakness. The second phase of posters featured Kenny with messages based on his leader's address at the party's Ard Fheis, and specific promises: 'I'll make the criminals pay for their crimes,' 'I'll end the scandal of patients on trolleys' and 'I'll sack the wasters of taxpayers' money'.

The strategy was a success insofar as the results of an *Irish Times* opinion poll confirmed. The May 2006 survey showed Fine Gael support hitting 28 per cent – the party's highest level since January 2000. 'Its an indicator that the sustained critique of the government by Labour and Fine Gael is having a fairly profound effect by now and possibly an indicator that the more robust approach of real solutions to real problems announced by Fine Gael is beginning to punch through,' Flannery said. Kenny gave a very strong Dáil performance during the controversy which followed the Supreme Court decision that statutory rape legislation was unconstitutional. And while the party went into the summer recess in good shape the reality was that opinion polls results had been patchy for the leader and his party while Kenny's performances in the Dáil chamber had lacked consistency. But then back in 2002 few believed Kenny would have made Fine Gael politically competitive. Yet through hard graft, solid organisational planning and a touch of luck, Fine Gael was part of the narrative on government formation ahead of the 2007 general election.

A key part of these campaigns were a series of nationwide public 'townhall' meetings with Kenny in attendance. The Fine Gael leader was always more comfortable in these settings away from the media gaze in the Dáil chamber and the lights of the television studios. After one of these 'townhall' meetings in Dublin in late June 2006, journalist Kathy Sheridan wrote: 'He may not have the presence of a Charlie, nor the whiff of smoky backroom intrigue of a Bertie, nor the inspirational, cerebral engagement of a Garret, but he forges an easy, honest rapport with his audience . . .' Kenny was buoyed up by the reaction he had got at the meeting and out of devilment he decided to call into Fagan's Pub in Drumcondra, where the Taoiseach generally went for a late evening pint. The unexpected visitor drew gasps from locals as he walked up to Ahern saying he was just finished another public meeting and was in the mood for a relaxing pint himself. The two men had a good humoured chat before Kenny departed leaving the message that he would go anywhere to get Fine Gael back into government.

At the start of the new parliamentary year in September 2006 all the political parties knew they were only months from a general election. Fine Gael had already selected most of its general election candidates. The party had raised in the region of €3m. Kenny and Rabbitte once more returned to Mullingar as they pledged to publish joint polices on crime, health and the economy. The two leaders set out five 'guiding principles' which they said would influence their approach to office: bring government back to the concerns of families and communities; deliver value for money; be accountable and accept responsibility for improving public services; do not allow concerns to be lost between government departments; and be decisive, positive and pro-active, not allowing problems to fester in the hope they would disappear.

The two leaders had, in early July 2006, visited Belfast as part of a strategy of showing their good working relationship. The two parties had also published a 55-page document entitled *The Buck Stops Here* on the mismanagement of public funds and delivering better value for taxpayers' money. The document recommended increasing the power of the Department of Finance in monitoring public spending and giving the Taoiseach and Tánaiste a more central role in setting targets for strategic priorities. Kenny said he would sack a minister from a Fine Gael-Labour coalition if they were involved in controversies similar to Martin Cullen over e-voting machines and Micheál Martin over illegal nursing home charges. He said it was a 'cardinal sin not to read a brief prepared for you' as a government minister.

There were also a number of social meetings between Kenny and Rabbitte. Their advisors organised several high profile photo-opportunities to provide the public with evidence of their good chemistry and to convey the message that they would work together as a team. The highlight of this activity came in September 2006 at a two-day meeting of the Fine Gael parliamentary party in Sligo. As political sketch-writer Miriam Lord recounted: 'And for my next trick . . . Enda Kenny brought the house down in Sligo last night when he produced a live Rabbitte from a hat to a chorus of astonished gasps from his audience.' The appearance of the Labour Party leader as guest of honour at the Fine Gael gathering had been a tightly controlled secret. 'Short of sawing Bertie Ahern in two and making Michael McDowell disappear in a puff of smoke, Enda couldn't have pulled off a better stunt,' Lord wrote.

The show of unity in Sligo generated considerable media attention and was followed by Kenny's attendance at a subsequent Labour Party gathering in Cork. 'I think it demonstrates the seriousness of our intent,' Kenny said. 'We have our own individual identities but we have agreed to set out a range of agreed policy decisions in the areas of crime, health and management of the economy.'

The alternative alliance presented the Fianna Fáil-PD coalition with a real challenge and there were concerns in the government about the renewed focus on the opposition benches. Interestingly, in his 2009 autobiography Bertie Ahern attempted to make little of the alternative: 'that was a house built on sand right from the start. It was always easy for us to exploit the differences between the two parties, and within each party, as they argued over the next few years about what a new government would be like. They spent so much time debating what they would do when they were in government that they completely forgot they had to try and kick us out first.' The assessment was a selective retelling of the political agenda in the run-in to the 2007 general election but helped with an attempt to revise the record of Ahern's performance at that time. If anything, Fine Gael and the Labour Party were hesitant about deepening their joint involvement beyond a number of core areas but nothing could take from the Fine Gael achievement in clawing back from the political abyss.

In just over four years as Fine Gael leader Kenny had transformed the fortunes of his party. Rabbitte's backing for a coalition deal had been important in restoring Fine Gael's credibility. But Kenny had also shown his mettle in reorganising his party and he had proven many of his critics wrong about his application and focus. 'There is a palpable mood for change among the electorate and we are building on that,' Kenny predicted, with the 2007 general election test only a handful of months away.

9
Getting Noticed

The elements needed to sustain a political party include money, organisation, leadership and identity. The totality of these factors is vital in maintaining a head office, employing full-time staff, attracting members, recruiting candidates and fighting elections. In addition, a party must have a clear identity to capture the public mood and, most likely in the modern media era, a recognisable leader with a strong personality. Having all these elements in place would be the optimum outcome but most parties exist with varying strengths and weaknesses in their financial outlook, membership numbers, organisational structure, quality of leadership and clarity of identity. In the post-FitzGerald era Fine Gael maintained an adequate organisation and a relatively large membership base (although size says nothing about activity levels). The party's financial position varied although it went from heavy indebtedness in the early 1990s to a strengthened bank balance when private and business donations increased following its return to government at the end of 1994. Under Kenny the party ended a ban on corporate donations and benefited from a very successful focus on party fundraising.

In the post-FitzGerald era, Fine Gael's biggest challenge has been with its leadership position and a lack of clarity over its political identity. The two issues have not been mutually exclusive. The German political thinker Max Weber placed political leadership into three categories – traditional, bureaucratic and charismatic.

Traditional leadership is derived from authority associated with a particular social group and the individual is usually born into the position. Bureaucratic leadership comes from attaining senior status having risen through the ranks of an organisation. Charismatic leadership is dependent upon personality and where a leader may have acquired status as a result of taking a stand on a significant issue.

Garret FitzGerald was probably the only leader of Fine Gael who could be classed in the charismatic category although he also had elements of the traditional given his family's involvement in political life, and also the bureaucratic, having worked his way up through the Fine Gael organisation from the early 1960s. FitzGerald trained as an economist but by the time he was elected to the Dáil in 1969 he had considerable real-world expertise. He was Minister for Foreign Affairs in the 1973-77 Fine Gael-Labour coalition. During his period as party leader from 1977 to 1987 he associated the party with a liberal outlook and initially delivered unprecedented electoral success. FitzGerald, for all his academic training and fascination with detail, had charisma and populist appeal.

The men before FitzGerald all had a different approach to the role of leader. Although fine, able and principled politicians, none could reasonably be described as charismatic. W.T. Cosgrave was a senior and respected member of the republican movement who assumed a leadership role following the deaths of Michael Collins and Arthur Griffith. With the exception of the 1933-35 period he led Cumann na nGaedheal and Fine Gael from 1922 to 1944. Cosgrave was very much a traditional and bureaucratic leader. He was conservative and lacked charisma in contrast to Eamon De Valera, which was one of the reasons why he was replaced when Cumann na nGaedheal recast itself as Fine Gael. The first party leader, Eoin O'Duffy, was backed for the job because of his populist appeal but the former chief of police and quasi-fascist was unreliable and ill-suited to the role of party political leader. O'Duffy was replaced by Cosgrave who was eventually followed by Richard

Mulcahy, another member from the revolutionary period. Mulcahy led Fine Gael from 1944 to 1959 and, like Cosgrave, his leadership had elements of the traditional and the bureaucratic but lacked powerful personal charisma. Mulcahy was 73 years of age when he stood down as Fine Gael leader in 1959 but for the following six years the party was led by a man whose political style was more suited to the House of Commons in the nineteenth century than to political engagement in the emerging television era. James Dillon was a fine public speaker but he was not the type of leader Fine Gael needed to take the party into 1960s. He was succeeded in 1965 by Liam Cosgrave – son of W.T. Cosgrave and another politician from the traditional and bureaucratic leadership strain.

The first three post-1987 leaders had all served as senior ministers in the 1980s. They all initially at least had the support of a significant section of the party's public representatives. But each still faced internal resistance. None delivered electoral success for the party. Neither Alan Dukes nor Michael Noonan won a general election or served as Taoiseach. John Bruton enjoyed a two and a half year term as Taoiseach – due to the formation of the Rainbow coalition in the absence of an election – but he contested two general elections as party leader and failed to enter government immediately after each contest. Dukes and Noonan were considered to be from the social democratic wing of Fine Gael and very much associated with FitzGerald's liberalism. Bruton was seen as more conservative but like Dukes and Noonan he was essentially a right-of-centre politician on economic matters. Of the three men, Noonan came to the role based on perceived charisma but the view of his party colleagues was not reflected in the public response to his leadership. Dukes resigned before a motion of no confidence was passed, Bruton was removed after a leadership heave while Noonan resigned following an electoral meltdown. What is interesting about Dukes, Bruton and Noonan is that they spoke about their party in ideological terms. Unlike the pragmatism of Fianna Fáil, Fine Gael engaged in debates about political identity and ideological positioning. This debate continued in the post-Berlin Wall world and the changing contemporary Ireland where there was a blurring of political persuasion.

By way of contrast, Kenny has shown no interest in these debates. Unlike previous incumbents, Kenny came to the Fine Gael leadership without having held senior ministerial positions or a perception that he was a big political beast. Kenny was, in some respects, the political leader who came from nowhere. He was not a traditional leader associated with any particular bloc or strand of thinking within Fine Gael – even in the 1980s he straddled the liberal and conservative groups which existed uneasily within FitzGerald's Fine Gael. Neither could the bureaucratic leadership tag be applied to Kenny who despite his longevity in the party had not acquired a mantle of authority among his peers even when he contested for the top position. Throughout his career Kenny had not been associated with any particular national issues – he had never taken a stand on any significant topic. But it would be wrong to assume that Kenny got the job simply because he was the last man standing following the 2002 electoral meltdown. The parliamentary party may have been depleted but they had a choice of four very different politicians. Kenny was the candidate who offered Fine Gael a leadership driven by a combination of competency and personality rather than ideology. If anything in backing Kenny, Fine Gael selected a politician closer to the pragmatic and populist leaders associated with its main rival, Fianna Fáil.

Once he became leader in 2002 Kenny worked hard to project himself as a national politician leading a united team – a man who would be a capable Taoiseach. The model was very much chairman rather than chief, and Kenny's workload was huge as the Fine Gael organisation was rebuilt and party members focused on achieving the party's elusive objective – electoral success. But the opinion polls were still mixed. Kenny's performance in the Dáil chamber was inconsistent and his media interviews unconvincing. There was a sense that perhaps the personable Kenny just did not have the qualities needed to lead Fine Gael back into government – competency. From the criticisms directed at Kenny, that quality was variously described as charisma, judgement, experience and intelligence. In a *Sunday Independent* interview in March 2004 Aengus Fanning asked: 'Why does a personable, youthful, humane and able politician like Enda grasp to himself the poisoned chalice of leading Fine Gael out of the wilderness into the promised land of a place in government?'

For some, Kenny was too nice for the job – not tough enough. Others simply believed he was incompetent. Fianna Fáil opponents – Brian Cowen, in particular – claimed that Kenny did not have the brainpower to succeed, or as Bertie Ahern put it, 'part of the problem was that a lot of people didn't think the "Taoiseach-in-waiting" was up to the job.' This viewpoint was also evident in some media comment. For example, when Fine Gael challenged the government's policy on continuing to allow the United States military to use Shannon airport in the absence of a United Nations resolution on the war with Iraq there was a hostile response from columnist Kevin Myers who targeted Kenny and tapped into doubts about his leadership ability.

'In the – admittedly – unlikely event that the US wins, what will its response be if we closed down Shannon? Do you know, Enda? No? OK, for the sake of the leader of Fine Gael, who probably would have trouble identifying an Orange pipe band in the Vatican, we're going to make that question just a little easier, with multiple choice answers. So if we take sides against a firm friend which is the mightiest country in the world, one which has a GDP five times that of Britain and France combined, at the end of the war will a victorious US government: (a) Declare an aid package for Ireland worth $10billion? (b) Lift all import duties on Irish goods? (c) Announce Irish passport-holders need no visas to enter the US? (d) Name Ireland as a hostile power in time of war, with fierce economic consequences? It's a hard question for someone like Enda Kenny to answer, I know, but here's a hint: its not (a); and nor is it (b). You want another clue? OK, its not (c) either. Which leaves, well? Which one? You still don't know, Enda? Well, it's the letter on the cap you used to wear at school. [...] From Fine Gael, the party which made the Irish Free State, one might have expected rather more measured wisdom. But not, clearly, under Enda Kenny's sublime leadership.'

The column was met with fury in Fine Gael and a right-of-reply was extracted from *The Irish Times* in which Kenny concluded, 'Kevin Myer's personalised and vindictive attack . . . did not contribute anything to the very serious issues of this debate.' But Myers had touched upon a core challenge which Kenny faced – large sections of the national media did not take his leadership seriously. He certainly confronted his critics with continuous electoral successes. But the doubts about his ability, his competence in running a government, persisted. 'There is an embarrassed public suspicion that there isn't much to Enda Kenny,' Vincent Browne wrote in July 2003. Five years later Browne again claimed Fine Gael was in denial about its leadership problem: 'They refuse to acknowledge what is evident to everyone in the country, it seems, that Kenny as a prospective taoiseach has no credibility. But Kenny, in spite of this and his likeability, just is not credible as an alternative Taoiseach.' Browne had to issue an apology in October 2010 when he suggested following a poor opinion showing for Fine Gael that Kenny should go into a dark room with a gun and a bottle of whiskey.

But Browne was not the only media critic. In the aftermath of the 2004 local and European elections Fintan O'Toole referred to 'the great unspoken problem' – the prospect of Enda Kenny becoming Taoiseach was the biggest obstacle to the formation of an alternative government. Prior to the 2007 general election, O'Toole noted 'the preconception about Enda Kenny was that he is a bit lightweight, that he rose without trace through a quarter of a century as a professional politician, that he is no match for wily Bertie.'

But how fair were these conclusions? The role of party leader is significant when there is little to differentiate the main political parties. General election campaigns increasingly revolve around the choice for Taoiseach – with the focus on the leaders of Fianna Fáil and Fine Gael. Kenny has had to learn leadership on the job. 'I don't take myself too seriously, and never have. I feel I've learned a lot in the past two years,' he admitted in 2004. Senior officials argued that higher expectations were set for Kenny than for the leader of Fianna Fáil who occupied the office of Taoiseach, and had the benefit of huge support services which came from being in government. 'They say that opposition leadership is the lousiest job in politics. You are up against the might and the Machiavellianism of government every day. But the sun shines. If you are driven by a sense of commitment that you are in politics to make a difference, that is a great reservoir of strength,' Kenny asserted.

But with the focus on Kenny's personal leadership skills – or absence of them – what was missed was the extent to which he had recast Fine Gael into a highly pragmatic and populist electoral party. He identified with a handful of themes – trust and honesty in pubic life as well as crime, health and value of money. He rejected all attempts to define a political ideology for Fine Gael or indeed for himself or even to nominate his position on the traditional left-centre-right political spectrum. 'I've never liked the terms of left and right and centre; as far as I'm concerned the Fine Gael party has been a centre party, with a strong social conviction,' he says. 'My belief is that everybody's walk of life, everybody's job, is impacted upon by politics, whether it's the school system, the health system, the transport system, the crime situation, everybody's house, where we live, where we die – it's all impacted upon by politics.' The various marketing campaigns gave little away – 'I'll put you first' and 'It's time for truth in politics. For a change' – the slogans provided no clues about Kenny's politics.

At a Fine Gael parliamentary party meeting in Kilkenny in September 2004 Kenny was asked about his political outlook and whether his party's political position was on the left or on the right. The reply was vague and non-committal as he mentioned the need for 'a strong economy and clear fiscal policies' before adding that 'obviously everybody agrees on this'. He said the 'main battlegrounds' were 'obviously in the areas of justice, health, education and fiscal policy.' When pressed about his ideological position on these policy areas, Kenny spoke about 'the distance between announcements that are made on these issues and the reality of people's lives' which was the concern of Fine Gael. He gave the example of an 87-year-old woman who had a concern about a particular issue – she did not care whether a government was from the left or the right so long as her problems were addressed. In replying to an observation that his challenge was to persuade those on the left to support Fine Gael, Kenny said that he was 'driven by a sense of government being right or wrong', rather then being consumed with government of the right or of the left. 'I think there has been a great centralisation in Ireland over recent years, it is difficult to be individual and apart and still relevant on the political. I tried to do that very clearly on issues like benchmarking, Iraq, neutrality, drink and crime, bin charges, or whatever, and stand up and say our piece. So that people see Fine Gael has addressed the issues and that we are clear.'

Kenny has not been the stereotypical Fine Gael leader. He displayed no desire to be considered a political heavyweight and remarkably for a national politician he has shown little ego in trying to project grand thoughts about Irish society. When asked about his political beliefs, Kenny talked about decency and fairness not social democracy or christian democracy. Perhaps because of this absence of old-style political ideology, as discussed previously, he allowed Fine Gael to comfortably move into the non-ideological space where Fianna Fáil has long been positioned and prospered. Fine Gael under Kenny now perfectly matched Fianna Fáil as a political party fixed in the centre with the ability to move position on all issues as opportunity necessitated. Kenny mirrored the Irish electorate in the same way that many Fianna Fáil leaders have successfully done. 'He is a pragmatic politician who deals with problems as they arise,' one colleague says. The positioning also fits with the analysis in the 2002 Flannery Report which said Fine Gael under Kenny had to move to 'the progressive centre'. In an interview for this book, Kenny described himself as a 'conservative pragmatist'. But these terms carry no real political definition, and they are not linked with any coherent body of beliefs. According to

Frank Flannery, 'he doesn't have ideology but I don't think ideology is relevant. The global economy has narrowed down the options available to a government of a country. Ideology is not terribly important anymore. And Enda suits Ireland very well. What you have to do now is keep the county competitive so as to provide a decent standard of public services for your citizens. And that has nothing to do with ideology.'

One of the fascinating features of the Flannery Report was how Fine Gael was defined against Fianna Fáil. For most of the history of twentieth century Ireland, Fine Gael grappled with how to be different from its larger rival. But Kenny approached the conundrum of co-existing catch-all parties from a very different perspective – he has turned Fine Gael into Fianna Fáil. A similar line of thinking was evident in the confidential election strategy document '2010-2011 Election Plan' where again considerable thought was given to creating difference from Fianna Fáil and replacing it as the dominant political party: 'The normal way for a political party to define itself is by reference to ideology. But in Ireland the three main political parties are, like the electorate, broadly centrist in views.'

Kenny's approach has been about winning votes and gaining power – once there, he has promised higher levels of competency and to do a better job than his Fianna Fáil rival. 'Fianna Fáil really do not have any values other than party values, and they don't have any view of politics other than the three-monthly view ahead. Mine is different, and I want to approach politics in an entirely different way.' In his opinion, Fine Gael is the party of the people; Fianna Fáil is the party of the insiders.

Kenny succeeded in the elections he contested. His message to Fine Gael from the outset of his leadership was, 'we can win'. Brian Hayes, a parliamentary party member under Bruton, Noonan and Kenny noticed the difference. 'He has made Fine Gael less like a party of barristers. He has instilled the attitude that we can win.' From the outset of the Kenny leadership, Fine Gael has sought to woo the floating middle class voter, many of whom have little political consciousness. 'The starting point is no longer where the politician stands but from where the voter is looking at him/her. We are not telling them what they like or what they should like – they are telling us,' the Flannery Report concluded. The party's traditional values were summarised as defender of the institutions of the State, puts national interests ahead of electoral considerations, moderate nationalism, honesty and integrity, pragmatic on policy issues but strong on fiscal rectitude, liberal on church-State issues, and the 'just society'.

'What is required now is to bring these traditional values to bear on the major issues of the 21st century and develop new ideas that set and dominate the political agenda.' The task was to build a new political identity with greater relevance to an electorate which was more individualistic, more self-confident, more materialistic, more cosmopolitan and more internationally-minded. In short, the target market was the floating middle class voter. This audience was defined as well educated 40-year olds living in two-income households in urban Ireland and with a low-level interest in politics, somewhat cynical about the political process and with no interest in the past. Fine Gael's traditional values were irrelevant to this key constituency. Kenny's Fine Gael sought to develop politics driven by the ideas which interested these voters.

The party stripped its message down to a handful of key themes where the intention was to set the national agenda. In selling the electorate the new Fine Gael, the party wanted a language that resonated as the Flannery Report recommended: 'Use this new language to express old value – words such as progressive, ambition, aspirational, fair, generous, responsibility, healthy, human, community, education, family, homes, marriage, quality, living society, critical realism, balance, choice, priorities and environment.' The party's new values – or 'guiding principles' as they were called – included encouraging enterprise and ambition; compassion and fairness; equality of opportunity; articulating the hopes and aspirations of the new middle class; protection of the citizen; new radical policies to eradicate poverty; respect for individuals, while strengthening the community; committing to the welfare of one another; protection of the environment; passionate and constructive opposition to Fianna Fáil and others.

Fine Gael figures acknowledge that Kenny has shown little interest in his party's history. His approach is to deal with today and tomorrow – an aspect of his character which those close to him believe allowed him to overcome the poor opinion poll rating and negative media assessments about his leadership abilities. In the early stages of his leadership, a heavy focus was put on the theme of trust in politics which featured in initial billboard campaigns and was repeatedly worked into speeches. The target constituency was clearly defined at a national party conference in December 2003 – 'the vast silent majority. The quiet forgotten people of this country who work hard, rear their children, pay their taxes, contribute to their community, who still believe in the higher ideals, who balance their rights with their responsibilities.'

Kenny wanted to win back the middle classes to Fine Gael. Early focus group research revealed the concerns of this group – value for money, poor use of public spending, crime, anti-social behaviour. These issues were wrapped up in the theme of trust. To create difference from Fianna Fáil, Kenny repeated the statement that 'politicians are not all the same'. The message was straightforward: bad Fianna Fáil – good Fine Gael; unethical Fianna Fáil – ethical Fine Gael. 'It's time now for truth in politics. Time for politics of values. And of conscience. It's time. Because Ireland's democracy is being diminished. Because the people are being disengaged. Being disenfranchised by the lies and dishonesty of their government.'

The strategy played to the continuing embarrassing revelations associated with Fianna Fáil figures but also a public sense that Bertie Ahern's coalition had not been fully truthful about the state of the economy during the 2002 general election campaign. 'It is for discouraged, law-abiding citizens I want to inject new blood into the veins of the Irish body politic. Truth. And let that be the message that goes out from here tonight. Our truth has no limits. It will never promise people that hospital waiting lists will end, knowing the end won't be achieved. It will never promise 2,000 extra gardaí, or 200,000 more medical cards, with no intention of ever delivering them.'

'You see the big difference between our ethics and Fianna Fáil/PD ethics is . . . we have ethics,' Kenny told a party Ard Fheis in 2004. 'The Taoiseach told the Dáil that "those of us who are in here try to stay here. That is the code of ethics." That is the standard set by the Taoiseach of this country. But according to the principles cherished by Fine Gael in every generation we don't govern to rule. We govern to serve. Which is why we will always respect the equality of our people. Because Fine Gael believes in the dictum of Michael Collins: "On this we will be judged. On whether we have done the right thing in our conscience, or not."'

Kenny did not devote time to delving into policy detail. 'My style of leadership is not one of suppression, it's one of encouragement. It is one of putting people out front and picking a team of your best talents, adjusting them as the case might be. My effort has been to team build and let all these people who have ambition and talent and energy, let them vent that politically so that we can win the trust of the people and form the next government.'

But this approach left Kenny open to criticism that he did not have sufficient grasp of the issues – notably economic policy where he often seemed uncomfortable in media interviews. The space on the economy was filled by Richard Bruton who benefited from trust placed in his ability to deal with this subject. Bruton emerged as a national figure who connected with the middle-class voter which Fine Gael desperately needed. From the outset Bruton assumed considerable autonomy on economic matters. He ruled out increasing taxes on income or corporation taxes. He also said Fine Gael would not introduce property or wealth taxes. 'We do not believe that the issue is to raise extra taxation. The issue is to use resources effectively,' Bruton said. It was a theme which dominated Fine Gael policy up to – and beyond – the 2007 general election.

Bruton consistently attacked the record of Ahern, McCreevy

and Cowen. But he gained little traction for his dismissal of government claims to be running a low-tax economy. The Fianna Fáil-PD coalition had increased public expenditure prior to the 2002 general election but with declining tax revenues and increasing inflation, a spending reduction policy was implemented immediately after the contest was over. Fine Gael gained attention with its campaign on broken election promises. 'Since buying their way back to power with the people's money, they have scourged the country with a series of random and ill-thought out cutbacks,' Kenny said. 'The truth is, though, that his government and responsibility are complete strangers.'

Much of Fine Gael's thesis in the post-2002 period was ultimately proven to be correct as the economic recession from late 2008 onwards necessitated huge cuts in public expenditure. In a 2004 document, Who Cares? Bruton said the government had wasted the opportunity to improve public services in spite of increased spending. He continued an often lonely stance of attacking the economic policies of Fianna Fáil and the Progressive Democrats. Fine Gael was a persistent critic of the benchmarking process. The government refused to publish any data to justify the public sector pay awards. All supporting documents prepared by a 2002 review group were unpublished. But Fine Gael's persistent questioning forced the release of some information which put the final bill at over €1.2bn. The party gathered information from parliamentary questions that showed the pay awards in the education sector alone cost €300m. 'This money could have doubled the schools building programme,' Kenny said.

Fine Gael focused on what improvements had been promised in return for the payments. The party claimed benchmarking was a bad deal. Kenny said the process as constituted was 'a brilliant insight into how the government is running and ruining this country.' He said the explanation of how the process operated 'revealed a political vision more in keeping with the government of a rogue State.' Bruton called on the government not to pay the 2003 award. 'Benchmarking was the greatest wasted opportunity to get reform in the public service,' Bruton said. The Fine Gael attacks on bench-marking were effective – the party was connecting with a private sector support base. Opinion poll figures showed that while 43 per cent favoured the payments some 37 per cent were against while 20 per cent had no opinion. Almost 47 per cent of Fine Gael's sup-porters – and one third of supporters of the other main parties – wanted the payments withheld. The results met with a positive response when Kenny met his senior staff in Leinster House. 'It's been a long time since so many of the public agreed with Fine Gael about anything,' one remarked.

Fine Gael tabled a Dáil Private Members motion calling for the suspension of the payment of the remaining phase of benchmark-ing 'pending implementation of a serious reform package which would yield improvements in the quality of services delivered to the public, commensurate with the extra cost involved.' McCreevy challenged Fine Gael TDs not to accept the pay awards but even this glib response could not hide the fact that the Fine Gael stance generated the first serious government response to the party in the aftermath of the 2002 general election. The benchmarking process allowed Fine Gael to carve out some distinctive political space from the government parties, and also the Labour Party which was locked into its relationship with the trade union movement. The party's attacks on the secretive nature of the deal were effective, and time eventually proved Bruton and Kenny were correct as the legacy of the Ahern-McCreevy decision was the Cowen-Lenihan multi-billion strategy to cut public sector spending.

Feedback from Kenny's early constituency visits and informa-tion emerging from commissioned market research showed public anger at the cost of living and being charged high prices without corresponding high service. Fine Gael ran an aggressive campaign over several years on value for money. The party retained Dublin-based creative design agency Atomic who took Fine Gael topics and devised public campaign themes. Atomic's clients included Ben & Jerrys, eBookers and Café Sol, and Gerry Naughton in his previous role with the Institute of Chartered Accountants had worked with them. The agency was asked to give the Fine Gael campaign an edgy and contemporary look. Over a quarter of a million people logged onto a specially created website where they were encouraged to leave their stories. Party officials monitored the site and the relevant authorities were notified of recurring complaints. The first campaign targeted the insurance industry. The party claimed greater government action could improve competitiveness and save jobs. They also published publicity-friendly research comparing prices in the Irish branches of British multiples with their counterparts in the UK. The topics were populist – the price of alcohol in pubs, chicken fillets in supermarkets and the cost of CDs. There were calls for the appointment of a 'consumer rights enforcer' to 'name and shame' retailers who charged excessive prices.

The campaign expanded to encompass value for taxpayers' money. A number of high-profile government projects generated controversy including a highly expensive computer payroll system in the health services, an ill-conceived electronic voting system and overruns on major infrastructure projects. The exchequer coffers were full from buoyant taxation revenue. Ahern's government had significant resources available for improvements in public services and infrastructure. Decision-making in government was easy, and ultimately very costly for Irish citizens. There was unease about the value delivered for the money spent. Fine Gael highlighted the lack of rigorous oversight in some public spending projects. The award of an additional €1.5m to the development of the Punchestown centre was a typical example. The centre was in the constituency of Finance Minister Charlie McCreevy. It was reported that McCreevy breached the State's own funding cap on the project after it went over-budget. Kenny told the Dáil that the government showed 'blatant disregard' for its own funding rules. The Punchestown controversy was minor in financial terms when set against other expensive projects which failed to deliver value for taxpayers' money including the faulty HSE computerised payroll system. The so-called PPARs system was eventually shelved but not after considerable public controversy. Kenny raised the issue repeatedly in the Dáil chamber as Ahern initially claimed the PPARS system had not been fully abandoned. 'I think the Taoiseach should leave down his shovel at this stage,' Kenny said.

Tapping into increased public disquiet about how public money was being used, Kenny said Fine Gael would reform the way money was spent in government with performance being the acid test of budget allocations and an intolerance of waste and incompetence in any Fine Gael-led government. 'No minister will run amok with the people's hard-earned money,' he said. 'Anyone responsible for the equivalent of PPARS will be shown the door.' Kenny claimed that even though Ireland was one of the richest countries in the world, people were being let down in terms of services and quality of life issues. The government was accused of the 'mother of all rip-offs' with a multitude of stealth taxes and backing for rising prices for gas and electricity. 'Isn't it time to stop State companies taking the consumer for a ride? Isn't it time to stop the government using them as silent tax collectors?'

Feedback from focus group research also showed a growing public unease about crime and in particular anti-social behaviour associated with over-consumption of alcohol. From early in Kenny's tenure as leader, Fine Gael adopted a hard-line and populist approach to criminal behaviour. The party proposed tagging offenders and applying curfews while a network of civic wardens would act as 'social caretakers' in high-risk communities monitoring activity and visiting the vulnerable and the elderly. The language was emotive but picked up on the words used in the focus group sessions and from those who attended the party's ongoing series of regional meetings. In his first major party speech in late 2003 Kenny said Ireland had 'streets that are unsafe any hour of the day or night' while 'organised crime [was] threatening our democracy and our State.'

Once more working with Atomic the party devised a 'Safe Streets' campaign but whereas the rip-off campaign had no local dimension the anti-social behaviour campaign was linked into constituencies with public meetings and a touring party photographic exhibition with images of ugly late night scenes. The 2006 Ard Fheis heard plenty of tough-talking on crime with proposals to restrict bail, electronic tags for bail applicants and so-called 'drunk tanks' for anyone arriving drunk at accident and emergency units. Kenny's language, almost tabloid, and the uncompromising message won both praise and criticism. 'For me a "drunk tank" is the proper place for anyone, young or old who, 10 or 12 vodka shots later, arrives legless at A&E, cheerleaders in tow, to wreak havoc on seriously ill people and those trying to care for them . . . The term "drunk tank" sends an unequivocal message: Fine Gael will not tolerate the habitual, rampant public drunkenness that has taken hold of communities all over Ireland. Arrive at A&E drunk and you will be shown to your proper place – a drunk tank. The beds will be kept for the real medical emergencies.'

There was even more controversy in the aftermath of a trial in which a Mayo farmer Padraig Nally was jailed for shooting dead traveller, John Ward. Nally came upon Ward at the rear of his house. He shot Ward, wounding him in the arm and then attacked him with a stick. As Ward was limping off the property, Nally returned to his house, got more gun cartridges, reloaded and followed Ward onto the road outside his house where he shot him dead. Nally was given a six-year prison sentence for the manslaughter of Ward. Fine Gael proactively intervened in the widespread public debate about the Nally case which was dominated by anti-traveller rhetoric and outrage over perceived high levels of crime.

The party denied its stance was anti-traveller as its public representatives weighted into the debate. Wexford TD Paul Keogh courted controversy when he suggested that the killing of Ward had been justified in the circumstances. Fine Gael said Keogh had been disciplined for his remarks but the intervention only supported party critics that it was playing politics in stirring up local fears about crime. Kenny did not comment directly on the Nally case as he confined his remarks to discussing Fine Gael proposals which backed changing the law on burglary and trespass in favour of victims of crime. Kenny claimed the existing law was unbalanced – a position challenged by several legal experts – 'if a burglar has a base-ball bat and a house owner has a shotgun, the house owner is expected to leave aside the shotgun, get a baseball bat and have an equal contest.' His language was often emotive and highly charged. 'It is difficult to appreciate the terror and concern of somebody whose house has been robbed,' he said. He said that when some-body discovered a burglar in their home in the small hours of the morning they 'must make a decision either to retreat and leave the burglars to do their business or defend his or her home, property and in many cases family.' The policy was condemned by traveller representatives and groups such as the Irish Council for Civil Liberties which accused Fine Gael of hysteria and promoting a 'murderer's charter'. The party had, however, tapped into public concern. The tough-talking measures were popular.

In the aftermath of the 2002 general election, Fine Gael needed to create new talking points about itself besides the media narrative of electoral meltdown and patchy opinion poll results. Several of the controversial policy campaigns were adopted to get people thinking about the party in a different context. Some of the posi-tions including the crime proposals and the attitude to the bench-marking pay awards courted controversy. A similar outcome arose when Kenny expressed reservations about what he saw as position-ing Shannon 'as a key link in the supply chain of military action' when the US-led military action started in Iraq. Kenny called on the government to withdraw landing and over-flight services from the US military because the war on Iraq did not have the mandate of the United Nations. 'Since pre-emptive action by the US gravely undermines the primacy and legitimacy of the UN, Ireland's enlightened self-interest is best expressed by refusal to facilitate, through the use of Shannon, such pre-emptive action,' Kenny claimed. He warned that one of the consequences of the govern-ment support for the US might be to make Ireland a target for ter-rorist counter strikes. 'Not only is that a real and present danger; it is a real and future danger, if Ireland attracts the enmity of nations such as North Korea by its action in relation to Shannon.' The stance did not receive universal support from within Fine Gael but the party once more created some policy difference and became part of the narrative of political discourse.

Fine Gael also generated controversy when Kenny proposed an overhaul of how Irish was taught in schools, a stance which remained in place until the 2011 general election. The party said an 'in-depth review of the teaching and market value of Irish' was overdue and questioned the value of having Irish as a compulsory subject in the Leaving Certificate examination. There was an immediate response from Irish language lobby groups which criticised Kenny's proposal but there was also positive feedback on radio phone-in programmes and in the letters pages of the national newspapers. One opinion poll showed that two-thirds of voters backed the proposal to end the compulsory Irish requirement. Kenny asked how was it that fewer second level students attempted the higher level Irish paper in the Leaving Cert examinations than in French, German, Spanish and Italian 'Why are students so much more confident in continental languages studied for five years, as opposed to Irish studied for 13?' Official figures which showed that €500m was invested annually in the teaching of Irish, with 1,500 hours of tuition devoted to the language at primary and secondary level. 'As it stands most children and young people spend up to 13 years studying Irish at primary and secondary level, and yet a large number of them leave school without having achieved anything resembling a reasonable command of the language.'

Fine Gael policies also targeted those people pushed out of the housing market in the property boom. Its measures were once more populist and straightforward with an SSIA-type scheme for those saving for house deposits while considerable attention was paid to stamp duty payments which was a big topic prior to the 2007 general election but did not become a serious election issue. There was a similar motiation in the party's 2011 election manifesto proposal to target mortgage interest relief at those who had taken out home loans in the peak years of the property boom.

Kenny enjoyed his best period in the Dáil in the early summer months of 2006 in the wake of a political crisis created by a Supreme Court decision that 1935 statutory rape legislation was unconstitutional. The law had made it an offence to have sex with a girl under 15. The opposition raised the likelihood that if an offence was deemed unconstitutional then the trial and conviction under the legislation was invalid as was any subsequent imprisonment. Public concern increased when it emerged that there were people who were on bail charged under the legislation. The prospect was raised of convicted rapists of young children being freed due to the Supreme Court decision. But the situation took on additional seriousness when a court case taken under the now unconstitutional legislative provisions was adjourned.

The government promised to have legislation ready by mid-June 2006. But widespread outrage and anger met a court decision to free a man – known as Mr A – convicted under the unconstitutional law for raping a 12-year-old girl. The case was raised in the Dáil. Kenny's contribution was marked by conviction and displayed a resolve not previously evident. For the first time since his election as Fine Gael leader he seriously commanded the chamber. In a raised voice he asked what was the government's plan of action. 'He filled a young girl of Confirmation age with drink and had sex with her. That person will be out in society.'

The 41-year-old man had confessed to raping the 12-year-old girl having plied her with vodka and other alcoholic drinks. The girl was a friend of the man's daughter. He was sentenced to three years imprisonment, which he was still serving, when he successfully challenged his continued detention in the aftermath of the Supreme Court ruling. Under sustained political pressure – and growing public anger – the government said emergency legislation would be drafted over the June bank holiday weekend and that the Dáil, which had not been due to sit the following week, would be recalled if the legislation was ready.

The government side met with the main opposition parties to try to find a consensus. The initial attempt to reduce the age of consent for sexual activity to 14 years was opposed by Fine Gael which favoured 17 years as the age of consent for boys and girls. Kenny was insistent that the lower age level was too young and sent out inappropriate signals about the age for acceptable sexual activity between teenagers. With the government in crisis, Kenny caught the public mood, and possibly also led it. 'As a public representative and a father, I am appalled by today's decision by the High Court which releases a pervert back into society,' Kenny said. 'The fact that a person who deliberately plied a young girl of confirmation age with alcohol and then had sex with her has now been released back into society at time when this government has failed to see such a scenario coming is an appalling example of incompetence in respect of protecting young people. Who is in charge on the government benches? Why did the Minister for Justice state last week that there was no gaping hole in the law and no need to rush serious legislation?'

It was a powerful speech, and in the Dáil chamber the Fine Gael leader had grabbed the attention of all sides. 'To conclude, let me say that in the last few days, people have been looking to the government to protect their children. But in the last number of years, I believe they have been looking for something just as important, and every bit as absent: leadership. Leadership that acts from courage and conscience. Leadership that makes the tough, often unpopular decisions. Leadership that is most notable by its absence in this government.'

The political intensity was removed from the crisis when the Supreme Court ordered the 41-year old rapist return to jail. But in the debate on the emergency government legislation Kenny revealed more about himself than previously. He was the father of three young children and his role as a parent had been the defining component in his personal value system. 'As a society, this is a conversation we must have. We should do a radical reconsideration of what is acceptable and desirable behaviour by parents, children and the government. Ultimately, it takes not just parents but society itself to rear a child. In a well-functioning society, there is no such thing as other people's children. All of them are ours, but we have lost touch with this view in the past 10 years. We must reconnect with it again.'

Kenny explained why he opposed the initial plan to lower the age of consent to 14 years. The consequences went beyond teenage pregnancy and the risk of sexual disease: 'The Minister's proposal to reduce the age of consent would effectively legalise sex between young teenagers who, in my view, are children. The mark of a civilised society is how we cherish our children and their childhoods. Not for one minute are we cherishing our children or the shrinking space of their childhoods by legalising sex between young teenagers. At that stage, they are physically able to have sex, which they do, just as they are physically able to drink a bottle of vodka, but they do not have the emotional or psychological maturity necessary to deal with the consequences of sex.'

In these June 2006 interventions in the Dáil it became clear that personal values defined as decency and fairness underpinned Kenny's politics rather than any great sense of an over-arching ideology or worldview. 'Obviously my first priority is my wife and children, and then the issue is how much time you devote to the job. But I also think that the cards in life only come your way once, and you should play them when they do come, and my commitment is total. I gave that to the party, to the Oireachtas members, and to the people I meet around the country. And for what it's worth, I work 20 hours a day so that I can say in the future that I gave it everything, and that we gave them that choice. Because that's the essence of democracy.'

Playing the cards of personality and competency Fine Gael under Kenny was positioned in the centre with opportunistic policy shifts where necessary. Kenny's conservatism came with a small 'c'. But ultimately pragmatism defined his decision-making. The Fine Gael identity become more pragmatic, more populist, and more like Fianna Fáil than under any previous party leader.

10
Election 2007

Just before 8am on Sunday 29 April 2007 Bertie Ahern arrived at Áras an Uachtaráin to ask President Mary McAleese to dissolve the 29th Dáil. A few hours later he made a brief statement signalling the formal start of the election campaign. 'No one knows what the outcome of this election will be. The people have a real choice and two very different alternatives before them. That choice will frame Ireland's future, and the consequences of this election will be felt for many years to come,' Ahern asserted. The mention of the Fine Gael-Labour alternative was a significant concession – Kenny was being recognised as challenger for the position of Taoiseach. Research continued to show that the public were uncertain about the Fine Gael leader – although Fine Gael had done well in presenting him as competent and as more trustworthy than Ahern – but the love-affair with Ahern was nearing an end. Between 1997 and 2002 in the TNS mrbi opinion poll series for *The Irish Times*, an average of 57 per cent expressed satisfaction with Ahern's government. But dissatisfaction with Ahern and his coalition government was higher in the post-2002 period. The government's satisfaction rating from 2002 to 2007 averaged at 41 per cent, in one poll the level fell below 30 per cent, and never hit the 57 per cent average from 1997-2002 although the satisfaction ratings increased in the final 18 months of the political cycle prior to the 2007 general election.

While satisfaction with Ahern also lagged that recorded from

1997 to 2002 he was still ahead of his Fine Gael rival. Kenny made up ground on Ahern over this five-year period recording steady if unspectacular progress. Following the 2004 European and local election Kenny matched the satisfaction ratings achieved by John Bruton while in the 12 months leading into the 2007 contest he was ahead of Michael Noonan's best ratings. Prior to polling day, the satisfaction gap between Ahern and Kenny was down to 12 points – five years previously Ahern had a 40-point advantage on Noonan.

Kenny had a real opportunity to create a lasting distinction with Ahern in the eyes of the public in the autumn of 2006. Ahern had been under sustained media pressure since September 2006 over personal payments he had received from businessmen when he was Minister for Finance in the mid-1990s. The Progressive Democrats initially looked like pulling out of government but the party's new leader Michael McDowell eventually opted to accept Ahern's assurances. Senior Fianna Fáil politicians strongly rallied behind Ahern.

When the controversy was debated in the Dáil, Kenny attacked Ahern but stopped short of calling for his resignation, and his speech lacked the passionate conviction which only a few months previously had set the tone during the statutory rape crisis. 'This is a bad day for accountability, the body politic and the Progressive Democrats. It is a good day for cynicism and hypocrisy,' Kenny said. 'It is a very important day for the deputy,' Fianna Fáil minister Dick Roche shouted across the Dáil chamber. The Fine Gael leader took the bait. He responded to the heckler. 'Deputy Roche will get his comeuppance one of these days. He is probably the nastiest bit of goods of them all.' The unnecessary tangent seemed to sum up Fine Gael's uncertainty. Kenny was presenting a confused message because if Ahern's behaviour was so serious surely then he should go, but the main opposition party declined to pursue the resignation route. Kenny's staff were confronted with the question: what exactly had Ahern done wrong? The public information was incomplete and rather than offering clarity, Ahern's responses only added further confusion. In a RTÉ television interview with Bryan

Dobson at the end of September, Ahern offered an explanation for how payments totalling IR£39,000 had been given to him in the early 1990s when he was Finance Minister. He spoke about the breakdown of his marriage and school fees for his two daughters. He also revealed that there had been more money – cash received while at a function in Manchester.

A significant number of issues remained unresolved arising from Ahern's interview but his performance generated public sympathy over his domestic circumstances. A majority did not accept his version of events but satisfaction ratings for the Taoiseach and the government increased in a series of opinion polls. Senior Fine Gael figures were desolate. There was opposition resentment at media criticism of its handling of the affair. Ahern knew the line of inquiry being pursued by the Mahon Tribunal so he had had months to prepare his version of events; the opposition had to deliver an immediate assessment. The party managed to come within three points of Fianna Fáil in a May 2006 opinion poll but in the aftermath of the Ahern payments controversy the gap widened once more. Support for Fine Gael fell by six points to 20 per cent in a Millward Brown IMS survey in the Sunday Tribune in October 2006. The party polled poorly in urban areas and slipped to third place behind Fianna Fáil and Labour in Dublin. Since the previous Sunday Tribune poll in early September, satisfaction with Kenny declined by eight points to 38 per cent, while there had been a significant increase in his dissatisfaction rating which, at 42 per cent, was up 13 points. There was further bad news for the alternative coalition with support for the Labour Party declining by two points to 10 per cent.

The main consequence of the poll findings was to make the opposition parties highly reluctant to pursue the payments controversy during the 2007 general election campaign when more damning evidence about Ahern's financial circumstances reached the public domain through media leaks. Kenny argued that as he personally did not have access to the evidence he would not level damning charges against Ahern – and that the Mahon Tribunal should be allowed to do its job. He was also very clear with his staff that Fine Gael was not going to make political gain from Ahern's family situation. So as long as the Fianna Fáil leader continued to insist that his marital breakdown explained the payments, Kenny was not willing to delve further into the controversy until the tribunal of inquiry put more information on the public record.

Kenny's party decided that the only way forward was to stick to its pre-arranged election strategy. As communications director Ciarán Conlon later explained, 'It's recognised that Bertie Ahern is a very popular leader. You're dealing with somebody who has been there for 10 years. It's a difficult battle when you're the opposition and you're saying we can do the job. The only way you can prove that is if you have the job. But Enda Kenny is the most popular Fine Gael leader in two decades. The last comparable figure would be Garret FitzGerald. All we can do, to use the old sporting analogy, is focus on our own game and make sure we get our best outcome. And I think we're headed for that, a 28 or 29 per cent result that will deliver 50-plus seats.' Outside consultants were brought in to advise on their campaign strategy. The party had had a relationship since 2004 with the Washington-based political consulting firm Greenberg Quinlan Rosner which offered an outside perspective and insights about new campaign strategies which had succeeded elsewhere.

The Fine Gael election strategy was outlined in a leaked memo sent to the party's creative design agency, Atomic in Dublin. The memo set out the party's thinking for a five-month campaign to a general election in May 2007. The objective was to 'generate space in the political marketplace, as it were, for FG propositions; define the issues we will fight the election on; establish political responsibility/link for failures/non-performance in key areas with Fianna Fáil and the PDs; create a template for a sustained blast of political activity through the first six/eight weeks of the new year . . .'

The key areas for the Fine Gael campaign were the by now familiar ones of crime, health and public sector waste. The political background to the Fine Gael election strategy was also laid out in the memo: 'To create space for our positive messages, we need to firmly place responsibility for failures in key areas at the doorstep of Fianna Fáil and the PDs. Fianna Fáil and the PDs will shamelessly revise targets, attempt to manipulate figures and repackage and re-announce proposals in the hope that the public will forget that they have had 10 years already to tackle the various problems. Some obvious examples of this are things like a stated reduction in class size targets being dropped, garda numbers ridiculously being presented with trainees included and revised timetables and budgets for the Port Tunnel being announced as if they are the original figures. This is the type of hypocrisy and poor delivery of promises that we need to highlight in the initial phase of the campaign.'

The government traditionally received a post-budget bounce in New Year opinion polls. Going into 2007, Ahern's coalition also had the benefit of the multi-billon euro national development plan and maturing SSIA saving accounts. Fine Gael strategists believed they had to do something different to capture the public imagination. A mock-up of a poster lampooning Michael McDowell was released to the media in early January 2007. The image was widely used and provided the party with thousands of euro worth of free publicity. A similar strategy had been successful prior to the 2004 local elections when a limited number of posters poking fun at government ministers generated huge free publicity. But at the official unveiling of the 2007 billboard campaign the McDowell image was dropped. The party feared being branded too negative with its highly personalised attack on the PD leader, and decided it had done well enough with its free pre-launch publicity.

The billboard campaign focused on key issues including crime and health. The first poster unveiled from the revised campaign featured a man putting up a poster for Fianna Fáil and the PDs listing big percentage increases in murder, rape and gun crime. And alongside the statistics was the ironic slogan 'Everything is just great!'

'The key message of this phase of the campaign is that Fianna Fáil and the PDs will brazenly try to gloss over their failures in these areas and try to hoodwink the electorate with the message that 'everything is just great,' Kenny said.

The billboard campaign was a relative success – and there was considerable media comment about Kenny's new hairstyle – but the party still started into 2007 somewhat nervously. The campaign had been distracted by stories about the last minute decision to drop McDowell as the central image of the campaign. Kenny's intervention in the immigration debate caused unforeseen controversy when the media latched onto the sentence, 'as a Celtic and Christian people, we understand better than most the special challenges of immigration and integrating communities' – there were accusations that Fine Gael was intent on using race as an election issue. The use of the phrase was unfortunate as there were many positive elements in the speech.

John Deasy also re-emerged to question Kenny's leadership. Deasy said it would represent a total failure if Fine Gael was not returned to power after the general election and in those circumstances he might himself be a contender for the position. Another young TD, Damien English from Meath West, also made an ill-considered intervention speculating about post-election options but the topic was closed down when senior party figures criticised Deasy in particular for his poorly timed comments. 'One of the great successes of Enda Kenny is that he rooted out the atmosphere of backbiting that was once in the party, and that is what makes it so depressing for people like myself, who are involved in trying to articulate an alternative, to see John Deasy deliberately doing this,' Richard Bruton said.

A series of pre-election rallies started in early February 2007 with Kenny once more on the road meeting the party faithful and pressing the case for an alternative government with the public. The themes of the Fine Gael election strategy were stressed – Kenny would lead a government that ended waste in public spending, brought crime under control and fixed the health services. 'I want Fine Gael to win the election, not just to change the government. I want us to win so that we can change the country. I want us to win to solve Ireland's problems and get this country working the way it should,' Kenny told a gathering of over 700 supporters in Cork.

'In the next 100 days, I want your passion to be contagious. I want your enthusiasm to be infectious. And every time you pound on a pavement, knock on a door, kiss a baby, shake a hand or run from a dog, I want you to remember that the right man and the right woman is the one who seizes the moment. I want you to seize that moment for Fine Gael and for Ireland.'

Kenny was performing strongly on the hustings. Members of the public were greeting him by his first name. But his natural charm vanished when he arrived into a television or a radio studio. His personality was still not translating under the studio lights. His media persona was wooden. Private research commissioned by Fianna Fáil showed that the electorate were still uncertain about the competency of the Fine Gael leader. This information convinced the main government party that making Kenny the focus of sustained political and personal attack would undermine his credibility. The first monthly opinion poll of 2007 in the Red C *Sunday Business Post* series saw Fine Gael at 21 per cent – a lower level than the party's miserable 2002 performance. The only consolation was that the party was polling stronger in the TNS mrbi surveys which had the alternative coalitions neck and neck in public support.

Within the Labour Party hierarchy concerns about Kenny and Fine Gael persisted – the party also had access to research that showed voter uncertainty about an inexperienced candidate for the position of Taoiseach. But Rabbitte was locked into the Mullingar deal and the alternative coalition option was going to be presented to the voters. The two parties liaised about topics that they were planning to raise during leader's questions in the Dáil chamber and a number of joint policy documents were prepared and published including proposals for free health insurance for all children up to the age of 16 and free GP care for all children up to the age of five.

But there were some ongoing tensions. Fine Gael took exception to the smaller party saying Labour would be at the heart of an alternative government. Labour had issues with politicians from the larger party claiming that the alliance would be a Fine Gael-led government. In the end, the parties agreed to avoid language which antagonised each other. The two government parties continued to target the incompatibility of the two parties as an alternative coalition. McDowell also criticised Kenny for excluding the PDs as a potential government partner in favour of the Greens in what he predicted would be 'a ramshackle, contradictory affair'.

Fine Gael's research showed the party would not succeed in arguments about the economy, which remained the strongest issue for Ahern's government. But the public was much less happy with the progress achieved in policy areas such as health and crime. 'We can't win on the economy,' Michael Ring told one parliamentary party meeting early in 2007, 'so don't play on their pitch, drag them over onto our pitch.'

Fine Gael once more proposed a number of populist policies including random drug and alcohol testing in secondary schools. Kenny raised the issue in the Dáil. 'Cocaine, cannabis, heroin and ecstasy are available in every village, every parish, every townland, every city in this country now. Apparently, if you want a snort, or a shot of this, you will get it within 10 or 15 minutes anywhere. So much for zero-tolerance.' But Fine Gael made less headway on crime than other policies mainly because every time the party published a new initiative it was seized upon by McDowell. When the party gained headlines for its stance on the public's right to deal with intruders on private property the PDs published a bill in the Seanad in the name of one of its senators which, the PDs insisted, was not actually party policy.

Private research confirmed that the government was particularly vulnerable on heath and showed an overwhelming public belief that there had been a failure to deliver on past promises. Almost half of Kenny's contributions during leaders questions in the Dáil from the start of 2007 were taken up with the health services. Even when the news agenda was elsewhere – and party TDs wanted other issues raised – Kenny stuck with the strategy of focusing on the health services which would dominate the party's general election campaign. The government faced ongoing problems in the health services, particularly with overcrowding in A&E units. Kenny visited Beaumont hospital in Dublin and challenged Ahern to do likewise. 'I see hospitals being built on 24-hour shifts around the country, but regarding the most important buildings of all, hospitals, where people have no place at the inn, the Government has broken its commitments.'

The party also targeted first-time property buyers with reductions in stamp duty while extra tax relief was concentrated on one-income families and carers. The package was announced in mid-March 2007 when government ministers were abroad on St Patrick's Day trips. Government minister Seamus Brennan accused the opposition parties of making promises on 'an unprecedented scale' but then at the Fianna Fáil Ard Fheis in late March, Ahern doled out a long list of pledges. As subsequent developments ultimately showed, each of the main parties had based their spending plans on over-ambitious economic projections – Fine Gael's growth forecast was 4.2 per cent which was more-or-less similar to the estimate in the Fianna Fáil manifesto.

Part of Frank Flannery's job was to 'talk up' the party's electoral prospects. He made presentations to various Fine Gael groups, briefed the media and accepted invites onto television and radio programmes, and all with the singular objective of selling a message that Fine Gael would win seats – and plenty of them – in the general election. Flannery painted a benign scenario for Fine Gael – and based his predictions on numerous caveats in individual constituencies – but he gained helpful headlines about the party winning up to 30 additional seats. Even when newspaper opinion polls put Fine Gael not far off the 2002 general election level, Flannery insisted that with a 28 per cent vote share the party would win 51 seats.

Fine Gael was careful not to offend its potential coalition partner, the Labour Party, in its predictions. Party strategists insisted that the massive seat gains could be made without taking Labour

Party seats. This scenario was dependent upon a massive Fianna Fáil meltdown. But getting a Fine Gael 30-seat gain into the general election narrative was important. After the 2002 general election, the combined Fine Gael-Labour seat total was 52 seats – with the addition of Flannery's 30 seats suddenly the two parties were in the region of a parliamentary majority. Fine Gael gained a new credibility when print journalists wrote up Flannery's comments and the broadcast media discussed the possibility of such an eventuality. But the scenario was unlikely in the context of Fine Gael's insistence that its seats gains would not damage the Labour Party and also the requirement for Fianna Fáil losses which even the worst opinion poll results for the party were not predicting. But Flannery's job was not to worry about previous contests – he was exclusively focused on winning back Fine Gael seats lost in 2002.

Fine Gael's Organisation of Candidate Selection Committee played a central role in the 2007 campaign as the party nationally assumed greater control over candidate strategy although in reality Hogan and Flannery were most influential in candidate selection. The party sought to be far more ruthless than previously in its candidate selection policy. It sought to replicate the Fianna Fáil strategy of only running the same number of candidates as targeted seats in constituencies. Flannery had available the results of extensive party polling which was estimated to have cost in excess of €150,000. The results were acted upon. For example, ongoing polling in Donegal South West showed the party's candidate Terence Slowey was unlikely to win a seat. The outgoing TD Dinny McGinley was persuaded to change his retirement plans and Slowy stood aside. A similar intervention was made in Galway West where Padraic McCormack was successfully pressed upon to reverse his decision to retire. Data from private party polling was also used in Dublin North-East when it became clear that Brody Sweeney was struggling and as a result local councillor Terence Flanagan was added to the ticket.

The party's 'one member, one vote' system meant that there were big attendances at many selection conventions. The gathering in

Clare attracted over 2,000 members while there were 1,500 in attendance in Laois-Offaly and Cork North West and in the region of 1,000 in Cavan-Monaghan, Galway East and Mayo. But the conventions threw up some problems for the national organisation. In several constituencies the local delegates opted for candidates who the private polling showed were not in a strong position to win seats. Favoured candidates did not emerge from conventions in places like Clare, Galway East and Dun Laoghaire. The national organisation was forced to add stronger candidates which meant in several constituencies the party had too many candidates. Over-nomination ultimately cost the party seats in Carlow-Kilkenny and in Sligo-Leitrim. In the end Fine Gael nominated 91 candidates – 37 were running for the Dáil for the first time. Only 15 were women (16 per cent which was as unfavourable as the 13 per cent on the Fianna Fáil candidate list).

The 2007 Ard Fheis was a weekend long pre-election rally under the theme 'For A Better Ireland'. Kenny asked voters to enter into a five-year contract with him. 'If you enter into this contract with me, you give me a mandate for a better Ireland and I will deliver it,' Kenny said. It was probably his best performance as party leader. The idea for a contract borrowed heavily from the Republican Party in the United States and their 1994 Contract With America which committed the party to specific policy actions. Kenny promised not to seek re-election as Taoiseach if he did not achieve his targets, a stance which sought to raise the failure of Ahern's team to accept ministerial responsibility.

The need to counter a latent public and media negativity towards Kenny was central to the scripting of his pre-election Ard Fheis address. In a short film shown to delegates before the leaders speech Kenny said, 'Its like what Mohammed Ali said about Sonny Listen. "He's a nice guy, but he's in my job."' The idea for the film was also to present a more rounded image of the Fine Gael leader. Kenny offered integrity over the broken promises of the Ahern administration. There was a focus on family and background – a man grounded in his community, somebody the people could trust in contrast to the celebrity soap opera that engulfed Bertie Ahern and the payments scandal. During the 30-minute address, Kenny made reference to his father and to his grandfather, James McGinley, a lighthouse keeper working on the west coast. 'He kept his contract and he used it to look out for people, to make their journey better, to bring them home safely.' As the party leader concluded speaking, rather than parliamentary party colleagues milling around him, the television viewers were presented with Fionnuala O'Kelly coming on stage to congratulate her husband.

Fine Gael hit 31 per cent in a TNS mrbi opinion poll in late April 2007 – the highest level achieved by the party since 1989. The combined Fine Gael-Labour vote was four points ahead of Fianna Fáil and the PDs – the lead increased to ten points when the Green Party was included. Fianna Fáil faced a battle but there was still some uncertainty about switching from the incumbent after 10 years of considerable economic growth for an untested and inexperienced alternative.

Ahern went into the 2007 election campaign with many advantages. He had been Taoiseach for a decade, serving two full terms, the economy was still performing well and he had played an acknowledged role in the peace process in Northern Ireland. The SSIA saving accounts matured between May 2006 and April 2007 and savers were benefiting from the 25 per cent bonus on their five-year savings. But the shadow of the Mahon Tribunal hung over the Fianna Fáil leader – new details about his personal finances were expected to be revealed at a sitting scheduled for the day after the election was called – and from the outset of the election campaign the great unknowns about Ahern's finances impacted upon Fianna Fáil.

With the Taoiseach's early Sunday morning run to Áras an Uachtaráin kept from most of his own cabinet colleagues – some only discovered the general election had been called from the radio news – it was not unsurprising that Kenny officially only heard of the announcement after 6 a.m.. He immediately took an early flight from Knock Airport to Dublin. 'Fine Gael is in the hunt for every seat that we can get. We mean business this time,' he said at his opening media conference. Ahern refused to take questions at his first media briefing, departing after reading a short script. Fianna Fáil denied that the Taoiseach's dawn raid on the Áras had been designed to prevent the tribunal going ahead. In any event the Mahon tribunal adjourned its hearings but sufficient material was already in the public domain for the subject to dominate initial media briefings. Ahern was under pressure, and his ministerial colleagues and political advisors seemed to have no idea about how to deal with the ongoing controversy.

The media relentlessly pursued the story in the first half of the campaign, and with some legitimacy as subsequent controversial tribunal evidence revealed. Ahern and his finances was the only front-page story in the *Irish Daily Mail* for nine consecutive days from the start of the campaign. As had been the experience the previous autumn, the revelations about Ahern's personal finances raised more questions than they answered. The public was presented with the situation that a senior politician who had been Minister for Finance had no bank account and kept large piles of cash in a safe in his office. There were further unusual financial transactions regarding Ahern's purchase of a house, as well as stories about several foreign currencies and the involvement of a UK-based businessman and Celia Larkin, Ahern's former partner.

Ahern initially insisted that he would not make any public comment on his finances before appearing at the tribunal after the general election. But more revelations made their way into the public domain and when questioned about his relationship with stockbroker Padraic O'Connor, Ahern remained tight-lipped for six seconds. The silence was only broken by a press officer's interjection: 'next question please'.

The public did not believe the explanations Ahern offered about his personal finances. But still Kenny and the other opposition leaders avoided the payments controversy. Direct questions about Ahern were fudged: 'I hope that the Mahon tribunal in due course will have clarity and the answers to all these questions. But if there is confusion now, perhaps the matter should be directed at the Taoiseach.' There was a row with tit-for-tat allegations about who was responsible for leaking the tribunal documents. Kenny rejected a Fianna Fáil claim that 'someone high up in Fine Gael' was responsible. 'They should point the finger at someone across the cabinet table,' Kenny responded. When asked how he knew the leak came from the cabinet – and the inference was from Michael McDowell – Kenny weakly replied, 'I know what I know and I see what I see.' Fine Gael did not know how best to handle the Ahern controversy. The strategy involved no direct confrontation with Ahern but as the issue was a live media story Kenny could not decline to comment. 'The people of Ireland are sick and tired of listening to the ins and outs of Bertie's house,' Kenny said mid-way through the campaign.

Ahern eventually issued another lengthy statement but it was only in subsequent questions with journalists that he revealed that he made a payment to the Revenue Commissions in relation to monies received in the 1990s. 'I made a full declaration. I think I'll get most of that back,' Ahern declared. Kenny's response remained consistent with his party's non-engagement policy. 'I haven't got involved in this row and I'm not going to do so now.' Having made a big play of trust and integrity, Fine Gael was reluctant to openly call Ahern a liar and directly confront the huge ethical issues involved and the considerable inconsistencies revealed. If Ahern was not fit to hold the office of Taoiseach, Kenny was not willing to say so in public. Opinion polls showed that over half the electorate thought the Ahern's finances were an election issue. But Fine Gael feared provoking a backlash of sympathy for Ahern as had happened the previous autumn. Kenny would only go so far as to say that the Taoiseach's explanations were 'another in a catalogue of bizarre comments'.

The opening week-and-a-half of the election campaign had been a disaster for Ahern. The Fianna Fáil campaign was a shambles and even the best efforts of party advisors in claiming that the feedback from the constituencies was positive could not hide a lack of cohesion at national level. Ministers were contradicting each other over policy – at one event a senior advisor was forced to intervene to clarify the confused answers of party politicians – while even Brian Cowen's tongue-in-cheek remark about slowly roasting the opposition on a 'barbie' seemed inappropriate. The party's manifesto launch was hijacked by journalist Vincent Browne who publicly questioned Ahern about the inconsistencies in his personal finances.

Ahern's lengthy statement on Sunday 13 May 2007 took some of the heat out of the payments controversy and he was fortunate in that two days later he departed for London were he was to address a joint sitting of the Houses of Parliament. Kenny attended the Westminster event although the other party leaders did not take up the invitations, and possibly the optics did not help the Fine Gael leader who was removed from his high pace campaigning to play the role of onlooker as Ahern addressed members of the House of Commons and the House of Lords. The peace process did not sway many voters on the doorsteps, but the impressive visuals from Westminster – and from Stormont earlier in the campaign at the establishment of the new power-sharing executive – provided Ahern with two golden opportunities to play statesman during the election campaign. The events only served to reinforce Ahern's greater experience over Kenny, and it was little surprise when a subsequent TNS mrbi opinion poll showed 59 per cent saying Ahern was better positioned to represent the country over 25 per cent who backed Kenny.

Nevertheless, Kenny's satisfaction rating increased to a new high of 47 per cent – up six per cent – in a mid-campaign TNS mrbi poll although he still lagged behind the other party leaders including Ahern at 54 per cent and Rabbitte at 50 per cent. Fianna Fáil was up two per cent to 36 while Fine Gael was down three points to 28 per cent. But throughout the campaign the opinion polls delivered mixed messages for all the parties. A mid-election Red C survey had Fine Gael up three percentage points to 29 per cent with Fianna Fáil's support falling by two points to 35 per cent. After a disastrous start to the election campaign the survey results showed that Fianna Fáil was still in the game but there was increasing confidence in Fine Gael that its alternative alliance could win. It was a remarkable turnaround from the 2002 general election as Kenny recalled at the start of the 2007 campaign: 'Four and a half years ago people had written the obituary of the Fine Gael party, written off completely and starting into oblivion. Now we have rebuilt the engine and have tested it in the local elections and the European elections and a stunning victory in the Meath by-election with massive results. They are past victories now. We have honed that engine since, and we have travelled incessantly in the 43 constituencies in this country and the trend in the way people are thinking is that they want rid of this government and their time is up. They have had 10 years and they have failed in their duty and they are going to be thrown out.'

Voters heard a great deal about Fine Gael's 'Contract for a Better Ireland' which Kenny signed at the official start of the party's campaign. Fionnuala O'Kelly helped with a kiss. 'I'm hoping people will see the real Enda Kenny on the election trail,' O'Kelly said. 'There is a perception that he is wooden, but it's just not true. He's great fun, wonderful company, a fantastic mimic.' And she added, 'Sometimes I feel like saying to the critics, "leave him alone".'

The contract pledges were central to the party's election themes and brought together many of the areas which Fine Gael had already published and promoted. These included on health: 2,300 more acute hospital beds, free insurance for every child under 16, free GP visits for every child under five; on justice: 2,000 more gardaí, tougher sentences and an end to automatic reduction in sentences by 25 per cent; on education: access to a year of pre-school education for all children by expanding the number of public places and subsidising those who use independently-provided preschools; on immigration: appointment of a Minister for Immigration; on environment: specific targets for every government agency to reduce carbon footprints; on government waste: dismissal of any minister who wastes public money; on taxation:

cut standard rate from 20 per cent to 18 per cent, tax relief for families where someone stays at home to care for a child or a parent; on stamp duty: abolish stamp duty for all first-time buyers up to a ceiling of €450,000 and lower rates for every transaction.

There was more detail when the party published its election manifesto. At the press conference George Lee – future party TD but then RTÉ economics editor – said he was only half way through the 91-page document and he had already counted 569 promises. Lee asked: which ones will the voters actually get, especially when many of the promises had not been agreed with Fine Gael's potential coalition partners? 'These are proposals in the Fine Gael programme. Obviously all of them are not going to be implemented within the five-year period,' Kenny replied, acknowledging that the extra 2,300 hospital beds was 'a serious challenge.' He said the beds would be delivered over five years whereas the manifesto set out a seven-year timeframe. Somebody in Fianna Fáil took note of what was a serious weakness at the heart of the Fine Gael manifesto as the issue featured strongly in the subsequent leader's debate.

Fine Gael's strategy was to keep Kenny on the move with an energetic and confident campaign. 'Like a greyhound released from the traps, Fine Gael's wannabe-Taoiseach is careering around the country in a frenetic race for power,' was journalist Deaglán de Breadún's description after following Kenny on the canvass. 'Enda has had a rip-roaring start. We are all buoyed up by it,' Flannery said. Even Bertie Ahern commented on his progress: 'Enda, in my view, had been having it easy during the campaign, with almost all the focus on me.'

Kenny had spent five years campaigning but many journalists were only now seeing the public reaction to him for the first time. Hand shaking and back slapping came easy to him and the well-wishers were plentiful. Five years previously the voters had recoiled from Noonan; now they embraced his successor. Kenny arrived by helicopter in Limerick on one campaign stop. 'To be able to travel from Castlebar is certainly a privilege for me because generally I'm stuck in traffic as well as everyone else. I wouldn't say it's a dry run but you know we could get used to it, I suppose.'

The 2002 general election had been marked by Ahern's energetic campaigning but the 2007 contest was defined in its final stages by negative and personalised attacks by Brian Cowen. The then Tánaiste and Finance Minister led a Fianna Fáil attack on the economic policies of Fine Gael and the Labour Party. His performances galvanised the Fianna Fáil faithful after two weeks bogged down in the Ahern payments controversy and seeing Enda Kenny barnstorming across the country. But more significantly Cowen dragged the campaign narrative back to the issue of the economy, the one subject which Fine Gael feared most. The party's research showed that it would not win the economic debate – questions could be raised about the underlying strength of the economy but the national indicators were still very strong with unemployment under 5 per cent and jobs still being created. After the dizzy heights of the Celtic Tiger years the economic trends were downwards but in the summer of 2007 Ireland looked set for a soft landing. Blaming the government for poor policy decisions before a downturn hit was a hard message to sell on the doorsteps. Instead, Fine Gael strategists focused their efforts primarily on the health services, the other big issue with the voters.

The two main opposition parties had done well in highlighting the government's 'broken promises' after 2002. In the Dáil, Kenny had focused almost exclusively on the health services since the start of 2007. A Millard Brown IMS poll in the *Sunday Independent* in April 2007 asked whether the health services had got better or worse since the previous election in 2002 – 61 per cent said worse, only 16 per cent said better. A slight majority (51 per cent) was happy with the government's performance in handling the economy against 44 per cent who were dissatisfied. Health and crime were voter-winners for Fine Gael over Fianna Fáil whereas Ahern's party was still viewed as better to manage the economy.

Fianna Fáil was on the ropes and the party was facing an electoral defeat when the Finance Minister came out thundering about the economic policies of Fine Gael and Labour. As a strategy to move the news agenda away from Ahern's finances the attacks worked especially as the headline-grabbing intervention coincided with the Taoiseach's departure to London for his Westminster address. Cowen claimed the opposition was engaged in a 'con job' over their uncosted spending plans. Fine Gael and Labour were going to 'bust the budget or else bust their promises' because 'their figures just don't stack up', he warned.

Cowen claimed that most workers would pay more tax under the Fine Gael plans. Fianna Fáil newspaper adverts repeated the highly contentious allegation. Fine Gael felt Cowen was telling blatant lies. 'The politics of fear,' Richard Bruton said. But the claim was repeated often enough in the final stages of the campaign that it lodged with many voters. Cowen succeeded in creating some doubt. His party also engaged in an attempted character assassination of the Fine Gael leader by raising questions not just about Kenny's experience but also his ability.

The pre-planned trips to Northern Ireland to witness the establishment of the new power-sharing executive and to London to address a sitting of the joint Houses of Parliament Ahern allowed Fianna Fáil to play up Kenny's relative lack of experience of high office. When Kenny offered to appoint an intermediary in the nurses' dispute, Ahern questioned why the Fine Gael leader would by-pass the normal industrial relations channels such as the Labour Court. 'Anyone who knows anything about industrial relations would not say that,' Ahern said. On the campaign trail Kenny attempted to counter the Fianna Fáil jibes: 'I do not have experience of wasting public money on projects that don't stand up, on electronic voting machines that are now being stored at a million quid a year at your expense and on all the other projects that never saw the light of day.'

Twenty-four hours before the televised leaders debate between Kenny and Ahern, Fianna Fáil used its party political broadcast slot on RTÉ to stress the experience gap between the two men. The four minute film featured high-profile backing for Ahern from former US president Bill Clinton, former US senator George Mitchell and incumbent British Prime Minister Tony Blair. All three praised Ahern's role in the peace process in Northern Ireland. Much to Fianna Fáil's annoyance, Kenny had already received the backing of German Chancellor Angela Merkel through their membership of the same European political grouping but the subliminal impact of political leaders like Clinton and Blair – so well known to an Irish audience – could not have been underestimated. Fianna Fáil had had its best days of the general election campaign immediately before the party leader's debate. Cowen had succeeded in getting the economy onto the news agenda while the Westminster address and the Fianna Fáil political broadcast had stressed the best achievements of Ahern's decade-long tenure as Taoiseach.

The 2007 debate was held a week before polling and Kenny was at a certain disadvantage. Ahern had experienced two of these debates previously, and by 2007 he had a wealth of governmental experience after 10 years as Taoiseach. But as the Fine Gael leader arrived at the RTÉ studios he looked incredibly relaxed with his jacket swung over his shoulder. He was treating the debate as just another element of the campaign: 'Like facing into the 18th with a nine-iron from 157 yards with no fear.' Asked if he was nervous he left open the possibility that Fine Gael was considering confronting the payments issues: 'Not in the slightest – in this business a clear conscience is a formidable weapon.'

The leaders' debate has become the major set-piece event in recent general elections in Ireland even if it does not influence as many minds as the extensive media coverage would suggest. The 2007 debate achieved a higher audience level than the two previous debates in 1997 and 2002. Moderated by Miriam O'Callaghan, the debate had an average audience of 941,000 – a national share of 63 per cent. Throughout the course of the programme the debate had an audience reach of 1.4m viewers.

Each leader made a two-minute introductory address from a podium before taking their seats on either side of O'Callaghan. Ahern stressed the record of his government. Kenny said it was time to change from a 'tired government that breaks its word' and reiterated his contract pledge not to seek re-election as Taoiseach if the promises such as 2,300 extra hospital beds and 2,000 extra gardaí were not delivered.

Kenny was asked about his lack of ministerial ability and his ability to be Taoiseach. He said the role was about 'decisiveness and having a vision for the country in order to pick the team to deliver in government.' As had by now become his form, Ahern ducked and dived around the questions about his personal finances. 'I put all of my personal records for the best part of 20 years out there,' he said. 'They were fair questions to be asked and they were fair questions to be answered.' He fell back on blaming his marital separation for his unusual finances. 'To rent a house, I hope, is not a crime, or to take loans from personal friends or not to have bank accounts.' O'Callaghan gave Kenny the opportunity but he again refused to make political capital from the controversy. 'It's not for me to cast judgement on any man or anybody . . . I am not adjudicating on the integrity of Bertie Ahern . . . We have set up a formal tribunal to ascertain facts,' he said.

Both leaders stressed the positives of their respective policy positions while seeking to undermine their opponent's pledges. There was little engagement during the first 20 minutes but the exchanges became more combative when the discussion turned to the health services. Ahern floundered in claiming there was no crisis in the health services. Kenny spoke about Fine Gael's promise to provide 2,300 extra hospital beds but Ahern responded that Fine Gael's costings only contained money for 500 beds. Kenny countered that there was sufficient money if the political will existed and that he would reprioritise some of the €2.4bn allocated for acute hospital development in the National Development Plan. Ahern pointed out that such a move would mean a reduction in other health services. 'You're either using it for beds, or you're abandoning the other issues,' Ahern claimed. The Fianna Fáil leader was on tricky ground given the lack of specifics on hospital beds in the government's national plan. But Fine Gael leader never got his response out strongly enough either in the debate or in subsequent discussions over the following days.

Viewers would have been lost in a statistical haze as the two leaders argued over various issues, particularly garda numbers and precisely how many additional gardaí Fine Gael was promising. Kenny's contract was emphatic – 2,000 more gardaí to bring the size of the force to 15,000 from a total of just over 13,000 in May 2007. But as the total number of gardaí was expected to be 14,000 by December 2007, Ahern attacked the credibility of the Fine Gael proposal claiming the party was really only promising 1,000 additional members of the force. But when Ahern referred to a Fianna Fáil plan for 2,000 extra gardaí, Kenny argued that this was merely a repeat of an unfulfilled promise from the previous election contest. Kenny stumbled when he said his party's spokesperson 'did not have the official statistics' with him when he accepted that his claims about a doubling in crime were unfounded. Ahern repeated Fianna Fáil assertions that Fine Gael's tax plans would benefit the rich and tried to manipulate Kenny's response as accepting his point. But when Ahern remarked, 'we are the party which has made the construction industry' Kenny interjected, 'You are also the party which has benefited from the construction industry.'

The Fine Gael leader went into the debate not necessarily needing to win but he had to ensure he was not beaten. And as O'Callaghan thanked the two politicians and wished them well for the remainder of the campaign it was clear that Kenny had held his own with Ahern; no knock-out blows had been delivered by his more experienced opponent. Kenny had scored some decent points. The immediate assessment is interesting as the impact of the debate on the final week of the campaign has been highly contested. Pat Rabbitte described the event as a 'boring, score draw.' Mary Harney thought both leaders had performed well but that Ahern had 'shaded' a victory.

In the *Irish Independent*, Fionan Sheehan and Gene McKenna concluded that, 'Mr Ahern slightly shaded the exchanges in the TV showdown. But he could not deliver the clear victory observers believed he needed to pull back the Fine Gael leader's advantage in the general election. Mr Ahern was constantly harassed by an uncharacteristically combative and fresh-looking Mr Kenny.' Stephen Collins wrote in *The Irish Times*: 'The great debate of the election ended with Enda Kenny scoring on confidence and the clarity of his message on services and accountability while the Taoiseach scored on points of detail.' Miriam Lord also in *The Irish Times* wrote: 'Given Fianna Fáil's spluttering campaign to date, it was being said that Taoiseach Ahern needed to land a killer blow to stop the resurgent Kenny in his tracks. He didn't do it. Instead, Bertie's performance was typical of his party's surprising approach to this most surprising campaign: lacklustre, hesitant and uncertain. As for Enda: he didn't exactly cover himself in glory either, but he didn't crash in flames. His handlers will be very pleased. Here's a verdict we got on the phone as soon as it ended: "Enda's tie is nicer and their shirts are the same."'

Kenny hit the hustings in County Donegal on the morning after the debate. 'As Muhammad Ali used to say, 'Do I look as if I was marked?' was his response to questions about the outcome. Five floating voters were interviewed in one newspaper. They all thought Kenny was outscored by Ahern when the discussion turned to the economy and that he over-stressed the 'contract'. Four of the five said the debate would not make a difference in how they would vote while one of the group said she would vote for Fine Gael. But according to an TNS mrbi opinion poll Ahern had a comfortable victory with 32 per cent saying the Taoiseach won the debate, 13 per cent for Kenny, 14 per cent said neither and 41 per cent either did not know, did not watch the debate or had no opinion.

Fianna Fáil went into overdrive with an avalanche of claims about the strength of Ahern's performance and very focused attacks on Fine Gael's tax and hospital proposals, and on Kenny's experience and ability. The timing of the debate fits with growing support for Fianna Fáil in the final week of the campaign. The strength of the Fianna Fáil communication strategy influenced the media narrative to such an extent that four years later some commentators were writing about Kenny having been 'trounced' in the 2007 debate. This experience was not unusual – post-debate media analysis has been shown elsewhere to change the public's initial assessment of the debate performance of candidates.

The evidence from the RTÉ/Lansdowne exit poll was not consistent with the view that the television debate ultimately won the 2007 election for Fianna Fáil. Political scientist Michael Marsh observed that those who did not watch the debate were more likely to vote Fianna Fáil than those who did. In addition, there was no evidence that those who decided their voting choice near the end of the campaign, and after watching the debate, disportionately voted for Fianna Fáil. Some 41 per cent of late deciders who did not watch the debate voted for Fianna Fáil against 35 per cent who did see it; whereas among early deciders 47 per cent non-viewers voted for Fianna Fáil against 38 per cent among viewers. There was also no evidence that those who made up their mind in the final week of the campaign and thought Ahern won the debate were more likely to support Fianna Fáil.

The debate may not have been directly important in influencing voters but it certainly impacted upon the morale of Fianna Fáil party workers. For the first time since the campaign got underway Fianna Fáil engaged in the election debate with confidence and without the overhang of the Ahern payments controversy. The party also buoyed up when two leading media commentators supported Ahern on RTÉ's *Late Late Show* in an unplanned but controversial part of the national broadcaster's election coverage.

Fianna Fáil was clinging to power and it was willing to throw whatever mud was necessary to discredit its opponents. In the final stages of the campaign Fine Gael had to deal with attempts to smear Kenny and his senior advisor, Frank Flannery. Allegations of financial impropriety at the Rehab Group – where Flannery had been employed from the mid-1970s until his retirement in December 2006 – were contained in documents circulated to some journalists during the campaign. The allegations were false as were incorrect claims that large expenses had been drawn from the charity and that new auditing procedures were implemented following an internal inquiry. The allegations were totally dismissed by Rehab and gained no significant media traction but it was very clear that the people responsible were intent on damaging Fine Gael – the documents also mentioned that several Rehab directors were well-known figures in Fine Gael. Flannery had taken on a high profile role in the campaign and was a regular presence at the party's media conferences. Any controversy involving the party's senior strategist would have been both distracting and damaging.

The party's media advisors had to deal with a second smear story and they went into overdrive to keep an unfounded and nasty rumour about Kenny out of the national press. A growing internal belief that the party was facing a dirty tricks campaign was heightened when queries were received from freelance journalists who did not normally cover politics. The potentially damaging rumours had also started to circulate in wider media circles. Having consulted with Kenny the Fine Gael team decided not to engage with the subject – no comment would be provided – and considerable work was required to convince some newspapers that not only was the rumour totally untrue but that publication of a denial would play into the hands of those who were orchestrating what looked increasingly like an organised smear campaign. The source of the salacious story could not be traced to Fianna Fáil but Fine Gael officials continue to believe that the smear originated – as one advisors says – 'in a satellite of the Fianna Fáil election headquarters.'

In the public exchanges in the final days of the campaign Cowen increasingly targeted Kenny with highly personalised attacks. He said the Fine Gael leader had shown a 'flippant' approach to policy detail and figures. 'Mr Kenny thinks it will all just work out – he can do a double somersault and five flip-flops in a week and he will still land on his feet.' The Finance Minister attempted to convey the impression that Kenny was just not up to being Taoiseach. 'I don't think you can expect other people to be led by you if you don't know what you are taking about. And I'm sorry, Enda Kenny didn't know what he was taking about,' Cowen declared. 'Mr

Kenny is trying to run the country on the basis of 'I saw one saying this or another man saying that,' he added. Interestingly, one unsuccessful Fine Gael candidate, the businessman Brody Sweeney, later said that Fianna Fáil had done 'a great job' in making Kenny look 'completely incompetent'.

Fianna Fáil's final-week criticism of Fine Gael plans for extra hospital beds was disingenuous but it was also highly effective. 'We exposed the myth last night of the contract and that was clear to viewers,' Ahern said after the leaders' debate, 'there's no money for the beds except if you take money from cancer, from the children's hospital, from the capital development. So the issue is now clear.' The party insisted that Kenny had 'admitted' that Fine Gael could not afford to provide its promised hospital beds within the budgetary framework in its health manifesto. Fine Gael was slow to respond, and Kenny's party was for the first time in the campaign seriously on the backfoot as Fianna Fáil continued a high tempo and aggressive attack on the party and its leader. Cowen repeated his claim that the Fine Gael tax proposals were 'weighted towards the wealthiest' in society. Richard Bruton said the attack was 'propaganda' but it was hard to get away from the simple Fianna Fáil claim.

The inexperience on the party's frontbench was badly exposed in the final week of the 2007 campaign. Aside from Kenny, Bruton and Hogan, the party did not have politicians with the necessary experience to counter the hostility and aggression of their Fianna Fáil opponents. Many claims were made without response. There is no doubt that if Fine Gael had its 2011 frontbench during the 2007 campaign the party would have been in a significantly stronger position, and possibly would have been better able to counter the Fianna Fáil attacks. The government parties were themselves vulnerable on their hospital co-location plans but it was only in the very final stages of the campaign that Fine Gael focused on this weakness.

Kenny's contract certainly gave Fianna Fáil something tangible on which to focus their attacks as the party went all out to prevent an electoral defeat. 'Enda Kenny's contract is a fraud. It isn't worth the billboard it is written on,' Ahern asserted. 'The problem with Enda Kenny's contract is not only the promises in it, but what he leaves out as well. No mention of pensions, of schools, of transport. Not a word about farmers, or the peace process. And nowhere do we even see the word "jobs".'

Over a million euro was bet with Paddy Power bookmakers in the 2007 contest – a huge increase on the €75,000 from five years previously. Ahern had started the campaign as favourite to be the next Taoiseach but he was gradually overhauled by Kenny. By 18 May 2007, Kenny was favourite with the bookies at 4-5 while Ahern was 5-4. Most of the main bookmakers had Kenny as the frontrunner. However, the odds changed after the final TNS mrbi survey and by polling day Ahern was the clear favourite at 1-4 with Kenny a poor 11-4.

The TNS mrbi opinion poll showed an increase in Fianna Fáil support – by five points to 41 per cent – since a comparable survey 11 days previously. Fine Gael was down one point to 27 per cent. But the big loser was the Labour Party, down three points to 10 per cent which might suggest that Cowen's attacks had been effective in damaging the smaller party in the self-styled alliance for change. The respondents were also asked about the competency of the two leaders on key issues. Ahern was 25 per cent ahead of Kenny on the economy but the Fine Gael leader had a 10 point advantage on heath. Having flirted with the idea of change, it seemed many voters returned to Fianna Fáil rather than take a risk with a new governmental line-up.

When the final votes were counted in the 2007 general election Fine Gael's vote hit 27.3 per cent – an addition of 4.8 per cent on 2002. The performance gave the party 20 extra seats which was in the range of the party's private expectations. Flannery had not believed Fianna Fáil support would go above 40 per cent. His analysis was based on the premise that what was electorally good for Fianna Fáil was correspondingly bad for Fine Gael, and vice versa. Ahern's party won 41.6 per cent but with 77 seats the party lost four seats on 2002. The turnaround in Fine Gael fortunes from 2002 was dramatic. But the party had still not broken out of its post-1987 range but given the defeated and demoralised party Kenny had taken over five years previously the result was a massive personal achievement. 'You can't argue with the people,' Kenny said in Castlebar where he received a huge personal vote.

Fine Gael gained votes in all but eight constituencies. It lost no seats and saw its Dáil representation returned in Kerry South for the first time in 20 years, took two seats in Wicklow for the first time since 1982 and achieved a similar seat outcome in Clare for the first time since 1989. The party significantly increased its presence in the Dublin region. Only in three Dublin constituencies – and in Kildare South – was there now no Fine Gael TD compared to 13 constituencies in 2002.

Fine Gael's pre-election work in various constituencies led to the return of high profile politicians who had been defeated in 2002 including Charlie Flanagan in Laois-Offaly and Alan Shatter in Dublin South. Former minister Sean Barrett who had stood down at the 2002 general election made a comeback in Dun Laoghaire where the party had been without a TD. The party also capitalised on its high-profile MEPs with Simon Coveney opting to return to national politics but Mairead McGuinness lost out in Louth in what was probably a strategic mistake in not convincing the East MEP to run in Kildare South. Gay Mitchell, despite pressure to remain in national politics, opted to continue with his role in the European Parliament.

An analysis of party support in the different social classes showed that under Kenny, Fine Gael won back support in the AB middle class group and among farmers. The party won 30 per cent of the AB vote in 2007 (23 per cent in 2002) and 42 per cent of the farming vote (32 in 2002). But its gains were less impressive in the C1 lower middle class – up from 19 to 23 per cent – and gains in this category are significant as it totals one third of all voters. The party won 28 per cent of the C1 vote in 1997. By 2007 Fine Gael's share of the C1 support was seven points lower than its AB vote whereas Fianna Fáil C1 support was four points higher than its AB vote (41 against 37). Small changes in C1 support – given its large size – can have a big impact of party performance as Fine Gael experienced in opinion polls after the economic and financial crises in the autumn of 2008 – and in the 2011 general election.

Although Fianna Fáil and the PDs had lost seats in 2007, and now had a combined total of 80 TDs, Ahern was still set to form a new administration. Several independents had been elected who were open to dealing with Fianna Fáil while the Green Party was another possible partner and would guarantee an even more secure Dáil majority. But Fine Gael refused to concede that a Fianna Fáil-led coalition was a foregone conclusion. 'The figures stack up here . . . I can see distinct possibilities,' Kenny said. 'Do you want 15 years of one party in government or are we prepared to change that because 60 per cent of people voted against the government?' he asked.

Several members of the Fine Gael leadership argued that an anti-Fianna Fáil arrangement was a live possibility. 'Fine Gael, Labour and the Greens have 77. Fianna Fáil have 78, so it's practically a draw, and it's a question now of seeing what the attitude is of the other independents and parties to see if an alternative [can be found],' Phil Hogan said. Such an arrangement was fraught with difficulty – the three parties would have needed the support of the two Progressive Democrat TDs and several independents just to get to a majority in the Dáil. It would be a repeat of the situation in 1948 when a collection of parties and independents came together to remove Fianna Fáil from power. But unlike in 1948 Fianna Fáil was now open to forming a coalition government, and Ahern's party also had several options. The prospect of forming a Fine Gael coalition involving Labour, the Greens, the PDs and independents looked slim but Fine Gael pursued the possibility for several days after the election results were known.

Fine Gael made contact with the Green Party almost immediately after the final election results were known. Various permutations were discussed. Fine Gael believed the two PD TDs and at least three independents – Michael Lowry, Tony Gregory and Finian McGrath – could be brought within a multi-party arrangement which would have had 82 Dáil seats. The option of offering the position of Ceann Comhairle to a Fianna Fáil TD was considered which would have enhanced the alternative's Dáil prospects. Fine Gael actually made contact with four of the five independents – Gregory, McGrath, Lowry and former Fianna Fáil member, Jackie Healy-Rae although his support was not considered likely. Lowry said he would back a Fine Gael-led administration but he was unsure if the numbers would stack up to form a stable government. The independents knew a deal with Fianna Fáil offered great security which they all said was a priority.

The situation with Sinn Féin complicated the deliberations. In the lead-in to the 2007 general election, Kenny repeatedly warned about the possibility of a Fianna Fáil-Sinn Féin alliance and explicitly ruled out any arrangement between his party and Sinn Féin. Fine Gael could not sell a direct deal with Sinn Féin to many party deputies but those involved in the talks about a multi-party arrangement in 2007 feared Ahern could ultimately scupper their admittedly slim prospects by concluding an alternative arrangement with the four Sinn Féin TDs and independents Healy-Rae and Beverly Flynn. Two years later – in the summer of 2009 – a war of words developed between Kenny and Trevor Sargent about the nature of their contacts in 2007 and whether or not Kenny had asked the Green Party politician to contact Sinn Féin about their intentions on government formation. The Sinn Féin position on the vote for Taoiseach was vital if an alternative was a viable option to a Fianna Fáil coalition in 2007. Feelers were put out to four Sinn Féin TDs to see if the party was interested in some form of 'external relationship' with a Kenny-led government. But the party was not interested in supporting a government from the opposition benches. The possibility of including Sinn Féin in a rainbow arrangement was discussed but not seriously pursued. The numbers game was so tight than such a government would not have survived even the defection of a single Fine Gael TD unhappy at any deal with Sinn Féin.

During the 2002 leadership contest Kenny had been asked if he would involve Sinn Féin in a coalition government in 2007, if the numbers required it. Interestingly, he had not given an emphatic rejection to the idea: 'It's a long way ahead . . . The people who elected Sinn Féin TDs to the Dáil are the same people who elected me . . . 2007 is very far down the road and I do hope that by then the IRA will have been disbanded.' Such a move was, however, ruled out after 2002 and, while mirroring the Ahern's government's policy on Northern Ireland, Kenny was repeatedly critical of Sinn Féin, calling on the party to detail the income 'received from oil, petrol and diesel in the border areas, from narcotics through FARC and from various jobs done on post offices and banks through the years.' It was against this background that Frank Flannery caused controversy in 2009 when he described Sinn Féin as a 'legitimate party' that Fine Gael could do business with. Kenny was forced to defuse the row by publicly slapping down his closest advisor.

'He does not determine what Fine Gael policy is. He made a personal comment which has nothing to do with Fine Gael policy. Fine Gael policy was enunciated by me very clearly. End of story.' It was a difficult move given the hugely crucial role played by Flannery in all the electoral successes enjoyed by Fine Gael during Kenny's leadership. And his work had paid a handsome dividend in the 2007 general election.

In assessing the 2007 results, political scientist Michael Gallagher concluded that the Fine Gael performance could be assessed in two very different ways – as half full by those who saw the 2002 meltdown as signalling political oblivion; as half empty by those who saw the 20-seat gain as putting the party back to its uninspiring post-1987 level of support. For many of the team around Kenny the 2007 election was their first experience of a general election campaign. They had got many things right but an inability to deal with the avalanche of abuse from Fianna Fáil in the latter states of the campaign was a key weakness and possibly the party was too meek in dealing with the Ahern financial revelations. There was also some internal criticism that insufficient time had been devoted to properly testing key polices and that Kenny had gone into the leader's debate without what one staffer called 'a formula of words' to answer Ahern on potentially difficult policy areas.

Lessons were learnt from the 2007 campaign, particularly from the party's poor performance in the days before polling. The election strategy for the 2011 contest warned: 'FINE GAEL has traditionally not been strong in the last week of a campaign. Yet this is exactly when many of the swing voters decide how to vote. FINE GAEL must ensure that this time the last week is dominated by a strong FINE GAEL message and that we are not responding to the other parties.' Moreover, much great work was done ahead of the 2011 contest in preparing Kenny for the televised debates.

11
A Balancing Act

Enda Kenny had a tough decision to make in the aftermath of the 2007 general election. If he resigned immediately then his legacy would have been the man who saved Fine Gael from political oblivion. By staying as leader the only objective would be to lead Fine Gael into government, and a failure to do so after the next general election would mean the judgement of Kenny's tenure would be much harsher. The Mayo man signalled that he would remain as Fine Gael leader. He had the energy for another general election campaign. 'He has the advantage of being the "Peter Pan" of Irish politics. While everyone else goes grey or bald he appears to be more youthful,' Ivan Yates said. Kenny determined that the job had only been half done, and with the injection of new blood into the parliament he would finish the work. 'There was unfinished business,' Kenny says. 'I want to complete this work for Fine Gael and do a job for Ireland.' The ambition after 2007 was to break Fianna Fáil's stranglehold on power.

Several of the new Fine Gael TDs in 2007 were critical of the relative safety of the proposition the party had offered voters. Leo Varadkar, newly elected in Dublin West, sought more ambition: 'We did not win the policy debates. We showed an unwillingness to take clear positions. We did not demonstrate competence to run the economy. When our policies came under scrutiny we were, on occasion, unable to stand over our own promises – how and when would we deliver medical cards for every child under five; who would benefit most from our tax policies; how would we deliver 2,000 extra beds; whether the 2,000 extra gardaí were really extra at all etc? On other key issues we did not comprehensively research our policies as we should have done. For many voters, Fine Gael and Labour did not give sufficient reason to risk a change of government. In this context, thousands of voters took the decision to vote for the devil they knew in the closing days of the election campaign.'

Varadkar's was a fair analysis but one that failed to give sufficient consideration to the Fine Gael achievement in even being competitive in the 2007 contest when set against the work required over the previous five years. In truth, given where the party had started, it would have been unfair to have concluded that the 2002 contest was not a success for Fine Gael. Kenny – much derided by sections of the media and much lampooned by his political opponents – had delivered on the challenge set when he was elected party leader. He had overseen the implementation of a modern party structure. All the elements necessary to run a professional political organisation were in place. The horror stories told by those involved in the 2002 campaign were not repeated. Relations between the leader's office, headquarters in Mount Street and the press office were well managed while a huge reorganisation work programme in the constituencies had paid dividend. A comeback which probably should have taken two electoral tests had been achieved in a single general election, and Kenny had succeeded in making Fine Gael politically relevant and the results provided a platform for the subsequent contest.

The party leader faced a potentially tricky job in recasting his frontbench after the 2007 general election. He had to accommodate those who had worked hard over the previous five years alongside a collection of new ambitious deputies, and several experienced politicians who had returned to the national stage after an absence having lost their seats in 2002. Few of the outgoing team had established national profiles, and during the 2007 general election it was obvious that Kenny did not have from within his parliamentary party enough TDs with senior ministerial potential.

Eight frontbench members from 2002 were dropped. 'You're not going to like this but I have to make changes,' Kenny informed these colleagues who in effect now knew they would not be in cabinet if Fine Gael returned to office. The cull was undertaken with the minimum of public rancour, and no internal rump emerged to cause the party leader problems. The impact of the demotions was eased somewhat when Kenny allocated Fine Gael positions on a number of Oireachtas committees.

The party's deputy leader Richard Bruton remained as finance spokesperson and was the only member of the previous frontbench to retain the same job. The return of politicians who had lost out in 2002 provided Kenny with the opportunity to inject deeper experience into his frontbench team. There were positions for Alan Shatter, Michael Creed, Brian Hayes and Charlie Flanagan. Having opted for national politics over the European parliament Simon Coveney rejoined the frontbench. 'I have picked a team with a range of talents and experience that will directly mark government ministers as well as developing and advancing new Fine Gael policy,' Kenny said.

As he had done in 2002 with Deasy and Enright, the Fine Gael leader also took the opportunity to promote a number of new deputies. The health brief was given to James Reilly – a medical doctor and first time TD but a former president of the Irish Medical Organisation. Varadkar was appointed spokesperson on enterprise, trade and employment. Kenny also reorganised his backroom staff. Phil Hogan was relieved of his formal role as director of organisation having failed to bring in a running mate in the five-seat Carlow-Kilkenny constituency. Flannery was appointed as head of organisation and strategy, and having retired as Rehab chief executive he was able to give full-time attention to the party. Gerry Naughton moved on after the summer of 2008. He was replaced as Political Director by Michael McLaughlin, a long-time Fine Gael member, a onetime local elections candidate and market research executive. Economist Andrew McDowell was later promoted as head of research.

Kenny told his colleagues that the party needed to show 'a new aggressiveness' when dealing with Bertie Ahern's new administration. But the electoral success in winning an additional 20 seats brought its own internal challenges. Kenny had to manage a larger group with more experience, and equally a group of hungry, ambitious young TDs who wanted increased media profiles on key political programmes and expressed strong views about the narrow gap between success and failure in the recent election. They wanted a direct say about how the party was going to be run. New deputies like Leo Varadkar and Lucinda Creighton sought a new concentration on policy and image rather than organisation and leadership. And they wanted the party to be younger and more urban in its orientation. 'We will have to embrace urban and suburban Ireland, adopt a more modern cosmopolitan image and develop policies that will appeal to the hundreds of thousands of uncommitted swing voters in cities, county towns and commuter belts across Ireland,' Varadkar argued.

There had been increased bickering about the influence of party officials and staff working for Kenny, and calls for a more aggressive presentation of Fine Gael policy. The new TDs sought greater control over policy formation and party organisation which prior to 2007 had largely been driven by Kenny and his key personnel. These tensions surface not long after the 2007 general election and continued right up to the leadership heave in June 2010. Ulick Burke was annoyed by his lack of consultation in the recruitment of senator Ciaran Cannon from the Progressive Democrats who would be a rival candidate in the Galway East constituency. Kenny lost his cool with Burke saying he had 'gone out on a fucking limb' for him in the 2007 general election. Fidelma Healy-Eames, a Galway-based senator and Lucinda Creighton led further criticism of the party's strategy. 'People are looking for a steady pair of hands, in terms of who is going to lead the next government. So they're looking for reassurance. I think we could communicate a little bit better, even setting out policies in national newspapers and how we conduct our press conferences and launches." There was short shrift from Kenny, and eventually Creighton walked out of the meeting. 'These things happen in parties all the time,' Richard Bruton said when the episode appeared in the national media. Creighton also sought to smooth over the row. 'Enda and I had a cup of tea a couple of days later. He was more than respectful and nice. We talked about where the party was going,' the Dublin South East TD explained. Kenny listened to the complaints from some of his colleagues and responded but without diluting the influence of his core team. A number of internal committees were subsequently established to plan for the next general election – with party deputies heading up groups on candidate selection, communications and policy development but significantly all three committees report to a steering committee controlled by the party leader.

To be in government after the next general election Fine Gael strategists set an objective of winning more than 60 Dáil seats. Frank Flannery even spoke about breaking the 70-seat barrier. The party has started taking the necessary steps to win extra Dáil seats with the recruitment of new candidates and the promotion of councillors seen as future TDs. But the constituency activity has unsettled some incumbent deputies.

'That is going to make life uneasy for many of the 51 that we have. Because if you are going for a second seat or a third seat and you don't get it, the person that loses out may not be the new person you are running and may be one of the existing [TDs],' Flannery admitted. Relations have been more strained than at any time since 2002 and a new dynamic has played out within the enlarged parliamentary party. 'You must have a professional organisation, which is why Fine Gael has this role of director of organisation and why I am in it because I am bad enough of a bastard and tough enough to make really unpopular decisions,' Flannery said, and 'that has its own impact from time to time, which sometimes will take the form of an apoplectic member of the frontbench.'

Many of these internal tensions have arisen from what might best be described as the pressures of Fine Gael's new ambition in the wake of unpredicted, and unprecedented, changes in the political landscape since 2007. Against this new background, the stakes have risen – party deputies are now competing with each other for possible ministerial positions as Irish politics was on the cusp of an electoral transformation not experienced since the 1927-32 emergence of Fianna Fáil to the detriment of Cumann na nGaedheal, the parent party of Fine Gael.

During the autumn of 2006 and the first half of 2007 Fine Gael had tip-toed around the Ahern payments controversy. But throughout the Taoiseach's final year in office, Kenny rounded on the Fianna Fáil leader. For some it was a case of over-compensation for previous caution but with the publication of the opening statement of the Mahon tribunal in June 2008 the opposition parties grew in confidence in their approach to the Ahern's payments issue. With Ahern's tribunal evidence in the public domain from June 2008 Fine Gael and the Labour Party were more aware of the issues involved in the payments controversy. 'The people can't have this fantasy land where you have money flying around in bags, in hotel rooms, in wardrobes and in political constituency offices. This is the time for the Taoiseach to say where he got this money from, who paid it to him and why he accepted it,' Kenny asserted.

Ahern endured a tortuous number of months after the formation of his third government in June 2007. He argued that the opposition was 'playing the man and not the ball' but in truth he was responsible for the failure to provide consistent and understandable answers to the still-multiplying questions about his financial affairs. The ongoing revelations at the tribunal dominated the political agenda and fuelled speculation about his retirement as Taoiseach. Fianna Fáil's post-election opinion poll slump in the autumn of 2007 bottomed out early in 2008 but voters were divided on whether or not Ahern should resign immediately. One opinion poll early in 2008 showed that 44 per cent said yes but 46 per cent said no. A substantial majority of voters, however, did not accept that Ahern had given the full story about his personal finances.

The new parliamentary term opened in late September 2007

with a Fine Gael motion condemning the Fianna Fáil Taoiseach. Kenny delivered a powerful critique of the impact of Ahern's evasiveness. 'Who will lead the debate on right and wrong, on being truthful and accountable at all times, on what is acceptable and unacceptable? [...] I do not want the children of this country growing up where nothing is ever "right" or even "wrong"; where all kinds of behaviour are tolerated and accepted; where the truth is not respected, because now everything falls into the cursed, convenient no-mans-land of permissiveness, where anything will do because everything goes.'

Kenny's response was now based on three lines of attack – it was wrong for a senior politician to take money from business people for his own use; it questioned Ahern's cooperation with the tribunal and he said he did not believe Ahern's account. 'The Taoiseach's explanations of lodgements to his accounts over two years have been riddled with inconsistency and received with incredulity. He has changed his stories as the tribunal's investigations uncovered more and more hard facts,' Kenny said. Fine Gael senator Eugene Regan became the party's unofficial tribunal spokesperson. Regan with his legal training pounced on the growing inconsistencies in Ahern's evidence. Leo Varadkar also illustrated the new combative attitude when he spoke about 'perjury'. Ahern was accused of hiding from the tribunal and of not paying his taxes.

'We have a Taoiseach who can't explain why very substantial monies went through his accounts, backed up with blind allegiance from minister after minister, from his own party, the Greens and the PDs,' Kenny said. When Kenny accused Cowen of being 'an accomplice to the deceit that is emanating from Dublin Castle' the Fianna Fáil deputy leader rounded on his opponent, 'I don't need lectures from you on my standards'.

The Ahern controversy was crowding out the government's ability to move the agenda onto other issues. The post-2007 period was also proving to be the most challenging time to be in government in over a decade. The economy was slowing – house and car sales dropped significantly while the live register increased. In January

2008 Kenny accused the government of economic mismanagement. 'We now have a government that has blown the boom. We have a government that has us ill-prepared for the economic squalls and challenges that are on the way.' Ahern's government seemed to have lost its touch having approved a number of decisions that caused public outrage including significant pay hikes for top earners in the public sector and increased numbers of junior ministers. Despite a wish to remain in office for longer in his third term, the inevitable happened in May 2008 when Ahern resigned as Fianna Fáil leader and as Taoiseach.

His successor Brian Cowen arrived in a blaze of glory. Fianna Fáil hit 42 per cent in a TNS mrbi opinion poll. The party's new leader had the highest satisfaction rating of all his rivals while satisfaction with the government jumped 13 points to 48 per cent. Fine Gael's support slipped to its lowest rating in over three years – Kenny's satisfaction was down four points to 35 per cent, 12 points behind Cowen and on par with Eamon Gilmore, the new Labour Party leader.

Cowen had repeatedly shown contempt for the Fine Gael leader. In a number of personalised attacks during the 2007 general election, he questioned Kenny's ability. Early in 2008 during a debate on the Ahern payments controversy, Cowen remarked that Kenny was 'neither qualified nor able' to assess Ahern's guilt. Cowen's withering put-down related to the correctness of Fine Gael questioning Ahern's integrity but taken with previous remarks – and Cowen's general attitude in parliamentary dealings with Kenny – the meaning was clear: I don't rate you.

There was a general assumption that Kenny would find Cowen too formidable an opponent. 'I'm fed up of listening to that type of argument from you,' the new Taoiseach snarled at Kenny in the Dáil in November 2008. But the Fine Gael leader dealt with Cowen's aggression far better than he ever got to grips with the verbal meanderings from Ahern. 'Everything he has turned his hand to since becoming Taoiseach has turned into a disaster,' Kenny remarked.

Cowen's honeymoon was incredibly short. The Lisbon Treaty referendum was beaten within weeks of his arrival into the Taoiseach's office. Relations with Kenny were strained when during the campaign the new Taoiseach antagonised Fine Gael supporters with comments about their activity levels and a description of Fianna Fáil as the most European party in the State. Over the following months Cowen faced the whirlwind of an international financial crisis and the legacy of the economic decisions taken during his own tenure as Finance Minister in the Ahern era. The government's fortunes were hit on every front – a banking crisis, a deteriorating fiscal situation, rising unemployment, and the necessity for an early budget to stabilise worsening exchequer finances which was followed by embarrassing climb-downs on medical cards for over-70s, education cuts and the postponement of a promised cervical cancer vaccination programme.

Within five months of Cowen becoming Taoiseach the government's credibility was in tatters, and Fianna Fáil's much heralded boast about being the only party to safely manage the economy was in ruins. The party lost its mantle of competency. Kenny continued to remind Cowen that as Finance Minister he was responsible for a series of policy decisions which exacerbated the national economic situation. The previous Ahern-led government had prime-pumped the property sector and effectively allowed public spending to spiral out of control. Ahern had sneered at Fine Gael's warnings about generous benchmarking pay awards but within a matter of years Cowen was seeking pay cuts to take back monies given without any real productivity or efficiency gains in the public sector.

Support for Fianna Fáil and its new leader collapsed to the lowest levels recorded since the TNS mrbi *Irish Times* polling began in 1982. Satisfaction with Cowen halved to 26 per cent. The collapse in support for Fianna Fáil and for Cowen was not just a phenomenon confined to opinion polls in the autumn of 2008. Support continued to decline in 2009 – in one February 2009 opinion poll, dissatisfaction with the government's performance hit 82 per cent. In the wake of buoyant opposition poll ratings, Kenny claimed there was 'a sense of terror within government'.

Kenny's party was in prime position for the first time in the history of professional polling. From the latter stages of 2008 Fine Gael consistently headed Fianna Fáil in the opinion polls – the gap rising to over 10 points in some surveys. The party was achieving consistent ratings in the early 30s in the Red C *Sunday Business Post* series and in the spring of 2009 marked a new milestone in recording three consecutive 30-plus results in the TNS mrbi surveys. Fianna Fáil was punished not just for unpopular fiscal decisions but, more damagingly for its longer-term ability to turn around its electoral prospects, the party was also being blamed for making a bad situation much worse. The government was no longer seen as competent. And the replacement of Ahern with Cowen also damaged Fianna Fáil in the personality rankings – the new leader's party political aggressive approach was not well received by the public.

At his party conference in November 2008, Kenny attacked the government's economic record and controversially called for a suspension of the national pay deal. The party was prepared to alienate some public sector support – knowing it would most likely move in any event from Fianna Fáil to Labour.

'Wage restraint in the short term is preferable to job losses in the long-term,' Kenny said. He decided to take a 5 per cent cut in his TDs salary in October 2008. While the move caught his party colleagues by surprise it succeeded in removing Kenny from public criticism over political salaries and perks.

Following the autumn 2008 budget Kenny embarked upon a round of regional meetings. The party invested €100,000 in a 'Government Mistakes. You Pay' campaign. As in previous campaigns, an online presence was a key component to connect with party members and voters. But the task was easier now. In many ways, the government was doing the work for the opposition. Richard Bruton also consolidated his reputation, and was to the fore as Fine Gael proposed income cuts for State employees earning above €100,000 and a freeze in pay, bonuses and increments. The party called on the government to remove the boards and senior personnel in the financial institutions trading under a State guarantee scheme and also for changes at the financial regulatory authority. 'It is nothing personal,' Kenny said, 'we need to send out a message to the international markets that this country is taking a different direction and is not afraid to make decisive decisions.'

Fine Gael also adopted several opportunistic positions including opposing a move to withdraw an automatic entitlement to medical cards from the over-70s regardless of their income level. Thousands of elderly people protested outside Leinster House while inside the chamber the Dáil debated a Fine Gael motion seeking a reversal of the decision.

'Your Judas response to the elderly will be your epitaph,' Kenny said at the conclusion of the debate. With the government foundering, Fine Gael seemed to catch the public mood. And even with the focus on the economic crisis, the party did not lose sight of its populist crime agenda – Kenny proposed 25-year mandatory sentences for murder. In response to the gangland murder of an innocent bystander in the latter part of 2008, Kenny caught the public revulsion better than Cowen. 'This is war, Taoiseach, and it's a war that you do not appear to be winning,' Kenny told the Cowen in the Dáil.

Any lingering doubts about the solidity of the Fine Gael opinion poll support were dispelled with the results of the 2009 local and European elections and two by-elections in June 2009. Prior to polling Kenny had declared, 'We are the party of the future. Just as Fianna Fáil dominated politics for the past decade, I feel our opportunity, in this crisis, is coming to dominate Irish politics for the next ten years.'

Fianna Fáil had received a bloody nose at the local elections in 2002 – the party won 32 per cent of the first preference vote and lost more than 80 seats. The performance in 2009 was even worse as Fianna Fáil lost another 84 seats. The gap between Fianna Fáil and Fine Gael in local government politics was 105 seats in favour of Fianna Fáil in 1999. Five years later the gap was down to only nine seats. Following the 2009 local elections Fine Gael had 122 more local council seats than its long-time dominant rival. Fine Gael won 43 extra council seats taking its national total to 340 councillors. And for the first time since 1927 Fine Gael outperformed Fianna Fáil in a national election. Fianna Fáil under Cowen had been thumped by the voters, and, once more, in an electoral contest Kenny's Fine Gael enjoyed success. In a depressing day for Fianna Fáil the party also lost its European Parliament seat in Dublin and was totally out of contention in the two by-election contests. Fine Gael had gone into the European campaign confident of holding four of its five seats. The retirement of Avril Doyle weakened the party's chances of holding two seats in the three-seat East constituency. The party was always likely to struggle to repeat the 2004 success which proved to be the case. But Fine Gael had a victory in 2009 which generated even more media and public attention than the 2004 European success.

The by-election campaign in Dublin South had taken on a national significance when RTÉ's well-known economics editor George Lee announced his decision to seek the Fine Gael nomination. Lee had previously toyed with an invitation to stand for the party in Dun Laoghaire in the 2002 general election. The 2009 approach met with a more favourable response. Lee was one of a long list of names the party had identified as possible candidates for a variety of electoral contests. The RTÉ broadcaster was considered an ideal candidate for the Dublin South by-election caused by the death of long-time Fianna Fáil minister, Seamus Brennan. Frank Flannery and Tom Curran made the first approach to Lee and received a positive response. 'The reason I joined their party was simply their vision for a new Ireland and the way we should run the country. They were neither an extreme right or left party and have a pragmatic approach to dealing with problems. Their leadership style is that they are open to suggestions and willing to listen and understand people, which is so important in today's politics,' Lee said.

Lee's high public profile combined with his authority on economic matters meant the contest in Dublin South was as good as over before the campaign had even started. Recruiting Mairead McGuinness for the 2004 European elections was important to the development of Kenny's leadership as she joined at a time when the party was still rebuilding and needed the injection of faith in the future which her decision provided. But in 2009 the capture of Lee gave Fine Gael a massive credibility boost, and delivered into the party's ranks someone the public trusted as an economic expert at a time of unprecedented financial turmoil. Lee was elected on the first count in Dublin South. He received just over 27,000 first preferences – an impressive 53 per cent of the vote – while Paschal Donohoe increased his vote in Dublin Central and positioned himself as a very good bet for a Dáil seat at the next general election. 'His decision to stand for Fine Gael has created a phenomenon,' Kenny said about the new Dublin South TD with the prospect that Lee's high profile may be used to drum up excitement for Fine Gael at regional meetings prior to the general election.

The electoral contests in 2009 placed Fianna Fáil's hegemonic position under threat and if repeated in a general election the party would face a parliamentary cull akin to the 2002 Fine Gael meltdown. Yet, despite the upswing in support for Fine Gael, Kenny once more faced sniping at his performance and his ability to be Taoiseach. Like Pat Rabbitte before him, Eamon Gilmore produced sharper Dáil and media contributions than Kenny. Gilmore received much positive media comment for his performances but, again like Rabbitte, has not as yet managed to turn his higher personal satisfaction ratings into a tangible benefit for his party vis-à-vis Kenny. Despite an increase in its own support base, Labour remains behind Fine Gael in the ratings. The two parties continued to work on parliamentary tactics in Leinster House but with no prospect of a sequel to the Mullingar Accord: 'I don't think we will [repeat the pre-election alliance]. Eamon Gilmore has absolute right to keep his options open, he said that. I'm committing to making Fine Gael the largest party in the next Dáil . . . and [we will] put forward our own proposals,' Kenny said.

Fianna Fáil has also continued to target the Fine Gael leader, and to question his ability. Government minister Willie O'Dea in late summer 2008 described Kenny as 'the same tired puppet with the same people in the background jerking his strings'. Kenny was criticised for failing to show strong leadership, and for not winning confidence in his capabilities with the wider electorate. 'Some people are dissatisfied. But they don't want to say that. They all appear to be hearing in their constituencies that we've got the wrong man and Richard [Bruton] is doing the business,' one Fine Gael insider was quoted as saying in the *Irish Independent* in early 2009.

Comparisons were increasingly made with Bruton, who enjoyed a high profile with many assured performances during the economic crisis. A question in a TNS mrbi opinion poll in November 2008 found that when asked which of the most senior figures in Fine Gael would be a better leader in the economic downturn, 46 per cent opted for Bruton, 28 per cent for Kenny and 26 per cent had no opinion. The results led to the headline, 'new poll questions Kenny's leadership potential.' But the poll results failed to generate any negative reaction from within Fine Gael. 'There is the same chance of a change in leadership in Fine Gael as there is of Bertie Ahern coming back as Fianna Fáil leader,' Charlie Flanagan said. Bruton remained deeply loyal although he identified a key weakness for Kenny. 'I think that people who see him on the small box for 30 seconds don't see the full picture of Enda Kenny.'

Talk about replacing the Mayo man with his deputy leader failed, however, to recognise that Fine Gael had previously turned to apparent popular heavy hitters only to find when they were elevated to the top position that they did not have skills to lead the party. Fine Gael had learned the hard way that strong parliamentary performance and a good media profile does not automatically deliver electoral success. The leadership issue was raised with Brian Hayes as the results were being declared in the 2009 local and European election. The Dublin South West TD was exasperated at having the topic raised once more: 'What does Enda Kenny have to do? He wins another 40 seats at local authority level, he has a stunning victory in a Dublin by-election, we're going to be the biggest party at a European parliamentary level. What does this man have to do before people get off his back?' Hayes asked. It was a fair reaction to a question that has dogged Kenny since he surprised almost everyone in politics by putting his name forward for the leadership Fine Gael in 2001. 'I'm good at switching off the negative,' he said, 'Look, if you went around with the negative images and thoughts and all that, you'd pack it in and go and hide. You can't let it get to you.'

Kenny's personal satisfaction ratings remained poor – in an opinion poll in *The Irish Times* in early September 2009 only 29 per cent were satisfied with how he was doing his job. The figure was at first glance good when compared to the 15 per cent who were satisfied with Cowen's performance. But the Fianna Fáil leader was heading an increasingly discredited government, implementing a policy of severe fiscal cutbacks. More worryingly for many in Fine Gael was the 47 per cent who said they were satisfied with Eamon Gilmore – the highest of all the party leaders. But while the Fine Gael party figures were over 30 per cent, Kenny was secure. There was a relative stability in the party's opinion poll rating throughout most of 2009 and Kenny also had the benefit of having delivered strong European and local election results.

In the October 2009 Red C series for the *Sunday Business Post* Fine Gael was placed at 35 per cent – a ten-point lead over Fianna Fáil, with the Labour Party back in third place on 19 per cent. The following month Fine Gael support increased to its highest level since the Red C polling series began, as Fianna Fáil support levels indicated that the party was set to lose about half the 77 seats won in 2007. The party poll ratings were sufficient for Kenny to predict the possibility of an overall majority for Fine Gael in a radio interview on RTÉ. The radio appearance was overshadowed by media reports of a text message sent to Fine Gael members asking them to contact the radio station in support of the party leader.

Despite Fine Gael's position in the opinion polls there was still internal concern with Kenny's leadership. If anything, the period following the local and European elections in June 2009 fed those concerns. Kenny's poor personal satisfaction ratings were no surprise to many parliamentary party members who met strong resistance to their leader in their constituencies. The negativity was more pronounced in urban areas and among women voters. Fine Gael's key strategists agreed that the party suffered from months of drift in the aftermath of the local and European elections. The party representatives – and not just Kenny – performed poorly. They were reactive rather than proactive, and repeatedly seemed to be responding to other agendas rather than their own.

There was also growing annoyance within the parliamentary party at the lack of consultation on key policy and strategy decisions. The simmering resentment was very much directed at Kenny's team of advisors, who were viewed as having too much power – to the detriment of the majority of the party's elected representations. The mood worsened in late October 2009 when Kenny went public with a new party policy on political reform at the annual Fine Gael presidential dinner. The party leader announced his commitment to a referendum on the abolition of the Seanad, a reduction in the number of TDs and a review of the electoral system. The public would be consulted on the proposals within the first year of a Fine Gael government.

But there had been no consultation with Kenny's political colleagues. The announcement had been conveyed to members of the parliamentary party by text message earlier in the day. Nevertheless, prominent figures supported the move including Richard Bruton and several of the party's best performing senators, Frances Fitzgerald, Jerry Buttimer, Paschal Donohoe and Liam Twomey.

Despite this show of support, the announcement met with considerable annoyance from other parliamentary party members, especially due to the failure to canvass their opinion. Several senators went public with their outright opposition to the plan. 'I am a bit shocked really by what I heard. . . It's a bit of a bolt out of the blue,' John Paul Phelan admitted. Nicky McFadden bluntly responded: 'I have already made my feelings well known.' There was speculation that the announcement was an attempt to regain the political initiative after being outflanked by the Labour leader during the recent expenses controversy, which led to John O'Donoghue's resignation as Ceann Comhairle.

'Leadership is about leading. You can talk around these things for months,' Kenny explained in a subsequent radio interview. Further explanation was offered in a newspaper article in the leader's name, which described the move as 'the most fundamental change in our political system in 70 years.' Kenny asserted his right as leader to determine policy. He had taken a 'leadership decision,' the parliamentary party meeting was told in late October. The meeting lasted over three hours and there was strong opposition to the leader's actions. Even those who backed the proposal – or who were neutral on the idea – had reservations about the manner in which the decision had been taken, and then publicly announced.

There were continuing internal difficulties towards the end of 2009. Kenny faced criticism over his decision to back government proposals to reduce the blood alcohol limit. John Deasy tabled a motion at a parliamentary party meeting opposing the measure. Initially, the party hierarchy planned to call a vote on the parliamentary party motion and knock down Deasy's call for a free Dáil vote on the legislation. But as the meeting continued, it was clear that there was support for the alternative argument. A decision on the party's stance was deferred when it looked like the motion would be carried. These debates on political reform and drink driving created opportunities for some TDs and Senators to indirectly assert their position on the leadership issue. Many were still smarting over Kenny's solo-run on political reform and as some saw it, bouncing the party into favouring the abolition of the Seanad and reducing the size of the Dáil.

Familiar themes were again mentioned including poor communication between the leader and many of his parliamentary party colleagues, as well as the dominant influence of Kenny's backroom advisors. The Seanad announcement had arrived by text message. When the former PD senator Ciaran Cannon from Galway East joined Fine Gael, the party's sitting TD in the constituency – and other members of the parliamentary party – also received the news by text message. An increasing number of politicians were unhappy about not being consulted on major party decisions. 'We were telling them fair and straight you should consult with us rather than going on Friday afternoon TV to define party policy,' one TD was reported as saying.

12

George Lee

Bombshell. The word littered conversations in the environs of Leinster House and much wider afield on 8 February 2010. The reason was George Lee's dramatic decision to walk away from his nascent political career. There was genuine shock in Fine Gael circles. 'It beggars belief,' Lucinda Creighton said. Simon Coveney was 'annoyed'. Olivia Mitchell used the word, 'gobsmacked'. Enda Kenny, who had had pre-warning of Lee's decision, chose initially, at least, to remain silent.

Lee had been Fine Gael's big catch. His arrival had given the party the whiff of celebrity. The former RTÉ broadcaster was a national figure – an excellent communicator with a strong knowledge of economics; he was somebody the public trusted, as evidenced by the 27,768 people who gave him their first preference vote in the Dublin South by-election on 6 June 2009. But he had lasted a mere eight months as a Fine Gael public representative.

'I am unconstrained by RTÉ,' Lee had declared on the day of his election. But there were signs that he was not enjoying his new-found freedom and was struggling to adjust to the career transition from broadcasting to politics. Several of his Fine Gael colleagues were aware of the situation. Padraic McCormack spoke with Lee when he addressed a meeting in Galway in September 2009. 'I remember sitting down with him for a chat afterwards. He wasn't an easy man to get conversation going with but I asked him if he had any regrets about leaving his job in RTÉ and he replied, "Well, the jury is out on that one yet" – and he was only three months in the job at that stage.' Wexford TD Michael D'Arcy thought Lee's 'body language' was wrong before the Christmas 2009 break. But they all believed this was a normal enough feeling as Lee put down roots after his meteoric arrival onto the political stage.

Lee's impatience with his standing featured in a radio interview in mid-January 2010. Miriam O'Callaghan asked him about his ambitions to be a minister. She had posed a similar question the previous June when Lee was a guest on her summer television chat show. Then the newly elected Fine Gael TD replied: 'I'm number seven in a family of eight – I don't care who's at the top, I just want to contribute.' But the answer in January 2010 had a very different tone and gave a clear indication of Lee's frustration with his role in Fine Gael. 'I'm not making any assumptions but I will tell you this: I won't be hanging around for a decade for anything like that unless I have an influence. I'm not going to waste my life.' The *Irish Independent* picked up the remarks:'Sabre-rattling George sends a message to his leader,' the headline on the article read.

Kenny's delay in reshuffling his frontbench to create space for Lee had become a source of ongoing comment. Indeed, from the day of his election there was an expectation that Lee would assume a leading economic role within Fine Gael. His former RTÉ newsroom colleagues at a going-away party presented him with a briefcase which, they joked, he could use when he was a government minister. In the words of one parliamentary reporter Lee was, 'The golden boy of the opposition'. Miriam Lord dubbed him 'The People's Princess'.

In the immediate aftermath of the stunning by-election result in Dublin South, Kenny made it clear that an early frontbench reshuffle was unlikely. 'We'll consider these things in the times ahead,' he said. Moving Bruton from the finance position was not a realistic option so creating a new role in the general economic area was likely. Kenny had made room for newcomers previously, most recently for James Reilly and Leo Varadkar. But as Kenny saw it, Lee was very different from other new TDs – he did not need an immediate formal frontbench role to create profile or to develop policy.

Indeed, Lee's public profile was far in excess of any 'normal' arrival into Leinster House. Few TDs had access to the type of media platforms available to the Dublin South politician. He enjoyed frequent appearances on all national radio and television stations. For example, he was back in his former home in RTÉ within weeks of the by-election success as the first guest on the summer chat show hosted by Miriam O'Callaghan. The print media also eagerly reported on his utterances. He was in the unique position of being able to carve out media space for whatever stances he adopted.

Lee delivered his maiden speech shortly after 12 noon on 10 June 2009. There was more than the normal collection of deputies in the Dáil chamber – seats on the press gallery were filled like they would when the Taoiseach was taking questions from the leaders of the main opposition parties. The maiden speech was a solid performance from a professional communicator. 'The last couple of weeks have been a complete change of life for me. Given the outcome of the by-election, there is no going back now,' Lee predicted.

The new Dáil deputy disputed Cowen's insistence that his government continued to have a mandate to remain in office. 'I do not agree because I just received a mandate from the people of Dublin South that is equal to anybody's on the other side of the House. . . every member in this House has a mandate but nobody was given a mandate to govern from the people. The mandate for governing is an arrangement with the members of this House. . . based on a premise for the economy which turned out to be false. The government has an agreement but not a mandate to govern.'

The speech provided a review of the national economic environment but was light on specific policy detail, although it did contain a number of strong sound bites. 'We have heard a lot about rescuing banks and the public finances but we have not heard enough about the plight of people,' Lee asserted. He expressed thanks for the welcome he had received the previous day from all sides in the

House, but had no difficulty throwing a punch at the government side: 'While I was here yesterday there were three ministers over there asleep. . . it is just not good enough, in my view, that people in this House can take that kind of attitude to the difficulty that people are suffering.'

Lee shared his speaking time with his new colleague Michael Ring. When the newly-elected deputy ran over time, Ring told the House: 'If he wants five more minutes I am happy to share it. This man has a bright future and I do not mind giving way to talent.' Lee took advantage of the additional time and then concluded his speech with another sharp remark: 'I got a message loud and clear from the people of Dublin South, which I know they want me to deliver to the government of the 30th Dáil, and that message is, "Come in number 30, your time is up."'

The speech was widely covered by the media with reports by political correspondents and parliamentary sketch writers. By way of contrast, the maiden speech by Maureen O'Sullivan, who had been elected in another by-election on the same day as Lee, – an equally thoughtful contribution – received only passing reference.

The June 2009 by-election results in Dublin South and Dublin Central did not help the government's parliamentary position but it still had a majority of Dáil seats. The combined government total came to 84 comprising 76 Fianna Fáil TDs, 6 Green representatives and 2 independents – Jackie Healy-Rae and Michael Lowry who had formal deals to support Cowen's coalition. The opposition side – boosted by the arrival of Lee and O'Sullivan – came to 81. The coalition won a confidence motion in early June 2009 by a margin of six votes. Cowen's government had taken a battering in the European and local elections but the conventional wisdom at that time was that the two coalition partners would stick together and would not consult the electorate again until early 2012.

Lee was certainly a powerful draw at party events. Fine Gael constituencies all over the country wanted him to speak at meetings. He was also a main attraction when accompanying Kenny to public events such as the national ploughing championships in late

September 2009. There were requests for autographs and every-body wanted their photograph taken with Fine Gael's new star. The party claimed over 800 applications were received for the position of parliamentary assistant to the new Dublin South TD.

A former party press officer Karl Brophy offered some strategic advice on how to handle the new recruit. Writing in *The Irish Times* Brophy concluded that, 'Lee is best deployed not in the media, where cynical former colleagues will delight in having him defend political hypocrisies, but on the stump, up and down the country, where voters will delight in actually meeting him. Kenny should be dispatching the former RTÉ economics editor to public meetings in every town and suburb in the country with thousands of party membership forms in his back pocket. The more members Fine Gael has, the more ownership of a political movement it will have devolved to the public and it will have guaranteed more votes whenever the general election does roll around.'

Kenny was happy not to burden his new recruit with the chores of a frontbench role. The strategy was to gradually introduce Lee to the workings of the party and political life. He had had after all no previous political experience, but there was no intention of allow-ing him to wilt on the sidelines. 'Everybody in the party has a real part to play. George Lee is an exceptional attraction to politics in so many ways. And I'll put it to you . . . the thing about George Lee and people like him is that you should not allow them to become part of – I won't use the word that John Kelly used years ago – but ruined by the pressure of party politics,' Kenny asserted.

The first sign that Kenny was preparing to move Lee into a frontline economic role came in early autumn 2009 with his appointment as chairperson of a new party committee on economic policy. The role, Kenny said, provided Lee with a remit to drive party policy. Lee did not, however, exploit the potential of the role, and the committee never met, not to mind ever publishing policy proposals. Neither was Lee an active participant at parliamentary party meetings, where he could have raised specific policies that he want to pursue. A new business forum also presented Lee with an opportunity to carve out a distinctive policy niche.

Under the banner 'Working Together,' Kenny said the purpose of the business forum was 'to outline the party's approach to addressing the economic crisis and job creation, but even more importantly, the meetings are designed to hear the views of business people on what they need to protect existing jobs and create new ones.' But the forum also allowed Fine Gael to showcase its new star attraction. Lee chaired the meetings and shared the platform with Kenny, Bruton, Varadkar, Coveney and Kieran O'Donnell, the party's deputy finance spokesperson. 'It's not like the country has stepped on a landmine, it's like the country has stepped on three landmines, one on top of another,' Lee told a forum audience in Dublin in early November 2009.

But despite this involvement Lee later said he was not enjoying his new political role. He saw Fine Gael as hawking him around the country and trading on his high public profile. As a broadcast journalist he was unaccustomed to sharing prime position. And without a frontbench position, he apparently did not consider himself a serious player. But he failed to take advantage of the enormous opportunities presented with the economic policy committee or to appreciate how easily he could exploit his media profile to promote specific policy preferences. He also seemed to have made little effort to build relationships within his new party. 'In the Dáil, TDs go for coffee and chat about politics, but you'd see George on his own most of the time,' Galway East TD Paul Connaughton said.

Lee's first significant public appearance as a Fine Gael deputy had actually come when Bruton was unavailable to attend the MacGill Summer School in County Donegal in July 2010. Lee's appearance was eagerly anticipated. The summer school speech attracted column inches that matched those given to another attendee, Finance Minister Brian Lenihan. Most established Fine Gael politicians could only look in envy at the profile of the rookie deputy. 'What Ireland needs is a new era of responsibility, an era where governments take responsibility and stand up for ordinary people in the face of powerful vested interests,' Lee asserted.

He added that this new era would ensure that 'banks are held to account for the massive public rescue effort they have been gifted with and are forced to play a far more active part in the restoration of credit flows throughout the economy.'

The substance of the speech was populist; the tone headline-grabbing. Little of what Lee had to say was particularly radical. His approach to policy was orthodox, and it was easy to see him being comfortable as a Fine Gael figure in government, or for that matter, in different times, in a Fianna Fáil-led administration. Over the following months Lee's Dáil contributions were widely covered by the media – and on numerous occasions his utterances were reported ahead of Fine Gael's finance spokesperson Richard Bruton. But Lee was firm in backing Bruton and Fine Gael economic policy from Fianna Fáil criticism and allegations of being unpatriotic. 'Now that Richard is exposing the huge double or quits gamble on bankers and developers that Fianna Fáil is proposing to take with the Irish economy, they are trying something similar again.' He was also astute in defending Fine Gael banking policy from attack by Brian Lenihan:

'Almost every independent expert in the land shares Fine Gael's opposition to the way the government is going about solving this crisis. Yet Fianna Fáil is asking us to trust them on this one. But this is the party whose leader repeatedly assured young Irish families back in 2005 and 2006 that house prices then were based on "strong economic fundamentals". We now know that at that time he was receiving exactly the opposite advice from the world's foremost experts on house prices and banking stability at the IMF. Why should the public trust them now?'

Lee adopted somewhat independent stances on the declining budget finances ahead of the December 2009 budget. Fianna Fáil claimed his view on the extent of the necessary fiscal correction – Lee said a €4bn correction was 'too much' – was at odds with Fine Gael policy. He warned that too sharp a correction risked further depressing the economy, but the difference with what Bruton was saying was marginal. 'He was, in effect, our de facto enterprise spokesman and he was excellent at selling Fine Gael policy. I would say his real skills were not in the policy area – he was good on policy but he was just such a superb communicator,' one party officer says.

By the time the Dáil had adjourned at Christmas 2009, Lee had been a TD for a mere six months. The Dáil had actually only met on 53 occasions since the by-election success. But Lee was unhappy with his lot. Early in 2010 Olivia O'Leary used her radio column on RTÉ to warn Fine Gael that they had to 'use or lose' their new recruit. 'If you are not going to use him, give him back to us,' O'Leary remarked. In early February in a reference to his high pro-file without a frontbench role, Miriam Lord wrote that 'George must be itching to get out of showbiz and into serious politics.'

Kenny had initially delayed reshuffling his frontbench until after a much-speculated change in Cowen's cabinet lineup but by the start of 2010, Cowen had still not moved any of his ministerial team. A number of Fine Gael TDs including Michael D'Arcy offered to approach Kenny on Lee's behalf. 'I went to speak with George on the basis that there were four backbench TDs who were prepared to go to Enda and ask him to promote George to the front bench,' D'Arcy recalled. Lee asked them to wait as he was due to meet Kenny himself. When D'Arcy asked how the meeting had gone: 'He gave me the impression that it had went in the right direction.' The direction was, however, back to RTÉ.

Lee met Kenny at the start of February to inform him of his intention to quit national politics. The party leader sought to change Lee's mind. The frontbench position on economic planning – which would have been secured within a matter of months – was put on the table but Lee turned it down. The offer was made 'under duress', he believed. The two men had a second meeting which ended with Lee saying he would consider his position over the weekend. Some Fine Gael strategists believe a letter was subse-quently sent to Kenny, but if such correspondence does exist it has never been published.

By Wednesday 8 February 2010, Lee had made his decision.

Kenny received a phone call around 12 noon from the Dublin South TD. Lee was confirming his plan to resign – immediately and not just from Fine Gael but also from Dáil Éireann. Within a few minutes Lee sent a letter of resignation to the Clerk of the Dáil.

A media statement was issued: 'I have done my best to play a positive contribution to the national debate and to efforts to find a solution for many of the country's economic problems. The reality, however, is that despite my best efforts, I have had virtually no influence or input into shaping Fine Gael's economic policies at this most critical time. The role I have been playing within the party has been very limited and I have found this to be personally unfulfilling.'

There was a real sense of bewilderment in Fine Gael – and, in truth, also in the other political parties. Most TDs saw the decision as premature and lacking judgement. Lee's constituency colleague Olivia Mitchell was one of many who sought to put some rationale on the decision. 'I think it was a kind of a shock to him the kind of life it was . . . I think he probably missed the immediate impact of the 20-second sound bite on TV, that it's not the same when you're in politics. It's a hard-slog. The daily life of a TD is not the same as the glamour of a TV career.'

Leo Varadkar caught the mood in Fine Gael in accepting that the decision was a bad one for the party but that Lee himself was throwing away a great opportunity despite not having been elevated immediately. 'But he was offered a frontbench position and he didn't want it. He chaired a policy committee which never sat and he never called a meeting of it. He wanted to be consulted on economic policy but he never produced a single paper so I think it's a sad day for all of us.'

Nevertheless, there was a consensus in Fine Gael that the journalist-turned-politician could have been handled better as he made the transition from RTÉ to Leinster House. 'He wasn't handled particularly well and he was wasn't managed particularly well. Hopefully there's a lesson for us in Fine Gael. You can't just throw people in at the deep end and let them sink or swim. You have to help and guide them,' Lucinda Creighton said.

There was an acceptance that Fine Gael would be damaged. Simon Coveney was blunt in his reaction: 'I don't care what the spin doctors in Fine Gael say. This is damaging to Fine Gael. This is a significant setback. It's not a mortal wound by any stretch of the imagination but it is a setback. There's no point in trying to spin it any other way.'

The bombshell announcement immediately altered the day's news agenda. Lee started explaining his dramatic decision on RTÉ Radio One's *News at One* and spent the rest of the day being interviewed on a variety of radio and television programmes, only finishing close to midnight with Vincent Browne on TV3.

As he did the rounds of television and radio studios it became increasingly obvious that there had not been a major difference of opinion with Fine Gael on any significant policy matter. If anything, Lee was offering no clear reason why he wanted out aside from an unhappiness that Fine Gael had sought to capitalise on his high public appeal. 'I'm not there to be used just for my celebrity or [to] draw a crowd,' he said.

He downplayed his appointment as chairperson of the party's economic policy committee and the national business forum. He said he was unhappy at being unable to make an input into the party's economic policy. He felt he was being cold-shouldered and had had 'minimal involvement' with Richard Bruton. 'I had a maximum of two or three conversations with Richard Bruton in a total nine months period. I don't know how my relationship is with [him],' he said.

Despite all the media interviews Lee gave on 8 February 2010, it was several days before any significant policy difference was mentioned. The following weekend in the *Sunday Independent*, Lee was highly critical of the approach being pursued by Kenny and Bruton:

'They are afraid to be different. Do they have any confidence to offer a real alternative? Do they even know what is going on? Looking back to the 2007 general election, they got it wrong. And they are sitting there with the same advisors telling them they're going to get it right, and anyone with a different idea gets shut out. We have a consensus economy; nobody has rocked the boat and look where we are. They lack confidence. All they can do is make it personal.'

Lee's exit had not been prompted by any significant policy or political difference, leading Fionnan Sheehan to later write in the *Irish Independent*: 'After a week of blanket coverage we still do not know what he had to offer, what his policies were and why he failed to grasp the basic essentials that confront any new member of Dáil Éireann.' A phone text survey on RTÉ's *Liveline* had garnered 16,000 responses with 83 per cent backing Lee. But the survey was a mere talking point and its unscientific nature meant it added little value to public discourse. The first serious measure of public opinion actually showed division over Lee's decision to exit politics. A Millward Brown/IMS survey on 14 February reported that 45 per cent thought Lee was correct to resign against 43 per cent who said he was wrong.

Lee's ability to automatically return to RTÉ also divided opinion. The one-year non-renewal leave of absence arrangement surprised many people. A clear impression had been given that the arrangement applied only to the by-election period and that having been elected to Dáil Éireann, Lee had severed his ties with RTÉ. In the words of a hard-hitting editorial in *The Irish Times*, 'Mr Lee can be comforted in the knowledge that he made a financially risk-free decision. He can return to RTÉ where his salary and pension are guaranteed.'

Eoghan Harris – who later wrote about the 'panic attack at the prospect of being permanently cut off from Montrose' – speculated that financial considerations and the long political working day might have influenced the decision. Lee took exception to comments by Brian Hayes that he had complained about 'a major reduction in his income' following his move from RTÉ into political life. Hayes had been director of elections for the Dublin South by-election and, like many in the party, felt a sense of betrayal at the premature resignation.

Lee had taken a salary cut in moving from RTÉ where it was widely reported he earned a minimum of €150,000 and, like other broadcasters at the national station, he had the ability to generate additional income from public appearances and other outside activities such as chairing conferences. As a backbench TD, Lee's basic salary was €92,000 and the job came with a generous expenses system. An appointment as a government minister would have returned Lee to his journalism salary but with Cowen's coalition having survived a very difficult end to 2009, it was thought likely a general election might be as far away as the spring of 2012.

Senior Fine Gael strategists were at their weekly Monday management meeting when the news broke. They immediately went into crisis mode. From the outset the view was to let Lee have his say. 'When we heard him on *Liveline* we knew the situation could be managed. His targets kept changing and the callers who supported him were attacking the political system not Enda Kenny or Fine Gael,' one official said, who also believed that the more Lee spoke, the less immediately damaging his resignation became for Kenny.

The party deliberately put Leo Varadkar forward as their representative on RTÉ's *Frontline* television programme, which cleared its agenda to deal with the resignation of the backbench opposition TD. Varadkar was a good choice – a young TD who had developed a clear policy niche since his election in 2007. The Dublin West deputy also undermined Lee when he revealed that he had asked for feedback on some policy proposals – but Lee had never responded.

The resignation of the Dublin South TD could not have come at a worse time for Kenny. The year had started badly with a number of poor media interviews and there was increasing discontent among a number of the parliamentary party. Kenny's initial reaction came in a written media statement. A decision was taken not to publicly criticise Lee. 'I had anticipated a very important role for George in the coming period with Fine Gael,' Kenny said. He later said he had 'held out brilliant opportunities for George Lee coming into politics' and that he was a 'serious contender' for ministerial office.

Lee, in a departing flourish, created an opportunity for Kenny's critics. There was, he said 'certainly lots of large mutterings at the moment in relation to the leader's position. It's not something I'm involved in. . . it's for other people to say how that will play out.' Kenny's advisors were keen to talk down speculation that the leader's internal critics were about to seize upon the embarrassment at losing Lee to mount a heave. As they monitored the media interviews they sensed that through his own words – and the lack of a significant political issue for his resignation – Lee was lessening the impact of the resignation. 'People outside Fine Gael would like there to be instability. The party has learned over the years that the stability that Enda Kenny has brought the party is important,' a Fine Gael advisor said when briefing the media.

But the departure of Lee only added another item to the list for those who were agitating for a leadership change. There was a growing belief within a section of the parliamentary party that the leadership issue had to be addressed one way or the other. Kenny's opponents believed that if Richard Bruton moved, the Mayo man would most likely stand aside. But Bruton had not signalled his intention to move against Kenny, a fact which Kenny's backers talked up even in the whirlwind of Lee's exit. 'Richard has offered nothing but the strongest support. He recognises cohesion, and he has been absolutely consistent in his support for the leader,' a Fine Gael spokesperson said.

The possibility of moving against Kenny was discussed but there was a general view – even among those who favoured a change – that the timing was wrong, and that an immediate heave based on Lee's resignation was not in the best interests of Fine Gael. Lucinda Creighton spoke for many of her colleagues in insisting that Kenny's role as leader could not be judged solely on the Lee debacle and that there were issues for party handlers in how they had dealt with the Dublin South TD.

The frontbench meeting in the aftermath of Lee's resignation lasted for almost two hours. Kenny was left in little doubt that several of his colleagues were deeply frustrated with his poor media performances and the damage arising from the Lee resignation. Brian Hayes bluntly told Kenny he had to 'up his game'. Simon Coveney warned that he needed to prepare better for set-piece media appearances and in the Dáil chamber. There was recognition for the work done since 2002 but the political situation had now moved on – Kenny had nothing to prove as Fine Gael leader, he now had to convince the wider public that he could be Taoiseach. Kenny heard honest assessments of his performance. He pledged to take the criticism from his colleagues on board. 'What I'm going to do now is be myself and I'm going to speak out from my heart on the issues that I believe Ireland needs for change,' Kenny said in the aftermath of the frontbench meeting.

The matter was also poured over at a meeting of the Fine Gael parliamentary party. The meeting ended with what Tom Hayes called full endorsement of Kenny's leadership. But not before several TDs and senators had openly set out their frustrations, among them Lucinda Creighton, John Paul Phelan and Damien English. Despite the government's weakened position the majority view was still that the coalition would limp on until 2012. Kenny's detractors were unconvinced about his ability to take the party into government. In truth, several frontbench members had given up on Kenny. A growing anti-Kenny camp believed that Bruton should replace Kenny. Many privately speculated that Kenny would step aside if Bruton withdrew his support.

There were divided loyalties among many Fine Gael TDs who had been supporters of the Mayo man but who had concluded that he had taken the party as far as he could. One frontbencher Simon Coveney had inadvertently kept the matter alive: 'He needs to step up to that mark and if he can't achieve it, well then there are the obvious consequences of that,' the Cork South Central TD told RTÉ. Another member of the frontbench, Denis Naughton had already sought several one-to-one meetings with Kenny where he expressed unease at his lacklustre media performances and inability to convince large sections of the public that he was Taoiseach material.

An appearance on the *Late Late Show* in January 2010 had offered Kenny exposure to a significant audience as well as a real opportunity to convince doubters about his ability to lead the country. An open-shirted Kenny initially came across as relaxed and was comfortable with questions about his family and personal life. The presenter Ryan Tubridy then moved the conversation onto political matters and sought to tease out Fine Gael's stance on various potential coalition partners. Kenny stressed his preference for a single party government. Without prompting, the Fine Gael leader raised his previous stance in ruling out a coalition arrangement with Sinn Féin. 'On what basis?' Tubridy asked. 'Well, obviously there were some matters that were not cleared up,' Kenny replied as Tubridy interjected: 'Like what?' 'Well obviously there were some details in relation to Northern Ireland activities,' Kenny said. Tubridy interjected again: 'Like what?' Kenny replied: 'Like activities that were, you know, related to republicanism.' Tubridy responded: 'I don't know what that means.'

The import of Kenny's reply about not doing a coalition deal with Sinn Féin was clear but the hesitant nature of his explanation and the rapid-fire interjections of the programme host did him no favours. Unusually for the subject matter under discussion the studio audience applauded Tubridy's interjections, which only added to the 'stop-start' nature of the exchange.

By stumbling through the answer on Sinn Féin, Kenny only provided ammunition for his critics to emphasise the now well-established perception of a nice man who was out of his depth. Fianna Fáil's Willie O'Dea later poked fun at Kenny's performance: 'He sought to cover over his embarrassment by beaming lovingly at the camera. And there it was. The single picture, the single frame that encapsulated the core Fine Gael message – smile over substance.'

Kenny's appearance had not been a disaster although few people would have been swayed from their previously held opinion about him. The full interview could best be described as lacklustre and low-key, but in the weeks to come the *Late Late* appearance would be judged on the basis of the minute-long sequence relating to Sinn Féin.

Interestingly, the first media mentions of the interview were far from damning of Kenny with Tubridy coming in for equal criticism. Writing in the *Sunday Independent* on 17 January 2010, Eoghan Harris observed that Tubridy had gotten 'cheap applause' from the studio audience for giving Kenny a 'hard time about not wanting to do business with Sinn Féin.' Elaine Byrne in *The Irish Times* on 19 January 2010 also took Tubridy to task for some of his soft-focus questions. 'Who cares if Kenny likes Bertie Ahern or not? Or whether or not he would have a pint with Brian Cowen? That personality-type politics and limited-media mindset has us where we are.'

However, in Leinster House the political journalists were united in their assessment that Kenny had performed poorly. The most generous assessment came from Stephen Collins, who captured the core conundrum of the Fine Gael leader: 'His performance on last week's *Late Late Show* showed once again that he has a problem with television, particularly light entertainment programmes."

Within Fine Gael, many parliamentary party members saw the interview as yet another missed opportunity for Kenny to convince the wider public of his leadership credentials. Their mood darkened even further when listening to Kenny on Newstalk's morning radio programme on 27 January 2010. There was little positive to take from the performance where, not for the first time in a set piece media interview, Kenny came across as ill-prepared, reinforcing the view that he was out of his depth. In response to a question on charging for water usage, Kenny said that Fine Gael did not have a position on the reintroduction of water charges. His reply was not just evasive but littered with incomplete sentences and stumbles.

Presenter: Are Fine Gael in favour of water charges or not?
EK: Fine Gael have, have, Fine Gael haven't, eh, Fine Gael

have not . . .

Presenter: Haven't thought about it yet?

EK: We haven't discussed this yet, but we, we haven't said that, eh, we have a particular view on this. Obviously, just a second, no . . .

Presenter: Gormley came forward this week and said he's going to meter the house. Yes or no?

EK: I have no problem with John Gormley metering water, eh, bringing in meters for water all over the country, but I'll say this to you: if you look at the question of public procurement, the savings that can be made in local authorities have yet to be determined and may run into hundreds of millions . . .

Presenter: You've got very adept at not answering straight questions. Voters are entitled to know: are you going to introduce water charges?

EK: Voters are entitled to know. Fine Gael prepared an alternative budget in December and we said that we agree with the principle of taking out four billion out of the Irish economy and we put together an alternative that did not involve water charges, that did not – I'm telling you now. You're not going to have any budget until next December ah, eh. We've already made the point that you shouldn't start screwing the lower paid by taking out extra, extra pay reductions on them. What we've got to do, Ivan, and you know this, is to invest in the Irish economy but cut out the waste and get people to get value for money. I agree water; water is a very scarce commodity and getting scarcer. God knows, in our country raining for six months, one half of the year to the other.

Kenny's performance contrasted with Richard Bruton's handling of the issue a few days later during a Today FM interview with Matt Cooper. 'I believe a very low water charge should be introduced as a method of encouraging efficient use,' Bruton replied.

The first month of 2010 was not yet over but Kenny and his advisors were already on the defensive. Kenny's continued leadership was a talking point once more in Leinster House. The two media appearances only reinforced the view among Kenny's internal detractors that Fine Gael needed to change leader. For a growing number of Fine Gael TDs and senators, Kenny was a liability in killing off Fianna Fáil. There was real concern in sections of Fine Gael that Fianna Fáil would ultimately regroup and somehow manage to overcome the post-2008 traumas to win another term in government. Having implemented its austerity budget, passed its banking policy into law and overcome the second Lisbon Treaty referendum, Cowen's government – unpopular as it was – looked increasingly like it could remain in office until the 2012 general election deadline.

Kenny felt the need to raise the interviews at a frontbench meeting as he moved to prevent a public airing of unhappiness over his leadership. Before business got underway at the weekly meeting Kenny spoke about the fallout. He accepted that his performances had not been good enough. His colleagues, who had not expected the matter to be raised, were surprised at the apology on offer and a promise to improve. Kenny told his colleagues that he felt like he had had a bad day on the football field. 'You have to up your game when you have a bad day,' he said. At the same time arrangements were also put in place for individual meetings with all the members of this parliamentary party.

The Kenny camp knew that the leader was increasingly vulnerable to a challenge. When asked if they thought Kenny would lead Fine Gael into the next general election some 49 per cent of respondents to a Millward Brown/IMS survey on 14 February 2009 said he would not; 38 per cent said he would. But in the heat of a great difficulty Kenny refused to panic, which ultimately strengthened his ability to head-off a potential heave. His critics underestimated his ability to see the danger of the position he was in – a characteristic which benefited the party leader when he was eventually challenged for his job.

As they considered their options there was another difficulty for the dissidents. Bruton declined to offer a challenge. He repeatedly said he had never ruled out becoming leader of Fine Gael. There was growing frustration that Kenny was depending upon his undoubted electoral successes to shore up his weakened position. Bruton took up this theme in his first remarks in the aftermath of the Lee resignation. Rejecting the view that Kenny had mishandled the situation, Bruton said: 'I think he acted very honourably. But he has to come out his corner fighting. I think that in the test of politics, it's your next game, not your last one, that matters.'

Bruton was walking a tightrope. His words of loyalty were laced with deep frustration with Kenny, and an increasing belief that he might not lead the party into government. 'I have always supported Enda Kenny's leadership. I have supported every leader in this party. I am absolutely committed. No one can question my loyalty to any leader that I have supported,' Bruton said. But crucially he said Fine Gael had to work very hard to regain ground lost to the Labour Party and to define its own policy agenda.

Bruton was waiting in the wings. In a *Hot Press* interview the previous summer he acknowledged there was a problem with Kenny's presentation skills. 'Yeah, he can be a bit wooden in the Dáil. People say that his 30-second sound bite is not crisp enough, and I think that's probably fair. But the 30-second sound bite was never the test of a good leader – and I don't think it should be now. But that's not to say that he couldn't polish up his 30-second sound bites! There's always room for doing that,' Bruton said.

Yet, whatever the view of his critics the Kenny camp's strongest retort was the party's consistently strong poll ratings. The party was still in front position in the first *Irish Times* poll of 2010. At 32 per cent Fine Gael support was up a single point putting the party eight points ahead of the Labour Party and 10 points clear of Fianna Fáil. Fine Gael had been consistently in front of Fianna Fáil in this series since the middle of 2008. The party's support was also spread evenly across all key demographic subgroups – above 25 per cent in all social groups with the exception of the unskilled/unemployed

(DE) cohort.

The first Red C poll of 2010 also showed Fine Gael on track to form a coalition government with the Labour Party while Fianna Fáil looked set to suffer significant losses. But the figures also indicated that a Fianna Fáil recovery might be underway – the party was up four points since the previous poll – and while Fine Gael was still in lead position its rating had slipped back two points. Fianna Fáil had not just clawed back some support but Cowen's satisfaction rating, having fallen to 15 per cent in September 2009, increased to 26 per cent by January 2010.

But even if Fianna Fáil failed to recover there were real concerns in Fine Gael that the party's position in the polls would ultimately be undermined by public antipathy to Kenny. There were nervous glances in the direction of Eamon Gilmore. The Labour leader's satisfaction rating hit 46 per cent in January 2010, and there was real concern in Fine Gael was that he could position his party to gain disproportionately from a Fianna Fáil collapse. Kenny's satisfaction ratings continued to show large sections of the public were unconvinced. It was, of course, possible for a leader with low satisfaction ratings to be elected Taoiseach – Albert Reynolds in 1992 was the obvious example.

The Kenny camp took some comfort from the decidedly mixed public reaction to Lee's resignation. They were also boosted by the first opinion poll after the resignation. The survey in the *Irish Independent* saw Fine Gael support increase by four points to 34 per cent – ahead of Fianna Fáil at 27 per cent and Labour at 19 per cent – although satisfaction with Kenny remained poor, down three points to 26 per cent. Kenny's colleagues continued to defend him in public. Fergus O'Dowd told *The Examiner*: 'His leadership is very strong, he has built a very strong team around him and I think he will definitely be the next Taoiseach.' Within a matter of weeks, O'Dowd and many other Fine Gael public representatives adopted a very different stance in seeking to instigate a 'palace coup' in replacing Kenny with Richard Bruton.

Bruton was not actively agitating against Kenny but he was

increasingly frustrated and there was a sense that he was readying himself to take over as party leader. In an interview with *Business & Finance* magazine in early March 2010 he repeated his assessment of Kenny's poor media skills – he would never be the 'master of the 30-second sound bite or the media's darling.' And while professing loyalty to Kenny and saying a vacancy was unlikely before the next general election, he kept alive the idea of leading Fine Gael: 'I have never made any secret of the fact that I would love to lead the party.'

The leadership issue was also kept alive by the media. A questions was posed in the Red C series in February 2010: 'Would you be more likely to vote for Fine Gael if Kenny was no longer party leader?' The survey reported 43 per cent saying they would consider switching their support to Fine Gael with a new leader, against 35 per cent who said no and 22 per cent who did not express an opinion.

There was also a renewed sense of defiance within the parliamentary party. Many TDs and Senators were still smarting from the lack of consultation on key policy decisions. Kenny had pre-empted the party's political reform policy document to announce moves to abolish the Seanad and reduce the number of Dáil deputies. Unhappiness at that decision, and the manner in which they had been informed of the decision, lingered. There was considerable sensitivity about the package of reforms and the approach the party hierarchy was now opting for on other elements of the plan. The draft policy document on political reform, which was being fronted by Phil Hogan, met resistance when it was discussed at several meetings of the party's frontbench in early 2010.

There was opposition to the idea of introducing a list system to guarantee that a number of people from outside the political process would be members of Dáil Éireann. The draft document suggested that 15 seats from the newly reduced Dáil membership of 146 would be filled by a list system. The proposal would be put to the people in a referendum. But the frontbench in mid-February 2010 rejected the idea. Yet when another draft of the document was discussed some weeks later, the list proposal was still included in the raft of reform measures.

Around the same time another proposal from the document – to introduce quotas of women candidates – came before the parliamentary party. Kenny supported the idea which would set targets to ensure 20 per cent of party candidates at the next local elections were women with a 25 per cent threshold at European parliament contests. Lucinda Creighton, who considered the proposal ill-judged, opposed the move. 'You really have to look at other things like the long hours, childcare and how [women] are treated in the political environment. There are no anti-bullying, or anti-discrimination measures nor any human resources systems in place in any of the political parties. Unless you deal with those, the rest is window dressing to make us sound progressive,' the Dublin South East TD said.

Creighton pushed the proposal to a vote. It was an unusual move, as votes were not generally taken on such proposals at parliamentary party meetings. Despite Kenny's backing the quota idea was rejected on a show of hands by 18 votes to 14. When the final version of the document – New Politics – eventually went to the Fine Gael national conference in Killarney several weeks later, the two contentious proposals had been dropped. But the rebellion was about more than the issue of candidate quotas or the introduction of a list system. A message was being sent about the lack of consultation and an increasing unease about Kenny's leadership in the aftermath of the Lee affair.

Yet by the time the party faithful gathered for the Fine Gael national conference in Killarney in late March, much of the media spotlight had been taken off Kenny's poor start to 2010 and the loss of George Lee. The national agenda continued to be dominated by the economic collapse and the government's inept handling of the banking crisis. The survival of the Fianna Fáil-Green coalition had not been helped by the resignations of Willie O'Dea and Trevor Sargent in controversial circumstances and the departure of Green senator Deirdre De Burca in a row with her party.

There had been considerable disruption in the Dáil chamber in mid-February when Kenny accused O'Dea of perjury. Kenny asked if it was ethically correct for the Defence Minister to submit a false affidavit to the High Court for political gain. 'Standards in the country have dropped because the government harbors a perjurer at the cabinet table. I want to offer the Tánaiste the opportunity to answer my question, yes or no.'

The government responded with a motion of confidence in the Defence Minister. Cowen raised the matter of the timing of Fine Gael's no confidence motion. 'Is it because of the traumas Deputy Kenny and his party endured last week?' Cowen asked with reference to the Lee resignation. 'The refusal of the Taoiseach and his colleagues to demand any accountability for this behaviour was the reason that I tabled a motion of no confidence in Deputy O'Dea,' Kenny responded.

The Fianna Fáil-Green government clung to the hope that it could consolidate its position in 2010 and start to work its way out of a hugely challenging economic and political environment. But the opposition parties continued their attacks on the government's response to the economic and banking crisis. Kenny predicted that the establishment of the National Asset Management Agency (NAMA) would be the most expensive lie ever told to the Irish people and would continue crony capitalism in Ireland.

Against this backdrop it was no surprise that under the theme 'Getting Ireland back to work,' the Fine Gael conference in late Mach 2010 had the feel of a pre-election rally. Kenny focused on getting growth back into the economy, reforming the health services and transforming the political system. He delivered a solid if unspectacular performance in his televised address. 'This country is finished with slogans and repeated photo opportunities. This country is ready for the best and the most hard-working government in the history of the state,' Kenny declared.

The man who should have been the star of the weekend was not present. 'We had been preparing for a "George-fest",' a party organiser admits. But instead of being at the top table George Lee was preparing for his return to RTÉ. His name was left unmentioned. Instead, during his speech Kenny name-checked several of his frontbench colleagues including Coveney and Reilly in a deliberate strategy to promote the idea of a strong party leadership. Kenny also took the time to refer to his deputy leader by name: 'in Richard Bruton I know I have the right man to run the Department of Finance at this critical time for this country.'

13
Leadership Heave

Talk about a leadership heave intensified towards the end of 2009. George Lee's abrupt exit from national politics in early February 2010 presented an opportunity to move against Kenny. The idea was canvassed among a small group within the parliamentary party but ultimately, they decided that the timing was wrong. 'We weren't going to give Lee the satisfaction of justifying his decision with the departure of the party leader,' one of Kenny's leading critics explained in the aftermath of the 2011 general election.

Fine Gael was at 30 per cent in the May Red C poll – a decline of three points, having also fallen by two points the previous month. The 30 per cent level was Fine Gael's lowest rating in a Red C poll since February 2009. Over that timeframe Labour – now at 22 per cent – had made 'dramatic gains' according to pollsters in their analysis of the figures. There was renewed pressure on Kenny. 'Fine Gael has dropped five points in opinion polls in the last two months as party leader Enda Kenny's new image has failed to take off,' a story in the *Irish Independent* declared on 31 May 2010.

The poll offered a glimmer of hope for the main government party. Fianna Fáil's support was up by a single point to 24 per cent – and while that type of figure pointed to electoral disaster, there was hope that the party's support levels had steadied. The party had a solid base of support, which its leadership hierarchy still believed it could build upon in the months ahead. By the start of the summer of 2010 the belief that Cowen might lead a fight back lingered in Fianna Fáil. It was a desperate hope that was never realised, but that very hope worried many in Fine Gael.

Cowen's run of bad luck and poor judgement continued, with a mishandling of the restructuring of pensions arrangements for former ministers. A much-trailed speech in early May 2010 setting out the government's role in the economic and banking crisis failed to deliver the expected public response. 'Sorry is a word Fianna Fáil do not recognise,' Kenny said following Cowen's lengthy speech. 'He expects everybody else to accept responsibility for it but not him. He hasn't the courage to come out and say, "Yes I made a mistake", apologise to the Irish people and do what I can to rectify it. It's another example of hands being washed by those in charge, a refusal to accept responsibility for their part in destroying the Irish economy and heaping economic woes and depression upon so many people.'

At that stage Cowen had the luxury of another two years in office, which his ardent backers believed would be sufficient time to spur Fianna Fáil support back towards the levels enjoyed in previous elections. There were periodic strong performances from the Fianna Fáil leader, but these were ultimately undermined by a lack of consistency coupled with growing public anger at the ever-worsening economic situation. Many in the party were bracing themselves for an electoral meltdown and they seemed paralysed about how to respond.

Fine Gael minds were focused on the increase in support for the Labour Party. Two years previous, Gilmore's party had poll ratings in the region of 10 per cent but that figure had doubled in the intervening period. Within Fine Gael the party's 30 per cent poll rating was a key threshold, especially given the depths of government unpopularity. Fine Gael won 27.3 per cent in 2007 but Fianna Fáil's vote had subsequently collapsed. Those agitating for a leadership change in Fine Gael argued that in the event of a series of poor poll results, Bruton would have no choice but to act. It seemed apparent that Kenny was now leading Fine Gael from opinion poll to opinion poll; one poor result could provide room for the long-talked-about heave. Despite this, there was outward support for Kenny, as Leo Varadkar remarked at the end of April 2010: 'Certainly there was a wobble around the day George Lee left, but at this stage he's more secure than at any time I've been in the party.'

Kenny may have survived the ire of his critics at frontbench and parliamentary party meetings in the aftermath of Lee's departure, but discussion about the leadership issue continued in private. Coveney and Hayes – among other members of the frontbench – were exasperated by a lack of consultation on key decisions and had doubts about Kenny's ability to capitalise on the government's unpopularity. There was an internal row with Richard Bruton about the issuing of a media statement on the EU's stance on taxation policy. Meanwhile, Kenny was continuing to blow hot and cold in his media appearances, and in the Dáil chamber. Politicians like Billy Timmins and Denis Naughton were growing restless. Recognised critics like John Deasy, Lucinda Creighton and Damien English continued to talk about an urgent need for change at the top.

Bruton was being put under pressure to act. His supporters formulated a plan. The dissidents were confident that they had the support of a majority of the members of Kenny's frontbench. They would ambush Kenny at a frontbench meeting. One-by-one they would declare their lack of support in his leadership. The theory was – having heard the view of a majority of his senior party colleagues directly to his face – Kenny would have no choice but to resign. Bruton had lived through the bloodletting, which forced the three previous leaders from the post and he was still reluctant to move against Kenny. But this plan had a certain appeal in that, if successful, it avoided a messy leadership battle and the bitter fall-out evident in previous heaves.

The results of opinion polls in the Red C series increased the likelihood of a heave before the summer recess. Impatience with Bruton was increasing within the dissident camp. The leading agitators believed that the prize would automatically be Bruton's if he moved against Kenny. Plan B was less attractive but was available if Bruton continued to procrastinate. Plan B involved another TD challenging for the leadership although it was accepted that such action would inevitably lead to a bitter contest which risked damaging the party.

The position of Kenny's opponents was significantly strengthened with the results of an opinion poll in *The Irish Times* on 11 June 2010. Fine Gael was down four points to 28 per cent – the first time since June 2008 that the party's support in the series had dipped below 30 per cent. Kenny's already poor satisfaction ratings fell further – down seven points to 24 per cent – his lowest rating since becoming party leader in 2002. Worse still for Fine Gael was the Labour performance; Gilmore's party was up eight points to 32 per cent. 'Labour now the biggest party in State for first time, poll shows', the front-page headline in the newspaper declared.

The accompanying news article made for depressing reading for Fine Gael: 'The Labour surge has taken place all over the State with the party increasing its lead over all other parties in Dublin, in joint first in the rest of Leinster and just one point off the lead in Munster. Fianna Fáil has dropped back to the record low it reached last September, while the standing of the government and Taoiseach has fallen sharply over the past six months. There is also bad news for Fine Gael, with the party dropping back to its lowest rating in two years and leader Enda Kenny falling back in terms of satisfaction rating.'

Fine Gael was a single point better off than at the 2007 general election despite facing the most unpopular government in the history of the State. An analysis of the poll findings was worrying. Fine Gael's vote was solid in Connaught-Ulster; it was down marginally in Munster and the rest of Leinster but had declined significantly in the Dublin region where Labour recorded a commanding lead as the largest party in the capital.

The surge in support for Labour suddenly seemed to give credibility to the party's strategy of positioning Gilmore as an alternative choice for the next Taoiseach. But following two years of economic turmoil it was unclear why, at that particular point in time, the electorate had opted to move away from Fine Gael and reward Labour amid continuing anger towards Fianna Fáil. 'It is impossible to discern which recent events have propelled Labour into pole position,' Damian Loscher, the Managing Director of Ipsos MRBI noted. The possibility of a rogue poll did not feature in the wider political and media analysis although Loscher observed, 'the change vote by its nature is volatile and can float away from a party as easily as it gravitates towards it.'

Within Fine Gael, the politics of protest was seen as having paid dividend for the Labour Party, which had offered strong and vocal opposition to the government's fiscal austerity programme. The party's Election Strategy Committee discussed the situation in some detail over the following months as a strategy to counter Gilmore's party was formulated. 'How far we ultimately go in defining Labour is a political decision,' the confidential report concluded, but the gloves were off – 'Labour has certainly shown no hesitation in presenting us as little different to Fianna Fáil.' Fine Gael had dutifully published a raft of polices but the party was winning little credit. Its own private research showed that voters responded positively to the policies but few were really aware of what exactly Kenny's party was offering. For some in Fine Gael this was due to a communication deficit; to others the reason was down to a leadership deficit.

The headline figures from the Ipsos MRBI poll were broadcast on RTÉ's evening news on Thursday 10 June 2010. Richard Bruton had a pre-arranged interview on RTÉ's *Prime Time* to discuss the economic situation and two independent reports on the government's banking policy by Central Bank governor Patrick Honohan and international banking experts Klaus Regling and Max Watson. The reports largely blamed misguided national policy for the crisis. Cowen was very much in the dock for his performance as Minister for Finance.

Kenny tabled a motion of no confidence in Cowen in the aftermath of the publication of reports. But a few hours later Fine

Gael's own deputy leader was being asked about confidence in Kenny. Bruton was in the *Prime Time* studio. In light of the poor Fine Gael performance in *The Irish Times* poll, he was asked if he had confidence in his party leader. The Fine Gael deputy leader declined to answer. 'It's not about me. . . I'm just as much in the dock in terms of Fine Gael's failings. We're in the dock. We have to look at our whole performance as a party.'

'It's a straight yes or no,' Miriam O'Callaghan replied. Bruton gave a non-committal reply as he sought to evade providing a direct answer. 'It's not about me,' he said. 'Do you have confidence in the leader?' O'Callaghan asked.

The TDs who had been encouraging Bruton to move against Kenny were unaware of his intentions. Many like Brian Hayes, who had just arrived home from a leaflet drop, were left surprised at what they heard from their stalwart. Another senior party TD said, 'I was shocked really. The plan had been to wait until after the summer because we expected a run of poor polls which would have forced Kenny out.' A heave was on – perhaps, maybe – but Bruton had spoken to none of his main backers. Just over an hour later Bruton was in another television studio. Vincent Browne picked up where O'Callaghan left off. But again Bruton was evasive. He was even giddy as he accepted that he had leadership ambitions. 'In the swag bag of every corporal is a lieutenant's baton,' he said.

The leadership issue had simmered since the 2007 general election and had intensified in the latter half of 2009 when there was consistent talk about the possibility of a heave. That Bruton had walked himself and his supporters into a contest without better planning meant the opportunity to start the heave against Kenny with serious momentum was lost. Bruton went on the two television programmes without a clear message for his parliamentary party supporters, Fine Gael members and the wider public. There was no narrative as to why he should replace Kenny. If anything he seemed surprised to be asked about the ramifications of the opinion poll findings for the leadership of Fine Gael. He was giddy. He was evasive. This lack of preparation – and the lack of experience among many of the leading plotters – ultimately combined to reduce the effectiveness of the coup. But one thing was certain following Bruton's television interviews: the Kenny camp knew that an imminent challenge was now a possibility. 'But we still weren't certain. A lot of us watched Richard's interview and asked, "what does this mean?" To be honest there was no sense that a challenge was inevitable at that stage,' one Kenny advisor says.

The following day, Friday 11 June 2010, the opinion poll in *The Irish Times* dominated the news agenda. Media commentators and political pundits were wild with discussion of fundamental changes in the political landscape. Gilmore was now seen as a realistic contender for Taoiseach. The absence of a significant explanation for the surge in Labour support at that point in time was sidestepped in the analysis – as was evidence presented by Red C that this support was soft, or 'flakey' as the poll experts concluded.

Conventional wisdom at the time was that a general election was still two years away. There was continued speculation of a leadership heave in Fianna Fáil. Noel O'Flynn spoke of an 'electoral wipe-out,' but the party's dissidents ultimately failed to move against Cowen. In both Fianna Fáil and Fine Gael there was a sense of waiting for a challenger to emerge to the embattled incumbents. Cowen survived as his internal opponents refused to move against him until the eve of the general election campaign – a decision that ultimately cost Fianna Fáil dearly.

There was a different reaction in Fine Gael. The party had a bank of policies. It had constructively engaged with the economic turmoil and had signalled an appetite to deal with the gap between national income and expenditure. The failure to prosper from the collapse in Fianna Fáil support was attributed to Kenny's weakness as party leader. The results of the latest poll added substance to this argument.

Leo Varadkar and Frances Fitzgerald went public to support Kenny in the context of the poll findings. 'Enda has been leader of the party when we were on 19 per cent and also on 38 per cent in the polls. We don't change our leader on the basis of any one poll.

We've been ahead in 25 polls in a row for two years including one only 10 days ago, which had us in first place and Labour in third. I would not be talking about a seismic shift in the political landscape based on this one poll,' Varadkar argued. Fitzgerald added, 'this is not the election. This is a moment in time. The detailed work that has been done by the party will come into play when the real election is there.'

Following his Thursday evening television interviews Bruton went silent. He was at a wedding on Friday where many of those attending were Fine Gael members and supporters. But he remained publicly silent on the leadership issue. There was speculation of a challenge but nothing to confirm that a heave was underway. Some doubts persisted about Bruton's real intentions. 'I'd go with Richard but do you know what, I don't think Richard has the balls to go for it. If he doesn't, there is no one else around who will, or could,' one unnamed frontbench member told a weekend newspaper.

On Saturday Kenny and Bruton had the first of several telephone conversations about the leadership issue. Kenny sought to persuade Bruton not to instigate a leadership bid. The move would damage Fine Gael, Kenny argued. He asked Bruton for a public declaration of confidence in his leadership. Bruton could not deliver. The matter was left without resolution. They agreed to talk again the following day.

Bruton's challenge was now underway. He called his main supporters on the frontbench. The campaign was being organised by Hayes and Timmins. There was backing from backbenchers Paul Bradford, John Deasy, John Paul Phelan and Damien English. The Sunday newspapers were briefed. 'The knives are out for Enda. I expect a move to be made within the next two weeks,' one unnamed frontbench TD was reported as saying in the *Sunday Independent*. Another said, 'I like Enda but the game is up. End of story.'

Kenny's critics did not go public – they were keeping their powder dry for what they saw as the crucial Tuesday morning frontbench meeting. Hayes declined to comment while political reporters could not contact other rebels. But a core group of front-bench dissidents was quickly identified: Brian Hayes, Michael Creed, Billy Timmins, Olivia Mitchell and Denis Naughton. The main Sunday newspapers reported that Bruton could count on the support of a majority of frontbench members. Bruton supporters briefed journalists that there would be – as one put it – a 'seamless transfer of power' with Kenny voluntarily resigning in favour of Bruton without a contest.

The weekend strategy was largely focused on frontbench members. Bruton called his colleagues and spoke about the need for a changed approach and a new direction for the party. The strategy was to throw down the gauntlet at the Tuesday morning meeting. With a majority of the frontbench on their side, the view was that Kenny would have no choice but to stand aside – in effect, a blood-less coup.

The strategy seriously misread Kenny's intentions. The Mayo man let it be known that he had been elected by a vote of the par-liamentary party in 2002 and that he would remain as leader until such time as a majority of his colleagues cast their ballots against him. He had no intention of stepping aside like Alan Dukes had done in 1990. There would be no coronation. He reminded his col-leagues that Liam Cosgrave had survived an attempted heave in December 1972 and within a few months led the party into gov-ernment, while John Bruton had been challenged in late 1994 only to emerge as Taoiseach by the end of that same year.

Kenny drove from Castlebar to Dublin on Sunday morning. He met Bruton at Fine Gael headquarters. But his attempts to persuade Bruton to back off were still unsuccessful. Bruton would not offer a public declaration of confidence in the party leader. The finance spokesman emphasised that the party had previously been faced with questions about Kenny's ability and having listened to the Mayo man pledge to redouble his efforts his critics had backed away from a challenge. Now the time had come for a change, he argued. But Kenny rejected the case for a smooth and swift transition in power.

Kenny and his supporters moved quickly to consolidate their position. Phil Hogan was working the phones along with Paul Kehoe, James Reilly and Michael Ring, Maurice Cummins and Frances Fitzgerald. They accepted that at least half of Kenny's front-bench was in the Bruton camp although they were unsure about the intentions of Simon Coveney and Fergus O'Dowd. Leo Varadkar, who had publicly defended Kenny in the aftermath of the poll being published, opted for silence over the weekend. The Kenny camp put their attention onto the party's backbench TDs, Senators and members of the European Parliament.

They sought to undermine the Bruton strategy of dealing with the leadership question at the Tuesday morning frontbench meeting. The leadership was a matter for the entire parliamentary party. Meanwhile, loyal frontbench members issued public statements of support in a final attempt to persuade Bruton to call off the challenge. 'People have learned lessons from the past and we should not be having an internal discussion about our leader when we are on the verge of a general election. Enda will lead the party into the general election and the election results should be the only results by which leaders are judged,' Hogan declared.

Paul Kehoe warned that there was no appetite for a challenge. 'No one wants to go back to the bad old days of Fine Gael. No one wants to undo the absolutely Trojan work Enda Kenny has done over the last eight years.' It was a refrain that was repeated over and over by other Kenny supporters. Jim Higgins dismissed suggestions of a heave. 'I don't think anybody with the integrity of Richard Bruton would do this.' Kenny's supporters were publicly batting for their boss. 'There are no dark mutterings, and there are no dark doings going on against the Fine Gael leader,' James Reilly declared.

After a weekend of behind-the-scenes phone calls the Kenny camp was confident in its numbers. There were public endorsements for Kenny's leadership from frontbenchers Phil Hogan, Paul Kehoe, Alan Shatter, James Reilly, Jimmy Deenihan, Michael Ring,

Charlie Flanagan and Frances Fitzgerald. Coveney urged his colleagues against 'over-reacting to a single opinion poll,' although he did not offer support for Kenny's leadership.

The dramatic headline in Monday morning's *Irish Independent* read: 'Bruton tells Kenny: You no longer have my confidence.' The newspaper – correctly – speculated that the weekend conversation had effectively sparked a leadership challenge which would unravel over the following two days. 'The move is underway. He's doing it in the right way, which is not confrontational. Everybody wants this to happen as peacefully as possible,' one party figure was reported as saying.

Kenny and Bruton made contact again early on Monday but their conversation went over now-familiar ground. Bruton would not offer a public declaration of confidence in the party leader. Kenny was not resigning. The issue was expected to come to a head at the Tuesday morning meeting of the Fine Gael frontbench. The belief in the Bruton camp was that Kenny could not survive with his finance spokesperson opting to switch to the backbenches. One opponent said: 'He has been given every opportunity. Enough is enough. Does anybody seriously believe he can lead Fine Gael with Richard Bruton on the backbenches?'

The party leader consulted with this team of key supporters. They agreed to implement the strategy formulated over the previous 24 hours. Kenny would pre-empt the attempt to turn the frontbench meeting into a forum where the fate of his leadership would be decided. He would sack Bruton thus preventing his attendance at the crucial meeting. It was, Kenny said, 'an impossible position' with Bruton declining to offer a public pledge of loyalty.

But before Kenny contacted Bruton he made one other call – to Michael Noonan. The two men spoke by phone, and when Kenny briefed his key advisors about the outcome of the conversation there was confidence that Noonan would support the incumbent leader.

Noonan remained silent throughout the heave. His name appeared on several lists as an opponent of Kenny. Even his local newspaper, the *Limerick Leader*, reported that Noonan was expected to side with Bruton. For several months he had listened to the rumblings among the malcontents but had offered no encouragement to his colleagues. He said the timing of the heave was a surprise but explained that as a former leader expressing a preference would be inappropriate. 'I know how I'm voting. I'm just not telling anyone,' Noonan said publicly.

But two of Kenny's main supporters confirmed to this author that a deal had been agreed between the two men on the Monday afternoon. 'Enda would never make a decision like sacking Richard without working out the consequences and considering what he had to do next. His opponents too often overlooked those sharp political instincts,' one Kenny strategist, who was aware of the deal, said. Throughout the days of the heave as they canvassed for votes, the Kenny camp actively encouraged the idea that Noonan would be appointed as frontbench spokesperson on finance.

Kenny phoned Bruton again late on Monday afternoon to dismiss him as deputy leader and as the party's spokesperson on finance. He then contacted Padraic McCormack, the party chairman, to table a motion of confidence in his leadership. The motion was in Kenny's name and that of the party's whip Paul Keogh. The vote would take place in less than three days time at a meeting of the parliamentary party on Thursday.

The dramatic move to unseat the incumbent leader and his equally dramatic intention to remain in the position was now very much in the public domain. Kenny described the decision to sack his deputy leader as 'very regrettable and very disappointing'. There was a clear message to others on the frontbench who were considering declaring their opposition. He pledged widespread 'personnel changes' in the aftermath of the confidence motion. 'I want an end to this bickering. I want an end to this situation where there is a lack of clarity from some people about where the Fine Gael party is headed.'

'Over the weekend, some unnamed people have done huge damage to Fine Gael through their anonymous comments to the media which has resulted in an opinion poll dominating the news agenda at a time when all our energies should be focused on getting this government out of office,' Kenny said.

'Among the many huge challenges I faced when I was elected leader of Fine Gael was to heal the deep wounds left from previous internal conflict and leadership challenges. I was that solider. And I defended and supported Richard's brother John on three occasions. I know what is it like to have the internal conflict that leaves such devastating results for any political party.'

'I have worked patiently and sensitively to bind the party into a cohesive and united team and I am very disappointed that a small number of colleagues are determined to bring Fine Gael back to those old days,' Kenny said.

In the aftermath of his sacking, Bruton went public with his challenge. He had been a loyal deputy leader but 'at a certain point you have to decide is this working?'

'Everyone feels intensely loyal within Fine Gael but at some point loyalty to the country and loyalty to the people has to take precedence over an individual person.'

The challenger predicted he had the support needed to oust Kenny and openly questioned his ability to be Taoiseach: 'I believe he does not have the capacity to deal with the difficult problem that the country faces.' Kenny's poor command of economic policy was stressed. 'We have to restore economic security and we have to have a leader who people have faith in, and in his capacity to do that. And sadly, he hasn't been able to do that, despite huge other things that he has done for the party,' Bruton said.

Kenny now faced a crucial three days with a meeting of his frontbench (minus the now-sacked Bruton) on Tuesday morning and a parliamentary party meeting on Thursday to decide on his confidence motion. But by Monday night only three members of the parliamentary party had openly declared their opposition – Bruton, Fergus O'Dowd and John Paul Phelan. The incumbent had already garnered the public backing of 26 members of the parliamentary party. But crucially some 36 TDs and Senators had opted not to comment publicly. Nevertheless, on the Monday evening – three days before the crucial vote – Kenny's advisors were confident as they worked out the scorecards that they were within reach of the crucial 36 votes needed for victory.

The media was already characterising the contest as Dublin-versus-county and the posh-school set against the boys from the local tech. These were easy shorthand generalisations but fundamentally inaccurate. The two candidates shared support among the younger group of TDs – Bruton had more high-profile, younger TDs like Hayes and Coveney but Kenny had the likes of Joe Carey and Paul Keogh. Likewise, a number of leading women TDs were in the Bruton camp but Kenny was backed by the likes of Frances Fitzgerald, Catherine Byrne and Deirdre Clune. When it came to education there was an even spread of private school students and the holders of university degrees. 'In some ways, the leading protagonists in the Bruton camp bought into these media characterisations. But the one thing about Enda Kenny is that he always knows his electorate. Remember the 2001 leadership contest is the only election he has ever lost. He knew that taking the fight to the parliamentary party was his strongest card,' one Kenny strategist says.

Burton was also seen as having solid support in the Dublin region. But his opponent had already received the backing of senior Dublin TDs James Reilly, Sean Barrett and Alan Shatter. Dublin MEP Gay Mitchell also went public with his support for Kenny. 'It's really crazy when there's a vote of confidence in the government to be concentrating people's views on Fine Gael,' Mitchell declared.

The lack of planning in the anti-Kenny camp was seen in one small episode over the weekend as Bruton continued to withhold support. Bruton rang one of his supporters in the parliamentary party looking for a mobile phone number for Gay Mitchell. But while Bruton was looking for a contact number for Mitchell, the Kenny camp had already moved to secure the backing of not only the Dublin MEP, but also the three other Fine Gael MEPs.

There had been some surprise in the Bruton camp when Alan Shatter declared his support for Kenny. Shatter had bitter experience of two previous heaves when he was on the losing side and, in particular, the 1994 heave against Bruton when he was one of the leading plotters. The challenge was defeated, within months Bruton was Taoiseach and Shatter remained on the backbenches during the life of the 1994-97 Rainbow coalition. He had returned to Leinster House in 2007 having lost his seat in the meltdown election five years earlier. Colleagues say the two men quickly developed a strong mutual respect: Kenny admired Shatter's intellect and reliability; Shatter acknowledged the rebuilding work and sense of party unity. When Shatter informed Kenny of his decision, Phil Hogan laughed and said, 'Well, Alan at least you won't make it three in a row.'

The dissidents arranged an early morning meeting in the Green Isle Hotel in west Dublin to agree their approach for the crucial frontbench meeting. Bruton was also in attendance. The hotel was a good location for all concerned just off the motorway with good access for those travelling from outside Dublin. Seven frontbench members attended – Varadkar, Creed, Mitchell, Timmins, Naughton, Hayes and O'Dowd. Olwyn Enright participated via speakerphone.

Some on the frontbench like Hayes and Timmins had agitated for the heave. Others were forced to make a decision once the heave got underway. Leo Varadkar had defended Kenny on the Friday morning when the opinion poll was published. But he had remained silent over subsequent days. Varadkar had long held the view that Kenny would be fine as leader so long as Bruton was finance spokesperson – but when Bruton was sacked the Dublin West TD had been forced to reconsider his position. Similarly, Coveney, who was not at the Green Isle meeting, had also wavered. He had appealed for unity over the weekend but had not actually offered Kenny his public endorsement.

The meeting lasted almost two hours. Bruton went through the detail of his conversations with Kenny. They agreed on a strategy of spelling out one-by-one to Kenny at the 11 a.m. frontbench meeting the reasons why it was best for Fine Gael if he stood down as party leader. The group was confident of a positive outcome. They numbered nine of Kenny's team. There was consensus that the leader would be gone by teatime. They were about to conclude the perfect coup.

But for the second time in as many days Kenny gazumped his opponents. He was aware of the gathering in the Green Isle Hotel – news had then leaked to the media and the meeting ended in some farce as the plotters sought to leave the hotel complex without being photographed or door-stepped.

Kenny's strategy was straightforward: he would not allow the frontbench meeting get into a discussion about his leadership. He would seize the initiative. Accordingly, he opened the meeting with a hard-hitting response to the developments of the previous few days. There had been a failure of collective responsibility, Kenny said, and many of his critics around the table had not been pulling their weight in recent times. He made reference to a lack of work and support over the previous months. He said his door was always open if colleagues wanted to talk to him – and that criticism should be delivered in private, not in public and to the detriment of Fine Gael. They were hearing 'home truths' Kenny's spokesperson later said. Kenny also gave the meeting his version of the recent discussions with Bruton, and explained why he had been forced to sack his deputy leader. Bruton had shown enormous political misjudgment, he said.

The atmosphere in the room was tense as Kenny laid into his opponents who faced him in the parliamentary party room waiting for their turn to respond. They listened in silence for almost 20 minutes. But then suddenly Kenny announced that this was the last meeting of the current frontbench ahead of a reshuffle after he won the confidence motion. He was dissolving the frontbench. He said the decision on the leadership was for the Fine Gael parliamentary party and with that in mind, given the motion of confidence in two days' time, he was adjourning the frontbench meeting.

Kenny then picked up his papers and left the room. Michael Creed called after him to sit down and discuss the situation. But with Phil Hogan and Paul Keogh alongside him Kenny was gone. The dissidents were stunned that Kenny had effectively 'shut down' the meeting. Billy Timmins, who was also unhappy at the way events had unfolded, followed Kenny out onto the corridor and the two men had a short conversation in the leader's office.

The dissidents were once more on the back-foot and had again to regroup to work out an alternative approach. They now accepted that Kenny was not going to go voluntarily and that the decision would be taken at the parliamentary party meeting on Thursday. Kenny was giving his critics a master class in how to deal with a heave. His actions were comparable to Charlie Haughey's strategy during a 1983 heave, when he bought vital time in adjourning a crucial parliamentary party meeting following the death of a Fianna Fáil TD.

The drama continued throughout Tuesday. After a quick meeting the gang of nine decided that they would go public together – and that Denis Naughton would speak on their behalf at a media briefing at noon outside Leinster House. The nine frontbench members declared they no longer had confidence in Kenny to lead Fine Gael. The group comprised Enright, Mitchell, O'Dowd, Timmins, Varadkar, Hayes, Creed, Naughton and Coveney. They called on Kenny to withdraw his confidence motion and to stand down as party leader. 'We believe now is the time for Enda to step aside,' Naughton declared.

'We're disappointed that he didn't give the members of the frontbench the opportunity to speak with him,' he added. 'The majority of the frontbench, I can sadly say, isn't supportive of the party leader and we believe that is replicated throughout the parliamentary party. We are putting our political careers on the line in what we believe is in the interests of this country and in the best interests of the Fine Gael party.'

Naughton found the experience difficult – his voice trembled on several occasions as he spoke. He had backed Kenny for the leadership in his unsuccessful contest against Michael Noonan in 2001. But he had stressed his unhappiness and frustration with

Kenny's performances at private meetings with the party leader over many months. Like many of his colleagues, he had genuinely believed that the confidence vote would not happen, and that Kenny would rollover under pressure from his frontbench. It was a serious misjudgement.

Their message was clear: they still wanted Kenny to stand down. Olivia Mitchell spoke for many of her colleagues when she admitted that there was resistance to Kenny on the doorsteps. 'The public can't visualise Enda as Taoiseach,' Creed added. 'The public haven't faith in him. He's done a wonderful job for the party, but he doesn't seem to be able to make the bigger leap,' Enright said. The plotters also stressed Kenny's poor command of economic policy. 'When the phone rings at 3 a.m. with the call from the Central Bank to the Taoiseach's home, I would like to see Richard Bruton picking up that phone,' O'Dowd said.

They focused on Kenny's poor media performances. 'I think he has found it very difficult to communicate to people outside of the Fine Gael fold in an impressive way that gets large numbers believing in him as someone they can trust to take the country forward,' Coveney said. And they mentioned the recent opinion poll ratings. 'We have an opportunity to put Fianna Fáil out of office for a generation if we change leader and put in a person who has credibility with the Irish public,' Hayes said.

But despite the criticisms, Kenny had not gone in the manner they had predicted. The Mayo man had stood up to his opponents who had failed to appreciate the determination he had brought to the job of FG leader, and his determination now to hold onto that job. While the rebels stood before the media at one entrance to Leinster House, the leading members of Kenny's team, Phil Hogan and Paul Kehoe, briefed at the other entrance. The well-worn 'family at war' description for Fine Gael was being dusted down.

In the aftermath of the frontbench meeting Kenny was scheduled to speak in the Dáil chamber on his party's no-confidence motion in Brian Cowen. He had a brief few words with Bruton as the debate began. The two met and shook hands before taking their seats. Kenny was in his usual leader's position but Bruton was no longer in the adjacent position he had occupied over the previous eight years. James Reilly sat along side Kenny. Many Fine Gael members in the chamber spent their time sending text messages. It was reported that Leo Varadkar was reading a copy of the Fine Gael rulebook.

Fine Gael was self-destructing just as Fianna Fáil had to deal with a no-confidence motion in its party leader based on independent reports, which were highly critical of his tenure as Minister for Finance. The timing of the Fine Gael heave was deeply embarrassing for Kenny. Much of the sentiment in his script could have been directed at his leadership by his internal opponents. 'How can you claim that you have any moral authority to sit in that seat?' Kenny asked. There was one line in the prepared script that Kenny did not deliver. 'Only one honourable action remains to you. Go. Go now. In God's name, go.'

There was plenty of speculation as to why Kenny had tabled the motion of no confidence in the first place. Some said he had forewarning of the poll figures earlier on Thursday afternoon and the motion was a strategic attempt to put off his internals opponents. Others said he did not want to be upstaged by Eamon Gilmore, who might have followed a similar course. In any event, Fianna Fáil got off lightly with the confidence motion; not only was media attention distracted by the convulsions in Fine Gael, but the long-awaited Saville Inquiry report into the events of Bloody Sunday was also published on the same day.

The lobbying and canvassing continued in Leinster House. The decision was now in the hands of the party's 51 TDs, 15 Senators and 4 MEPs. On Wednesday morning one media report claimed Kenny had 34 supporters; his opponents totalled 26, with 10 crucial unknowns – some of whom were claimed by both sides.

Publicly the talk was of an amicable debate but internally the atmosphere was nasty. Kenny's supporters let it be known that in the event of their man being defeated, Bruton would not take the leadership without a contest. A rival for the position would emerge.

In such an eventuality, the election of a new leader was going to be a divisive and timely affair. A new electoral system had been introduced based on a college system with weighted votes for three party groups; the parliamentary party – TDs, Senators and MEPS (65 per cent); party membership (25 per cent) and party councillors (10 per cent).

As the canvassing continued there were offers of frontbench positions and deals on candidate strategy. There was speculation that Terence Flanagan (Dublin North East) and Tom Sheehan (Kerry South) had been promised no running mates in their respective three-seat constituencies. Lucinda Creighton claimed that the Kenny camp had offered her a job in exchange for her support. Hogan said it was untrue. Kenny held face-to-face meetings with many wavers. Senator Paschal Donohoe told Kenny he was backing Bruton. Pat Breen from Clare was also scratched off the Kenny list: 'This has been a very painful decision for me to make as I have worked very closely with Enda over the past number of years,' Breen said.

There was ongoing speculation about voters switching allegiances. The Kenny camp suffered a number of setbacks late on Wednesday. First, Kieran O'Donnell – who had been promoted to acting finance spokesperson earlier in the week – came out against Kenny. Charlie Flanagan was also about to change his mind. A few days previously he had strongly supported the party leader: 'A return to the divisive heaves of the 1980s and the 1990s would cause deep wounds. Enda Kenny is the leader of Fine Gael and he has my support. Fine Gael should be very mindful of past bloodbaths. This is not the time for internal strife that will undoubtedly leave serious wounds and long-term scars.'

Flanagan, who had been on the losing side in the 1994 heave against Bruton, became the eleventh member of the frontbench to withdraw support. The defection of Flanagan and O'Donnell was perceived as a last-minute blow to Kenny's survival prospects. 'Kieran's decision was a surprise, especially as he had accepted the frontbench appointment earlier in the week, but there was less surprise about Charlie. There were indications over the previous couple of days that he might be having second-thoughts,' a Kenny advisor said.

Bruton took to the Leinster House plinth and, in the company of nine frontbench members, he again called on Kenny to stand down. 'My message to Enda Kenny is obviously I would prefer if this motion didn't have to go ahead, a lot of people thought that this could be resolved internally,' Bruton admitted. Hogan also briefed the media surrounded by 21 TDs and Senators. He predicted a clear victory: 'Statements issued in favour of Enda Kenny are already in excess of the quota.' In a statement Kenny said: 'I look forward to winning the vote tomorrow and leading the party into another successful election as I have done on three previous occasions.'

Both sides were claiming they had the numbers for victory as they gathered in the main party meeting room in the basement of the Leinster House 2000 complex on 17 June 2010. Pictures of past Fine Gael leaders looked down from the walls. As few as 7 of the 70 parliamentary party members were thought to be unspoken for with Kenny seen possibly as having a slight lead on the Bruton camp. Kenny went into the meeting knowing he had tactically outplayed his opponents over the previous few days. Nevertheless, his leadership was on the line. The meeting lasted for four-and-a-half hours, broken only for a short period for a Dáil vote. Contributors were limited to four minutes but on several occasions Padraic McCormack had to remind speakers to bring their words to a close.

Kenny had tabled the motion so he was entitled to speak first and then to sum up at the end of the meeting. In his opening speech, Kenny set out his record as leader and the revitalisation of the party since 2002. 'We're on the brink of government,' he told his colleagues as he outlined the central policy planks for a Fine Gael-led government: overhauling the political system, reforming the health services along the lines of the Dutch system and creating employment through the party's proposed NewERA investment vehicle for infrastructure development.

Kenny had done serious preparation with his script – and even his critics said it was a very strong performance. At the end of the speech he was blunt in dealing with his opponents – several were identified by name. He took on criticisms uttered in public by Hayes, Creed and Naughton. He spoke about the dissent of the previous week. He told Varadkar: 'I stood by you.' Varadkar had unwisely said on *Prime Time* that if he stood down Kenny would still have an important role to play, and in a future Fine Gael government could be Minister for Foreign Affairs. 'Leo, I'm sorry. I cannot have a situation where you go on television and offer me the job of foreign affairs minister,' Kenny said.

Bruton made what was considered a measured speech, setting out the rationale for a leadership change. Like all who spoke against the confidence motion Bruton acknowledged Kenny's achievements as party leader. Many who were voting against Kenny said they were doing so reluctantly as they respected his record and work. Several spoke about how personally difficult it was to turn away from the Mayo man. But they were united in explaining the reason for wanting a new leader: the party was languishing in the polls. But the heave was not just about a single opinion poll, even if Fine Gael's recent break from a solid trend over the previous two years had presented the opportunity to move against Kenny. Simon Coveney was clear that the vote was not about rewarding past achievements. They were not casting judgement on Kenny's record but about the future of the party. Kenny's supporters questioned the timing of Bruton's move. Ciaran Cannon, who had been recruited into the party after the demise of the Progressive Democrats, raised some smiles when he spoke about the end of his former party. 'I was the last man to take out the gun and shoot myself as leader of the PDs.'

In his final contribution, Kenny spoke about returning to Mayo after being elected party leader in 2002. He recalled being greeted by 3,000 people in Castlebar and how what he remembered was not the bonfires, but the pride in their eyes. He referred to previous heaves when Fine Gael leaders had been 'demonised in the jobs but then eulogised after they had been ousted.' In his final words he declared: 'When I win this vote, I'll go on to be Taoiseach.' Most of those in the room rose from their seats. But it was still not clear if the standing ovation would equate with a majority of the votes in the secret ballot.

The votes were counted by Padraic McCormack and Paschal Donohoe, and shortly after 4.30 p.m. news emerged from the meeting that Kenny had won. Although the actual result was not announced – in keeping with Fine Gael policy – word quickly spread that the margin was 38 to 32. The anti-Kenny camp continue to believe the margin was as low as four votes but Kenny's supporters are adamant their man won by over ten votes.

'I'm thrilled and indeed very relieved that the motion of confidence has been approved and endorsed by the parliamentary party,' Kenny declared. 'For me, this is the end of any of the tensions that were building up. We move on from here as a completely united party.'

'There will be no more heaves,' Bruton asserted. 'This is an issue that had to be resolved for the party. I think Enda Kenny has demonstrated his resilience and I think the decision has been made – clearly that decision has to be respected.'

Kenny said there would be no vindictiveness. There was no gloating in public but the recriminations continued. Hard words had been spoken in private. The experience had been bruising for the newer members of the parliamentary party. Many younger TDs – the likes of Varadkar, Creighton, and Enright – had never been confronted by the raw politics of the previous week. Tactically they had been out-thought. They had also underestimated Kenny's steely determination. Lucinda Creighton later said: 'I'm glad it happened. I think it cleared the air and got us over an issue that had been bubbling there beneath the surface for quite some time, and I think Enda came out of it a lot stronger.'

Kenny proved himself to be a better party politician that his opponents. He was not the type of leader favoured by the professional middle-classes who wanted a newer, updated version of

Garret FitzGerald – urban rather than rural, intellectual rather than middle-of-the road. Richard Bruton was not their ideal choice but he was the best option available. Yet the party had opted to stay with Kenny.

Kenny's advisors talked of him as a 'championship player' who put in big performances for the important contests, but in the periods in-between he lost focus and found it difficult to maintain momentum. They argued that the 'championship player' analogy was confirmed by Kenny's record in winning elections, and that he had now delivered another successful performance in the leadership contest.

The heave undermined the idea of Kenny leading a focused and united team into government. It had been a central pillar of Fine Gael strategy. Bruton had previously described Kenny as a 'great team leader'. The George Lee debacle left some limited negative impression about Kenny as a team leader. But the heave damaged the concept, especially as so many of Kenny's own frontbench appointees had walked away. Kenny was aware that work was now needed to rebuild the party's reputation with the electorate.

Throughout the heave he had left open the possibility of re appointing rebels to his new frontbench. In the immediate aftermath of the result he stuck a conciliatory tone in response to questions about having Bruton and other opponents on this team. Bruton had repeatedly ruled out returning to the frontbench but after the result he was less emphatic. 'That's not a decision for today,' he said.

Some frontbenchers expected to be dropped – Hayes, Naughton and Mitchell were immediately signalled out, as were Creed, Flanagan and Timmins. Varadkar had already said he would be 'highly hypocritical' to turn around after the result and support Kenny. Several other leading opponents admitted they had no expectation of being reappointed. Coveney said he did not expect to be in favour with Kenny any time soon. Hayes said he would play any role Kenny wanted but he did not expect to be on the new frontbench.

Kenny opted to allow emotions settle before forming his new frontbench. The closer the announcement was to the Dáil summer recess the less time his colleagues would have to mull over recent events in the environs of Leinster House. He also signalled his preference for a low-key return to Mayo. There had been some adverse comments when Councillor Joe Mellet was captured on television cameras outside Leinster House shouting 'Up Mayo' when the confidence motion result was announced. There was to be no triumphalism, Kenny instructed. Initial plans for bonfires on the approach roads into Castlebar and a public rally were cancelled. The message was 'business as usual'.

14

Economic Collapse

Michael Noonan had delivered the set-piece budget day reply on ten previous occasions. As Fine Gael's finance spokesman, he had jousted with Ray MacSharry, Albert Reynolds and Charlie McCreevy. He was fully aware of the responsibility in being the first opposition deputy to respond to the Finance Minister's budget day speech. He also appreciated the sense of political theatre that defined the annual event.

But there was much that was different about the budget laid before the Dáil on 7 December 2011. Brian Lenihan had presided over the worst economic period in the history of the Irish State. And the imprint of the authorities in Washington, Brussels and Frankfurt was evident in the package of austerity measures outlined by the Minister for Finance.

A series of interventions by the Fianna Fáil-Green coalition to resolve the banking crisis had failed. They had ceded economic sovereignty to the International Monetary Fund and the authorities in Europe. The bailout of the Irish banks had cost billions and the implications were evident as Lenihan cut child benefit and other social welfare payments, and increased the tax take across an already declining economy.

As he came to the end of his speech, Lenihan sought to strike a positive note: 'We have been through a tumultuous two years culminating in our application for external assistance. Today's budget is our first step in ensuring that we can get back firmly on our own feet. It is a substantial down-payment on the journey back to economic health. We can emerge from this dark time as a stronger and fitter economy to provide sustainable jobs and decent public services for all our citizens.'

Noonan listened closely to the Minister's contribution. Little in the budget speech surprised him. The broad parameters were well-known and much of the content had been well-flagged. But when Noonan rose to speak, his initial assessment was damning: 'This is the budget of a puppet government, which is doing what it has been told to do by the IMF, the EU Commission and the European Central Bank. It is doing so in order that the State can draw down the bailout funds now that the country is insolvent.' Noonan used his initial remarks – when he had full media attention in the Dáil chamber – to lampoon Lenihan and lash out at the beleaguered coalition administration.

'I felt ashamed when I read the obsequious letters of the Minister for Finance when applying for assistance to Messrs. Juncker, Reynders, Rehn, and Trichet and separately to Mr. Strauss-Kahn of the IMF. The first two sentences in both of the Minister's letters reads as follows: "Ireland faces an economic crisis without parallel in its recent history. The problems of low growth, doubt about fiscal sustainability and a fragile banking sector are now feeding on each other, undermining confidence." What a self-indictment; the Minister's critics could not have done better. It is an absolute indictment of his own policies as set out in both of the letters he wrote to our new masters in Europe and in Washington.'

To the sound of 'hear, hear' from the opposition side of the Dáil chamber – most vocal from his Fine Gael colleagues – Noonan proceeded to paint the picture of a tired and jaded administration, ultimately overawed by the scale of the fiscal and banking crisis largely of its own making: 'If it was not so serious, it would be funny. When one reads the letters, they sound like confessions beaten out of him, as if one were reading a thriller. It is as if they water-boarded the Minister in Merrion Street and made him sign the letters, or perhaps they were motivated by the mock humility of the gombeen culture to think that he would get the €85 bn more easily if it was a handout.'

Paul Gogarty of the Green Party attempted to interject but without any success. On the government side Fianna Fáil TDs listened in silence as Noonan concluded: 'At times of crisis we tend to turn to the heroes of the past for inspiration – to Collins and Griffith, de Valera and Lemass. I know members on all sides of the House do that and therefore, I shall finish by reference to a quotation attributed to Michael Collins which we might all ponder. Collins said, "Give us the future. We have had enough of the past. Give us back our country to live in, to grow in, to love."'

Noonan's words had stung. 'His contribution was masterful,' a Fine Gael advisor said. That Noonan delivered the main opposition speech on 7 December 2010 was in itself a remarkable event – in a year of such dramatic political upheaval. Noonan had remained silent throughout the June 2010 heave. 'I didn't speak at the meeting of the parliamentary party. I didn't come down on any side beforehand and I wanted to keep it that way. I felt it would not have been appropriate as a former leader of the party so I wanted to stay out of it,' he said.

But, as mentioned previously, Kenny was convinced he had Noonan's vote, and two of Kenny's main supporters confirmed to this author that a deal had been agreed between the two men. The idea of Noonan's re-emergence to such a prominent role was never in the script. His short tenure as Fine Gael leader had been a disaster. He left behind a broken party. Neither was the Limerick man universally popular with his colleagues, although crucially he still commanded considerable respect from Fine Gael TDs and Senators.

Noonan's return undoubtedly had a certain appeal given the national focus on the economy, and it also offered reassurance to some wavers about the implications for the senior finance post in the event of Kenny winning the confidence motion. Once the leadership result was announced, Noonan immediately indicated his willingness to serve on the new frontbench. 'Everybody has to make themselves available in circumstances like these,' he said. The Limerick politician also encouraged the idea that room should be found for Richard Bruton.

Kenny had pledged to unite the party. A test of his intentions was going to be the composition of the new frontbench. He took some time to consider his options. Several of his opponents from the old frontline team indicated their willingness to serve again despite the harsh words spoken during the unsuccessful heave. The new line-up was eventually announced on 2 July 2010.

Kenny opted for experience – former minister Sean Barrett joined Noonan in returning to a frontline role. Barrett was given the high-profile foreign affairs position while, as had been well flagged, Noonan replaced Bruton as finance spokesperson. Limerick West TD Dan Neville was not alone when he said he looked forward to seeing Noonan 'demolishing the government'.

Bruton was given the next most senior economic position as spokesperson on enterprise, jobs and economic planning. He was also given responsibility for public sector reform. The unsuccessful challenger pledged his loyalty to the party leader: 'I believe Enda Kenny has proven his steel.' There would be no more heaves. The leadership issue was settled.

Kenny said he had tried to be inclusive. 'In the heat of battle, people will say things in electoral contest. When the electoral contests are over and concluded, we move on. That's what the Fine Gael party will do now,' he said. There would be no rump, and no more instability arising from the leadership issue: 'there's no long grass – it was all cut a couple of weeks ago.'

But despite expanding the frontbench from 19 to 21 members, Kenny wielded the axe as he took retribution on most of his chief opponents. Only five of the dissidents including Bruton were on the new frontbench – Coveney, Varadkar, O'Dowd and Flanagan. 'We had a view that Simon and Leo were not in the main gang. They were effectively presented with the situation: this train is leaving the station – its time to get on. The others were the ringleaders,' a Kenny advisor admitted. There was a clear signal that former loyalists O'Dowd and Flanagan were being retained on sufferance. The presence of Coveney and Varadkar also ensured the younger generation of Fine Gael TDs still had frontline representation. The new frontbench had an older age-profile as many of the 'young Turks' who had opposed Kenny were gone, including Naughton (37), Enright (36) and Hayes (40).

Kenny penalised most of his chief opponents. There was no frontbench return for Olivia Mitchell, Michael Creed, Brian Hayes, Denis Naughton, Billy Timmins or Olwyn Enright. Having recently announced that she was pregnant, Enright opted out for personal reasons, and later in the year announced her intention to leave national politics. Billy Timmins also asked not to be considered for the new frontbench although in any event, like Enright, he would not have been reappointed. Bruton expressed regret that his colleagues had been left out: 'I took this initiative. They put their necks on the line, and I feel let down for them. At a human level, of course it's tough.'

Many careers had been irrevocably damaged. Several politicians, who would have had realistic thoughts of a cabinet position in the event of Fine Gael entering government, knew they had fallen to the bottom of the pecking order. Those now on the outside accepted that they were facing a prolonged spell on the party's backbenches, and that if elected Taoiseach, Kenny would fill eight or nine cabinet positions from the colleagues on his new frontbench. And that is exactly what happened eight months later.

Key supporters were rewarded in the July 2010 reshuffle. James Reilly was the big winner. Although still only a first term TD, Reilly's reward for his loyalty and vigorous defense of Kenny was elevation to the position of deputy leader in conjunction with his existing role as health spokesperson. There were promotions for other loyalists: Alan Shatter (from children to justice), Jimmy Deenihan (from defence to tourism, culture and sport) and Michael Ring (from community and gaeltacht affairs to social protection). Phil Hogan was retained in his preferred brief in environment but was also appointed as director of elections. Paul Keogh also opted to remain in the same position as party whip but his standing as the leader's man was also significantly enhanced.

Kenny also found room for others who had backed his leadership: Catherine Byrne, Deirdre Clune, Andrew Doyle, Frank Feighan, John Perry and David Stanton. Perry and Staunton had served on previous frontbenches under Kenny as had Bernard Allen, who was appointed as chairman of the public accounts committee. Byrne, Doyle and Feighan were newcomers. Byrne's appointment was an attempt to compensate for the loss of Hayes and Mitchell in the Dublin region. The promotion of Doyle and Feighan was a double blow to their respective constituency colleagues who had opposed Kenny. Feighan and Naughten were TDs in Roscommon-South Leitrim while Doyle and Timmins were TDs in Wicklow. Not only were Naughton and Timmins off the frontbench, but their respective local rivals Feighan and Doyle had now leapfrogged them in the seniority stakes.

Kenny spoke of reconciliation but the atmosphere in the party remained poor. Many TDs were not talking to each other. 'There was a rawness,' one party insider said. But media attention was distracted with the return of Michael Noonan, who was widely seen as a highly credible replacement for Bruton. A cabinet minister in the 1982-87 FitzGerald-led coalition, he had also served as a minister in the 1994-97 Rainbow government. He was now returning to the leading opposition role as finance spokesperson which he had held previously – from 1987 to 1990, and again from 1997 to 2002.

The return was all the more remarkable given the scale of the 2002 defeat, not to mind the lack of a personal relationship between Kenny and Noonan. Many Fine Gael TDs acknowledge that Noonan never rated Kenny. The decision to dump Kenny from a frontline role in the aftermath of the 2001 leadership content was petty and vindictive, and one that did the Limerick man little credit. But Kenny had parked whatever personal feelings he felt at that time. 'Politics is not about friendships. It's been said that even in a party structure politics is a "game for sole traders,"' one Fine Gael inside said. The relationship between the two men proved successful, so much so that Kenny had sufficient trust in Noonan to appoint him as chairperson of his party's coalition negotiating team in late February 2011.

For Kenny these decisions were ultimately professional ones. He had after all, brought Noonan back in October 2004 as chairman of the Public Accounts Committee. The former leader also attended meetings of the party's frontbench. He was not reappointed after the 2007 election, but the decision was not because Kenny had dispensed with his services. 'I wasn't really in a fit position from about 2005 to take on a frontbench role,' Noonan explained.

His wife Florence had advanced Alzheimer's – and although only 66 years of age, in 2010 she had been living with the illness for 12 years. The illness only became public knowledge in late May 2010 when Noonan spoke for the first time about her condition on RTÉ television. A clearly emotional Noonan revealed how his wife had been diagnosed after continuing memory loss and how, as the disease became more advanced, it became increasingly difficult for him to provide the necessary care.

'I've moved from a situation where I was one of the carers of my wife at home to a situation where she's now in a nursing home and being cared for by professionals. I visit her every day I'm in Limerick,' Noonan explained. When he accepted the invitation to become spokesperson on finance Noonan admitted: 'My personal circumstances have changed. Things are different now.'

Longtime members of the parliamentary party saw a different Noonan in 2010 but not just because of the impact of his personal tragedy. Noonan's perspective on politics was also tempered by the fact that he was no longer driven by the ambition to lead Fine Gael. 'The monkey of the leadership wasn't on his back anymore. He wasn't watching or plotting – that was all gone and he was just interested in doing his own job,' one colleague said. Noonan was one of a group of Fine Gael figures who had ambitions to succeed Garret FitzGerald in 1987 but he had to watch as first Alan Dukes and later John Bruton filled the role. For many in the party throughout this period he was a negative, brooding force. Yet having realised his ambition in 2001, the Limerick man failed in the leadership position he had coveted for so long. 'Michael had the intelligence but he didn't cope very well with the pressure of being leader,' one colleague said. Noonan was the classic example of a good number two who lost his starring qualities when elevated to the premier position – something Fianna Fáil discovered also applied to Brian Cowen.

Noonan was more than just a credible replacement for Bruton. He filled the role of the party's elder statesman and over the following months, he ensured that the frontbench was fully informed about the evolving economic situation and the rationale for the Fine Gael response. He also allowed the two deputy spokespeople in finance – Damien English and Brian Hayes – significant media opportunities. English and Hayes had opposed Kenny, Hayes had been dropped from the frontbench, but both were intent on taking advantage of their new roles.

Noonan brought a sharp political edge to the finance brief. Whereas Bruton had been a hugely effective spokesperson, he had frequently failed to land a political punch on his opposite number. This 'nice guy' image was one of the reasons many members of the parliamentary party had actually doubted Bruton's suitability for the leadership role. By way of contrast Noonan was more robust, more abrasive, more aggressive.

Noonan had little ground to make up. Alongside his ministerial track record and experience as frontbench spokesperson, he had closely followed the recent financial debate. He had been a regular contributor to Dáil debates on the economy and had set out his own views earlier in 2010: 'We must find a way forward. The government has made a good attempt at fiscal correction. It has also brought in a new architecture for the banking sector. Whether we agree or disagree with that, it is now in play and I hope it works. However, the government has utterly failed in addressing the recession. The recession is not a subset of the fiscal or the banking problem; it is an issue in its own right and requires its own solutions.'

On the day the new frontbench was announced, Noonan immediately offered support for the broad thrust of Lenihan's fiscal plan and admitted that any new government would be obliged to adhere to the economic agenda implemented by the Fianna Fáil-Green coalition. 'We're stuck with a lot of what they've done now because a lot of it is irreversible,' the new finance spokesperson said.

But he was very keen to carve out distinctive space from the government parties. He criticised the unfairness in the cutbacks programme and pledged a new approach to the banking crisis. 'I think they've made an awful mess of the banking restructure,' he said. But significantly, he jettisoned his predecessor's 'good bank – bad bank' policy, which had failed to find public traction.

Noonan pledged vigorous opposition and started by describing Cowen as 'a bit of a disaster' and saying Lenihan was like 'the first mate on the Titanic.' There was also a blunt warning to the top executives in the beleaguered banks. 'If I were minister tomorrow morning, I'd say: "You've got six months". I'm not saying they were personally culpable but it happened on their watch.'

There was a harder attitude to the Labour Party – an issue which was the subject of considerable internal debate within Fine Gael, given the rival party's emergence as a serious player according to recent opinion polls. In early July 2010 Noonan called on Eamon Gilmore to outline his policy position before the general election. 'I think Labour have attracted a lot of new supporters and have become a kind of lightning conductor for the anger of the electorate. To turn their newfound support into core support, as the election approaches, they will have to be more explicit. But I'm not being critical of them. They have a different tactic, I suppose. It wouldn't be the tactic that I would follow.'

Noonan had an immediate impact – much of it positive for Fine Gael – although he was also responsible for the type of gaffe that would have had Kenny on the defensive with the media, and his internal critics had made similar remarks. Within weeks of his appointment, Noonan questioned the credibility of the 105,000 jobs promised in the party's NewERA policy document. 'Simon

Coveney was the author of that particular policy document and, if you look at it, the figure of 100,000 jobs doesn't appear anywhere in it. That seems to be some kind of public relations add-on that enthusiastic people attached to it,' Noonan said. The figure had actually been calculated by the party's research team following discussions with external experts. The number was derived from an independent economic formula to estimate employment creation based on infrastructure spending of €18bn. Noonan subsequently admitted that his remarks were incorrect: 'I handled that particular interview badly.'

The episode blew over quickly. Overall with the economy remaining the dominant national issue, Noonan added edge to Fine Gael's public profile. And with Reilly as a more visible deputy leader and Shatter in justice, the party seemed to benefit from the reshuffle of positions forced upon Kenny by the leadership heave. 'Noonan made a massive difference. It was a case of the right person in the right job at the right time. And, I guess, it could be said that it was another example of Kenny's luck,' one party official said. Another refers to the benefit Fine Gael got for the strengthened line-up with Noonan in finance, Bruton in enterprise and with a focus on public sector reform, and Varadkar having responsibility for the NewERA plan. 'Throughout the later half of 2010 the economy was the only issue being discussed by the broadcast media. There were a volume of television and radio programmes looking for our people, and we had a compelling trio in Noonan, Bruton and Varadkar supplemented by Brian Hayes and Damien English.'

Fine Gael favoured an approach which focused on spending cuts rather than tax increases. The party wanted better value from public sector spending – the mantra was 'more for less'. 'Salami-slicing the budgets of all departments by roughly equal amounts as our own government is doing, is a lazy, ineffective and damaging way to make savings,' Noonan observed.

Throughout the summer Fine Gael kept pressure on the government but in reality Cowen and his colleagues were having a horrendous time dealing with the consequences of their own decisions. In mid-July it was revealed that the government's financial advisors, Merrill Lynch, had warned that a blanket banking guarantee would be a 'mistake' and that Anglo-Irish and Irish Nationwide could have losses of over €10bn. Kenny claimed Cowen and his colleagues had not just ignored advice on the bank guarantee, but that 'they then sought to deceive the Oireachtas and the Irish public about the nature of the advice that had been offered to them. That deception continues to this very day.'

Cowen was still talking about achieving budget savings through cuts to current expenditure rather than having to increase taxes in late July 2010. At that stage the government was seeking to make savings of €3bn, but the external message was that the worst was over: 'Ireland has reached the bottom of its economic difficulties,' Cowen said. But the economic situation was actually worsening. A revised business plan from NAMA published in early July 2010 cut its projected seven-to-ten year profit on loans from the main banks from almost €5bn to €1bn. The deterioration – as NAMA reevaluated the information provided by the banks and determined that much of it did not stand up to scrutiny – once more exposed the risk Lenihan had taken on behalf of the taxpayer.

Differences within the government over the future of Anglo-Irish bank emerged in late August 2010. The Green Party had arrived at the view that winding down the failed bank might be a cheaper option for the State, rather than Lenihan's preference for dividing the operation into a 'good' and 'bad' bank. The two sides played down suggestions of division but there was little doubt that coherence and clarity were qualities the government's strategy lacked. The rising costs of the Anglo Irish rescue – and the scale of the funding needed for the other financial institutions – led to an increase in Irish bond yields in late August and early September. Interest rates on Irish bonds reached 5.9 per cent on 27 August. The markets were disbelievers when it came to Lenihan's banking strategy, and they were not alone: the European Commission would ultimately reject the government plan for the future of Anglo-Irish.

The cabinet met on 1 September 2010 for its first post-summer break meeting with news that Anglo-Irish had incurred losses of €8.2bn in the first half of 2010. The figure was the highest ever loss in Irish corporate history. Fine Gael called on the government to use the second anniversary of the bank guarantee to re-examine its policy and, in particular, its plan for the future of Anglo-Irish. Noonan reminded the public that in January 2009 Lenihan had confidently predicted that the cost of the Anglo-Irish nationalisation would be €4.5bn, but that by the summer of 2010 that figure had increased to €25bn, while Standards and Poor's estimated the final bill could hit €35bn. Not for the first time the government and the opposition clashed over the still-unexplained sequence of events on the night of the bank guarantee in September 2008.

The cost of the banking bailout was hurting the already precarious national finances. Negative sentiment about the government's ability to deal with the economic collapse was increasing. The IMF had warned that the budget in December 2010 would probably have to be more severe than Lenihan had previously indicated. Fine Gael predicted higher taxes and deeper spending cuts to pay for the bank rescue plan. By the second week in September, Lenihan signalled that even deeper spending reductions than the previously indicated €3bn were likely in the December budget.

Formal confirmation of just how badly wrong Lenihan had called the overall economic and banking situation came on 30 September 2010 when the government published its plans to bailout the banking system with a huge injection of public funds. The cost of the bank recapitalisation was put at between €45bn to €50bn. The final cost of the bailout at Anglo-Irish was now potentially €34bn – a huge difference from Lenihan's original estimate of €4.5bn. The decision took the national debt to 100 per cent of GDP and increased the budget deficit to 32 per cent of GDP.

In defending his actions, Lenihan told *The Financial Times*: 'Any Anglo failure would bring down the sovereign. It is systemically important not because of any intrinsic merit in the bank. I can assure [you] I don't see any. But because of its size relative to the national balance sheet. No country could contemplate the failure of such an institution.'

The government was also withdrawing from international money markets until early in 2011. The National Treasury Management Agency postponed auctions of government bonds in October and November. The cost of borrowing had become too high. 'We'll be back in January,' Lenihan predicted. 'The exchequer is fully funded until June 2011' quickly became the favoured mantra of government ministers and Fianna Fáil backbenchers. Lenihan accepted that the figures were 'horrendous,' but pledged that his decisions would 'bring the crisis to a closure'. Few people now believed him. The cost of the bailout had escalated to such an extent that Ireland's sovereign creditworthiness had been damaged and the State could no longer borrow money. The government had lost its authority, and any remaining trust with the people was in very short supply.

The opposition and the media dubbed 30 September 2010 as 'Black Thursday'. Noonan said the minister's banking strategy had collapsed and that he had made a 'calamitous mistake' in guaranteeing all of Anglo-Irish's liabilities. The latest injection into the banks was heavily criticised. 'The government, like a losing gambler, is doubling its bet in the vain hope of a win on the last race,' Noonan said. It was a view that was widely shared.

The implications for the December budget were obvious – a significant fiscal adjustment was needed. The previously mentioned €3bn figure was now the absolute minimum to bring the national deficit in order by the target date of 2014. At that stage, the Department of Finance was estimating growth of 3.25 per cent for 2011. The mandarins had been spectacularly wrong so often that few believed their figures.

Lenihan also announced his intention to publish a detailed four-year fiscal plan. He said that work on the document was underway and that it would be published in November. The multi-annual fiscal plan would cover 2011 to 2014 and the adjustments were aimed at allowing Ireland to meet the EU's 3 per cent deficit target over the four-year term.

The opposition immediately sought details on expenditure and taxation measures. Both Fine Gael and Labour said a new government would not be bound by the terms of the plan. Noonan said it was impossible to support the plan without knowledge of the background figures. He claimed that the European Commission was dictating the terms of Ireland's budgetary plan – a claim denied by the government.

Fianna Fáil appealed to the opposition to support the fiscal correction plan. Ministers sought a constructive reaction from their political rivals, and repeatedly said such a stance would be in the national interest. In a newfound spirit of inclusion, Enterprise Minister Batt O'Keeffe said there was no reason why the coalition would not take on board any good and practical opposition suggestions. It was the political survival strategy, which Fine Gael's Election Strategy Working Group had predicted, that Fianna Fáil would adopt.

Green Party leader John Gormley made what was ultimately a ham-fisted attempt to get cross-party support for how to deal with the budget crisis. His invitation to the opposition to talks with the two government parties met with a cool response. The fact that Cowen had already dismissed detailed talks with Fine Gael and Labour undermined Gormley's initiative from the outset. Noonan said the Taoiseach had already 'thrown a bucket of cold water over it.'

In late October 2010, Lenihan made another attempt to lock-in the opposition parties by sending them a letter to be signed by himself, Noonan and Joan Burton pledging to meet the targets in the four-year fiscal plan. The desire to link the opposition to the forthcoming budget was firmly underpinned by Fianna Fáil's political self-preservation.

Neither opposition party was willing to be embraced by Fianna Fáil in what was seen as a deliberate political strategy by the main government party to ensure blame was shared for unpalatable banking and fiscal policies. After spending over 13 years in opposition, neither Fine Gael nor Labour were overly enthusiastic about helping out Fianna Fáil now that the party was struggling with an economic crisis largely of its own making.

Fine Gael's Election Strategy Committee discussed but discounted the idea of a Tallaght Strategy: 'Our view is simple: If you are going to sup with the Devil make sure you use a long spoon. . .' The party committed to reducing the budget deficit to 3 per cent by 2014 and accepted the need for a four-year fiscal plan. But the party sought to create political space from Fianna Fáil by repeatedly stating that the overall 3 per cent deficit target should be met not just by spending and taxation measures but also by supporting growth and employment-creation measures. The central role of the NewERA investment plan for broadband, energy and water projects was stressed by Fine Gael spokespeople.

Noonan met with officials in the Department of Finance. Having had an initial briefing, he concluded that the fiscal adjustment needed in the four-year plan would be 'significantly higher' than previously indicated by the government. 'There are no soft options,' he admitted.

Lenihan's credibility was in tatters. He had been wrong so many times that few believed him anymore. The government envisaged a €15 billion correction by 2014, with some €6bn coming in 2011. The economic and fiscal background to the four-year plan included a €6bn reduction in 2011 followed by €3-4bn in 2012; €3-3.5bn in 2013 and €2-2.5bn in 2014. The reductions would cut the national deficit to the required 3 per cent by 2014. Cowen warned that passing the December budget was vital. To do otherwise would risk the State running out of money by the middle of 2011.

The opposition questioned the impact of the deficit reduction programme on employment and growth. The Labour Party rejected the adjustment approach favoured by the government. Fine Gael, however, accepted the overall budgetary figures but declined to offer support. Kenny was keen to stress that any new government would not be bound by individual proposals in the four-year plan. The party sought more details on the figures. At the end of October

2010, the Department of Finance was still forecasting average annual growth over the adjustment period of 2.75 per cent. 'We are not buying in. We need more information. We certainly need to know how the minister built up his forecast,' Noonan said.

The situation took another turn on 4 November 2010 when the government announced that it was postponing publication of its four-year plan until closer to the annual budget in early December. The move may have been to reduce the extent of dissent before the budget and also to ensure details in the plan did not dominate the Donegal South West by-election. The government was forced into another embarrassing action on the long-delayed by-election when the High Court ruled that a delay of 18 months was inordinate. Following the court judgement the by-election was set for 25 November 2010. Sinn Féin's Pearce Doherty eventually emerged as the victor in a contest which was totally overshadowed by developments in the national economic situation.

Throughout November 2010 the cost of Irish government borrowing increased to over 7 per cent. The gap with German rates was as high as five percentage points. The EU's Economic and Monetary Affairs Commissioner, Olli Rehn arrived in Dublin, and met with the opposition parties. Noonan told Rehn that a Fine Gael-led government would deliver the four-year adjustment plan. He said a new government would have a clear mandate to deliver the programme and would offer much greater political stability.

There was a real sense that Cowen's government was no longer master of its own destiny. On Sunday 21 November 2010 Lenihan confirmed that Ireland would be seeking an international financial rescue package. Negotiations had opened on a multi-billion euro bailout programme with a troika of the International Monetary Fund, the European Central Bank and the European Commission. Whatever small semblance of fiscal and economic credibility that Fianna Fáil still had was removed with this decision which brought with it external oversight of Ireland's economic affairs.

The twin track programme comprised two elements – plans to restructure and shrink the crisis-ridden Irish bank; and plans to reduce the gap between national income and national expenditure. Noonan said the government had relinquished national sovereignty. 'You are the person who holds constitutional obligation for the finances of the State,' Noonan reminded the beleaguered Minister for Finance.

The application had come after a period of appalling political misjudgment underpinned by the absence of a coherent communication strategy. From mid-November, sources in Europe – widely believed to be from the European Central Bank – started to brief against the Irish government. The announcements on 30 September, 'Black Thursday', had not delivered the required impact. The banking and fiscal situation in Ireland was judged to have reached the point where external intervention was necessary.

Pressure was being resisted in Dublin where the government was understandably keen to avoid the embarrassing and humiliating impasse of ceding economic decision-making to the International Monetary Fund and the European Central Bank. On 9 November Lenihan said Ireland had not lost its sovereignty and would not have to resort to the EU bailout fund. He gave a bullish interview to the BBC, in which he again refused to accept that the bank bailout was responsible for the country's economic woes.

Noonan said he thought there was substance in the bailout speculation: 'I think the Irish government are fighting a rearguard action for appearance purposes.' But government ministers continued to take their lead from Lenihan. The most exposed was Dermot Ahern who described speculation of talks being underway as a 'fiction'. The following day Cowen said an application for external support was not being made. 'I am just making the point that we will calmly and in a considered way deal with these issues in the days and weeks and months ahead,' the Taoiseach said. But Cowen was playing with words. He also said Ireland would work with its partners to find ways to bring stability to the financial markets.

Noonan was sharply critical, saying that the Taoiseach had to stop talking in riddles. It was a fair observation. Cowen only seemed capable of talking in official language – the words of the civil service. It was also increasingly evident that Lenihan had essentially been 'captured' by the system. His default position was to defend the Department of Finance from external criticism. Fianna Fáil was caught in a perfect storm and the party's hierarchy was unable to provide political leadership. Ministers seemed out-of-touch and after two years of unsuccessful battling economic turmoil, Cowen and his colleagues looked exhausted and sounded jaded. There was no energy in government. And through their denials – and what was increasingly seen as blustering by the Finance Minister – the public had not been treated like adults. There was an absence of any strategic thinking to the government's actions.

It took the intervention of Patrick Honohan on Thursday 18 November 2010 to bring some clarity to the situation. In a radio interview, the Governor of the Central Bank said that a substantial contingency capital fund could be made available to create confidence in the firepower available to protect the banking system. Lenihan finally confirmed that the IMF had arrived in Ireland. He told the Dáil that if a substantial contingency fund emerged from talks with the IMF and the EU, it would be a 'very desirable outcome.' Later he said he felt no shame in fighting for the country's interests.

But Noonan said Lenihan should be ashamed and that the entire government should share the shame. 'His colleagues, over the weekend with their incredible denials embarrassed the nation, and I am afraid their denials did not work. The other strategy the Minister has drawn from poker is bluff, and he is the greatest proponent of bluff I have ever seen in this House.'

Details of the bailout deal were eventually announced on Sunday 28 November 2010, and Fianna Fáil's already damaged reputation was dealt a fatal blow. The announcement on 'Black Thursday' had seriously undermined the ability of the party to recover any political ground prior to the general election. Defeat was a near certain probability from 30 September onwards. The actions of Cowen and Lenihan had diminished the authority of the their party and its claims to economic competence. But the ignominy of calling in the IMF and the bailout deal on the 28 November 2010 pushed the party firmly into electoral meltdown territory.

The government agreed a €85bn bailout deal with the IMF and the EU. Under the terms of the deal, Ireland contributed €17.5bn to the package by raiding the National Pension Reserve Fund and cash reserves at the NTMA. The balance of €67.5bn was provided by the external agencies – €45bn from the EU and bilateral loans from the United Kingdom and Sweden, with the IMF stumping up €22.5bn. The bulk of the funding – €50bn – was to cover national borrowing up to 2014 as austerity measures were implemented to reduce the gap between spending and revenue. The €35bn balance was set aside for yet another bailout of the banking system, the fourth injection of money in two years, which effectively brought the Irish banking system into State ownership.

The opposition parties were very critical of the terms of the bailout deal and what Eamon Gilmore described as a 'penal' rate of interest. Fine Gael said the deal was a 'hugely disappointing result for the country.' Noonan said: 'It's hard to imagine how this deal could have been much worse.'

'The government was cleaned out in the negotiations and has acted in the best interests of Ireland. At the very least we could have expected a low rate of interest on the loans, EU agreement on a jobs and growth package, and agreement to share the cost of rescuing the banks with the bondholders. The government came away with none of these.'

Brian Hayes described the bailout as 'Ireland's economic Iraq' but Lenihan defended the strategy. 'If the government has been reticent in making public comment, it has been in the interest of protecting the taxpayer,' the Finance Minister explained. But Lenihan's credibility was in tatters. 'We are the laughing stock of Europe,' Fianna Fáil TD Ned O'Keefe said as he called on the Finance Minister to resign.

The government signed a memorandum with the IMF and the EU which reaffirmed the need for €6bn in cutbacks in 2011 and a total of €15bn over the life of the four-year plan. The external agencies required regular updates on the country's progress in implementing the austerity programme. The dramatic decision of the Green Party to announce their intention to withdraw from government in early 2011 fundamentally changed the political situation. Gormley said his party would remain in government to ensure the passage of the December budget and related legislation. While the exact date of the general election remained unclear, it was now obvious that the voters would go to the polls in the initial months of 2011. The December budget brought only further bad news with increased income taxes, cuts in social welfare payments and a reduction in the minimum wage.

Kenny said the budget was the work of an exhausted government and lacked conviction, confidence and compassion. The public had reached a similar judgement. A post-budget opinion poll in *The Irish Times* indicated that dissatisfaction with the government had reached an unprecedented 90 per cent. The final Red C poll of 2010 indicated that Fine Gael's fortunes were on the increase as the electorate focused on the actual election. The party had seen a steady upward rise in its support over previous months and closed 2010 with 34 per cent of the first preference vote in the polling series. Support for the Labour Party had fallen back somewhat but Gilmore's party was also set for electoral gains with an estimated 23 per cent vote share. Support for Fianna Fáil, however, had collapsed. The economic turmoil had caused even more voters to desert the country's dominant political force. The Red C polling experts estimated that the worst-case scenario for Fianna Fáil was 13 per cent and that the best-case scenario was 19 per cent. The scene was set for the most dramatic contest in Irish electoral history and the realisation of Enda Kenny's strategy for Fine Gael to replace Fianna Fáil as the dominant political party in the Irish Republic.

Index